WRIGLEY FIELD

WRIGLEY FIELD

AN ORAL AND NARRATIVE HISTORY OF THE HOME OF THE CHICAGO CUBS

IRA BERKOW

with Special Interview Reporting by JOSH NOEL

Stewart, Tabori & Chang | New York

Published in 2014 by Stewart, Tabori & Chang
An imprint of ABRAMS

Library of Congress Control Number: 2013935994

ISBN: 978-1-58479-915-3

Editor: David Cashion
Designer: Danielle Young
Production Manager: Tina Cameron

The text of this book was composed in Century Gothic,
Chronicle Text, Clarendon, Gotham, Gotham Narrow,
Sentinel, and Serifa.

Printed and bound in China

10 9 8 7 6 5 4 3 2 1

Stewart, Tabori & Chang books are available at special
discounts when purchased in quantity for premiums and
promotions as well as fundraising or educational use. Special
editions can also be created to specification. For details,
contact specialsales@abramsbooks.com or the address below.

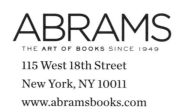

THE ART OF BOOKS SINCE 1949
115 West 18th Street
New York, NY 10011
www.abramsbooks.com

To Dolly and Howsie

CONTENTS

FOREWORD
BY KERRY WOOD

Coming into 2012, I figured I would get through the year, then reassess at the end of the season. I felt really good in the spring and tried to pace myself because I knew I was getting older. Then the season began and I felt OK, but I just wasn't getting results. I had a couple good games where I thought I was turning it around, but then the ball just wasn't coming out of my hand the way I wanted it to. I was battling myself, my body wasn't responding the way I wanted it to, and the results just weren't what I wanted. It all changes when you're not pitching well and you're putting your team in a hole. The younger players who watched me go through it will go through it themselves.

Those first two months were huge for me. If I couldn't get off to a good start, I knew it would be a long summer, because the wind at Wrigley would turn. The arm wasn't responding and recovering, and I couldn't pitch on back-to-back days. Physically, it didn't feel like it was worth spending two hours to get ready just to hurt the team.

By the end of April I was thinking that it would be my last season, but I was still planning to get through it. Then the end turned out to be closer than I thought. I tried to make adjustments, but I wasn't getting results. I tried new pitches, a couple sinkers here and there to go away from the lefties and down and in to the righties, just to show them something different. It wasn't working. I was going to try to get to the All-Star break, but I realized I didn't have the drive and the desire anymore. In May I made my decision.

I talked to [manager] Dale [Sveum] the night before my last game, and he asked me how I would like it to play out. I told him I hoped we would get a lead, I would put up a zero in the eighth inning, and Marmol would close it in the ninth. My dad said, "I never asked much of you, but you struck out the first hitter you faced. Can you strike out the last one?" I said I'd give it a shot.

My son spent that whole last day with me at Wrigley. We went up in the scoreboard and watched batting practice. He went up to the booth and got to say "Play ball!" when the game started. The main reason I continued to stick with the game is that I had a son, and I wanted him to remember what I did and to be old enough to remember being in the clubhouse and around the guys.

I knew going into the game that if I got up to warm up, I'd be put in and that would be it. When I started warming up in the eighth inning, I took in the fans a little bit more than usual, looking around and looking at the bleachers, knowing it would be the last time I would see the stadium from that point of view.

Usually when they would call for me, I would flip the ball to Lester Strode, the bull pen coach. That time I shook his hand and said, "I've enjoyed it, thanks for everything." On the mound I was business as usual. I struck out the one guy I faced on three pitches. I was ready for the next hitter, but Jamie Quirk [the bench coach who was filling in for Sveum after Sveum had been thrown out of the game] was walking out and it started to sink in. Then I was able to breathe and start thinking about things a little bit. All the infielders came to the mound to shake my hand. Adam Dunn was on first, and he told Bryan LaHair to tell me congratulations and that it's been good playing against me.

I started walking toward the dugout, and a couple guys—I think it was Matt Garza and Reed Johnson—pushed my son out to the top step and nudged him to run out to me. It was by far the coolest moment of my career to have my son run out to me in front of forty thousand people. It was poetic. It was a perfect ending.

I miss coming to the park in the morning and the energy of Wrigley Field and the neighborhood before a game. I miss waiting for batting practice to start and shagging balls in center field. It was like the game we played as kids. Those were the things I really missed when I left for Cleveland, and I really cherished them when I came back. But baseball wasn't who I was; it was what I did. I love the game and I respect it. It was part of my life. I'll always have those memories and I'm thankful for the opportunity. But I knew it would have to end at some time.

I was seventeen or eighteen years old when I first saw Wrigley Field, when I came up to sign a contract. I was just a nervous kid, on the field for batting practice and going into the clubhouse to meet the guys. Once the game started, my first full look at the field was from up in the press box. It was breathtaking. It was a different energy than I'd ever seen. The old band was playing in the seats, and it took me immediately to what I thought baseball was like in the old days. I grew up in Texas going to Rangers games at the old Arlington Stadium, but there's no history there. There's no band playing. You don't get that anywhere else but Wrigley Field. It's like it's out of a movie. For me, the band was the coolest thing, just the way they walk around and play between innings. In fact, I caught myself looking at them yesterday from the bull pen. Fourteen years later, I'm still looking at them.

I hated it the first couple of years here. It was too overwhelming for me—the city, the traffic, the people, the cab drivers, everything. I had Gracie [Mark Grace] take me under his wing. He was in love with Wrigley Field, knew all the stories and history, and he would talk about the guys who played here before us. You could see him work the crowd and the fans, and the way they accepted him. You don't see as much of that these days, but he was a good one to watch. He helped me embrace Wrigley Field and what it's about. It helped make things fine here, and made the field where I was most comfortable.

There's a microscope and intensity at Wrigley Field you don't have at many other stadiums. I like being on this field being surrounded by forty thousand screaming people. That's where I want to be, and that's what makes the game exciting. You go to, say, Colorado, you're far away from the fans. You get more time to think. It takes more concentration to stay focused. When you're

in the spotlight and in the middle of this electric crowd, it locks you in. Those visiting ballparks, they're wide open and they don't fill up. It feels empty and starts to look like a spring-training game by comparison. When you're here, you don't have to worry about staying focused. This atmosphere makes you focused. There's electricity. That's what I'm about.

Wrigley Field was one of the big reasons I came back to the Cubs as a free agent. I missed this atmosphere. There were other options, including a couple two-year deals, but I was at a point in my career where I had kids and had gone somewhere else—Cleveland—where I didn't have success and didn't enjoy going to work as much as I used to. I ran into Jim [Hendry, general manager] at Ron Santo's funeral, and I was at the point of thinking, if I can play another year or so, that'd be great, and if not, I was OK with being done. I knew I didn't want to drag the family around the country. Once I decided I was going to play again, the White Sox had an offer out, and I was real close to signing it if the Cubs said, "We can't give you anything"—which was their first reaction. But I wasn't asking for anything. We worked on it for a day. I met with Tom [Ricketts, principal owner] and Jim, and we got it done. There were some better offers, but I grew up here as a player, I live here, my kids are here, I love playing here, they were great to me when I was here, and I like the day games. It's baseball. For day games I get here at eight thirty and I'm home by five. It's a good fit for my family, and it's a good fit for me. This organization has given me everything I have and the opportunity to play, and loyalty is big to me.

Cleveland was tough. They made a financial decision to trade their big money guys away in my first season there. The stadium was empty and it was the first time in forever that I wasn't pitching in front of a full house at home. We can be struggling at Wrigley, and we're still sold out and we still have great fans that are supportive. Of course they boo when we play terribly, and it's not always easy when they're doing that. But that's the intensity of Wrigley Field, which is a good thing when things are going well.

In '03, '07, and '08, those winning seasons where we were playing well and getting into the postseason, it was special. The fans want to be part of a winning thing here so much. I think that's because it's been so long, but also because they can get close to us in such a small stadium. Fans get close to the players; we get close to the fans. We see the same season-ticket holders all the time. They feel like they know us, and we feel like we know them. We're

in a neighborhood here. There's that mentality, and you don't get that in a lot of places.

Fenway is the most comparable stadium to Wrigley. I didn't even get to pitch there until I'd been in baseball for ten years, so I never understood the comparison. I knew they were both old stadiums, but it's more than that. The fans are on top of you, the bull pens are wide open, and people can talk to you. It's that neighborhood feel. I'm sure they see the same faces again and again, like we do here. Wrigley Field has its share of tourists who put this on the vacation schedule, but these fans live and die with us, and when you're winning, there's not a better place to be.

I pitched at Wrigley during my first season with the Indians. It made me realize how much I missed it: the ivy, the field, and being so close to the stands. My family was here; my wife wanted the kids here because she thought my appearance was going to be big, and it was. The crowd was great—a standing ovation—and I'll never forget that. I wish I could've enjoyed it more, but I had to go out there and get my job done. But it was a cool thirty seconds, hearing that from the crowd. The game wasn't so great. I hadn't pitched in six or seven days, and I just knew I would come into Wrigley Field and have a save opportunity the first day—that's the way baseball works out. I didn't feel sharp, I wasn't fresh, and I hadn't thrown in a while. I had two save opportunities and blew both of 'em. In the first game, Derrek Lee hit a solo homer to tie it, and I gave up two or three runs the next day. I'm sure subconsciously I was nervous to be back. I won't say I felt nervous, but it probably did play into it a little bit. It was a rough couple of days. I was ready to get out of here.

Probably the most memorable game I pitched here was Game 7 against the Marlins in 2003. During Game 6, I was sitting here thinking, "I'm going to start Game 1 of the World Series." We were all happy in the dugout, getting ready to celebrate. I'm pretty sure they were putting plastic up in the clubhouse. Then obviously all that stuff happened. It happened so quick. Prior was cruising, and I didn't even think about the foul ball until everything started to unwind. I didn't see the play from the dugout, but I saw Alou's reaction, and then I went in and watched the replay. There wasn't any doubt the guy got in his way, but it's part of the game. You get breaks here and there. But you see Moisés flipping out and the umpires running down there to figure out what to do. It was a normal baseball play, and you just have to make the next pitch, but five or six pitches later, it seemed we were down. You can always hear the moans and the groans from the crowd and feel that attitude shift to negativity. We feed off that, no doubt. Well, we can feel it. We don't necessarily feed off negativity, but we can feel it. By the time Mark came out of the game, we were tied. I think it was Mike Mordecai who came in and, first pitch, hit a double and cleared the bases. Then the stadium was just quiet. The energy was gone. And that was it. As we were walking back to the clubhouse, I just thought, "Shit, I'm pitching tomorrow." I didn't have time to think, "Oh my God." I just thought that I had to pitch, and I had to end this.

I went home, went to sleep, and came in the next day and tried to keep everything the same. I didn't want to see the constant coverage and people in the streets doing what they should be doing—showing the excitement of the ballpark. I didn't want to get caught up in that. I knew once the game got started, it was going to be hard to control the adrenaline. I just stayed to myself, stayed to my routine, and got ready to go win a game. Game 7 was as loud as I've ever heard this stadium. When I hit the home run to tie it up—I still haven't heard the stadium as loud as that. I hit first base and was running to second and looked out at the bleachers, and everyone with a beer in their hand was in the air going crazy. I thought we had it at that time. I thought we were going to win. That was the highest moment of my career.

I just grinded through the next couple of innings and left in the seventh with the bases loaded. I don't remember if it was tied or if we were down by one. [The Marlins were up 6–5.] You don't remember the negative stuff. And it got away from us. We go through the whole season, we go through a mini–World Series with Atlanta, we go all the way to Game 7 with Florida after being up 3–1. We felt like we shouldn't even have been playing in that game. We were set to be the World Series favorite, and we didn't get it done.

The other big, memorable game, obviously, was my twenty-strikeout game. It was a day game, a Wednesday that was overcast. There were a lot of empty seats. I think there were fourteen thousand and some change in the stands, but I feel like I've met all forty thousand that were there. I remember warming up, thinking it wasn't going to be a good game. I wasn't throwing strikes in the bull pen. I was dragging, still getting used to the day games. I went out there in the first inning, thinking, "OK, well, here we go, let's see what happens." I struck out the side, but I still didn't feel like I was where I wanted to be. By the third inning, something changed and I definitely felt like I could throw the ball anywhere I wanted it to go. I was throwing my curveball, my slider, and my fastball—I was throwing all three pitches—where I wanted to throw them. By the fourth inning, I knew it was going to be a good day. There wasn't a lot of thought process. I stayed to myself in the dugout, and when I was out there, I was just in one of those zones. They were counting the strikeouts with *K*s in the outfield. I wasn't counting them, but I looked out there and saw a bunch of them at one point, and that was enough for me.

It started raining in the seventh. I remember it came down pretty good for a couple of minutes. I kept thinking the umpire was going to call the game, but he didn't. It was a one-run game, and I knew I hadn't walked anybody. I was just focused on staying aggressive and throwing strikes. After the rain, I was slipping seven, eight, nine inches when I landed and the ball was still going where I wanted it to go. It was just one of those days. I was never an accuracy and control guy, and there I was slipping nine inches and the ball was still going where I wanted. Everyone says about the fist pump when the game was over, "You knew you had the strikeout record, you did the fist pump." I was fist pumping because it was my first complete game and I didn't walk anybody. I hit [Craig] Biggio on a curveball, but I knew I didn't walk anybody. It was the only game that year where I didn't walk anybody. It was probably the only game of my career where I didn't walk anybody.

It's a special thing here. I've been here half my life, and I think the fans feel like they watched me grow up. I've had good years and horrible years and injured years, but when it comes down to it, I'm just a person like they are, and I think they know that. I have a cool job, but I have ups and downs like anyone. My son is growing up here, and hopefully, when I'm done pitching, he and I will be out in the stands watching the Cubs play at Wrigley Field.

PREFACE
BY FORMER U.S. SUPREME COURT
JUSTICE JOHN PAUL STEVENS

U.S. Supreme Court Justice John Paul Stevens prepares to throw out the first pitch, September 14, 2005.

U.S. Supreme Court justice Stephen Breyer and I had a brief conversation two days prior to the first game of the 2010 World Series, between the San Francisco Giants and the Texas Rangers.

"I'm rooting for the Giants in the World Series," said Justice Breyer. "I'm from San Francisco. But Giants fans say the name of the team should be the San Francisco Torture because of all the close games the team plays, and finally pulls out for victories."

"Torture?" I said.

"Torture," repeated Breyer.

"I'm from Chicago," I said.

Breyer looked at me for a fairly long moment. "I understand," he said, sympathetically.

I related the above to retired justice John Paul Stevens.

—Ira Berkow

The intimation, to be sure, was regarding the Cubs. Brother Breyer was aware of the Cubs' history, all right, the franchise that hadn't won a pennant since 1945 and hadn't won a world championship since 1908.

The Cubs television announcer Jack Brickhouse once remarked, "Well, anyone can have a bad century." I suppose it's true. It's a long time to have that kind of luck.

I'm a Cubs fan and have been since I was seven years old. As I write this, I am ninety years old. As a boy in Chicago I tried to listen to all the games I could on the radio. I had done that for two or three seasons, from 1927 to 1929, before I ever saw a game. I got hooked on listening to Hal Totten announce the Cubs games at home on WMAQ and Pat Flanagan, the WBBM announcer, who did the games when the Cubs were on the road, using the ticker-tape approach. You learn later when there was a delay in the transmission and the batter fouled off an inordinate number of pitches before the transmission was restored and he got a hit or made out.

The first game I ever went to was the opener of the 1929 World Series, Cubs versus Philadelphia A's, in Wrigley Field. I was nine years old. I was so excited. I had been following the team on the radio all season, and the Cubs had such powerful hitters. I was sitting behind home plate with my father, and that was the game in which Howard Ehmke, the A's pitcher, established the World Series record of thirteen strikeouts in a game. I had never *heard* of Howard Ehmke before this. He was near the end of his career and was a journeyman pitcher by then, and Connie Mack, the manager of the A's, surprised everyone by starting him. He beat us, 3–1. It was a tragedy for me, at my young age, my Cubs heroes going down in defeat like this. They went on to lose the Series, four games to one, which included Game 4 in Philadelphia when they were ahead

8–0 and the A's scored ten runs in the bottom of the seventh to win 10–8!

One of my heroes on that Cubs team was the outfielder Kiki Cuyler, a good hitter and excellent base stealer, but even more important for me, according to family legend he was a distant relative of ours. I've never been able to prove that in fact he was. But all the Cubs were heroes to me. Rogers Hornsby was a great hitter, Charlie Grimm a fancy-fielding first baseman, and they had those three outstanding pitchers, Guy Bush, Pat Malone, and Charlie Root. And the three fine outfielders, Cuyler; Riggs Stephenson, a steady batter; and Hack Wilson, who played center field, was a home-run slugger and made shoestring catches. Of course, when he missed, the ball would roll back to the center-field fence.

My dad also took me to the third game of the World Series in 1932, the Cubs' home opener in the Series against the Yankees after the first two games had been played in Yankee Stadium. That was the game when, in the fifth inning, Babe Ruth hit a home run into the center-field bleachers after he was alleged to have pointed, or called his shot. Well, I'm not sure he was calling his shot, but I can definitely say that he was pointing with his bat to the center-field scoreboard. I was sitting in the stands about fifteen rows up from third base. I know that Guy Bush, who wasn't pitching that afternoon, was taunting Ruth from the Cubs' dugout and came out of the dugout to razz him. I don't know if Ruth was saying to Bush that he was going to hit one out of the park or that he was going to knock Bush to the moon. But he definitely pointed, and he hit the next pitch out of the ballpark.

You know, I still have the scorecard of that game, framed and hanging on a wall in my chambers. The Yanks won that game, as it turned out, and, unfortunately, swept the Series from the Cubs, four games to none.

As I grew older and began my law career, I was away from Chicago a great deal and didn't follow the team as closely as I did as a kid. But I've always remained a fan—some loyalties don't just die hard, sometimes they don't die at all—and I've gone through one disappointing season after another in recent years.

As you mature, other things in life tend to hold your interest, and it seems that even when you are anticipating the bad news, it doesn't become catastrophic, year after year.

But I admire how Cubs fans continue to come out to the ballpark and root for the team, and often they stay even after the game, usually games the Cubs have won—they're motivated by any success of the team, they do demonstrate a lot of spirit but know that in the end it is just a game.

And yes, I think the ballpark has a lot to do with the avid fandom. I know that the ballpark has been designated a national landmark by the Illinois Historic Preservation Agency. The citation for such a landmark reads that it must be a place where "significant historical events occurred, where prominent Americans worked or lived . . . or that are outstanding examples of design or construction." I think all those elements apply to Wrigley Field. It is an inspiring ballpark; a lot of dramatic events indeed took place there. And it is beautiful. It's a very special place.

The ballpark has changed some since I first went there to see a game in 1929, when I was nine years old—there are stadium lights now, and there

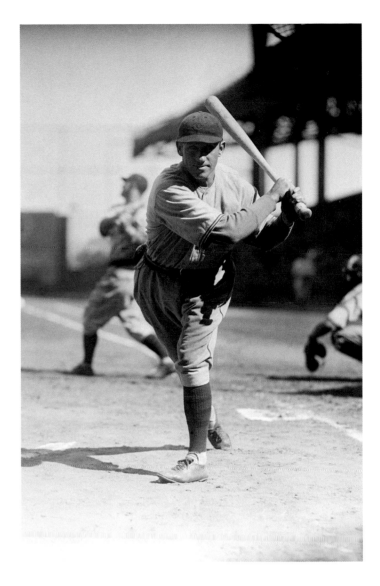

Cubs outfielder Kiki Cuyler, 1932.

are more seats across the street from left and right field—but it basically looks the same, the ivy on the outfield walls, the symmetry, the feel of it. It does stand the test of time.

I know there was a big controversy about whether Wrigley Field should have lights. Every major-league park had lights except Wrigley Field. I know it was Phil Wrigley's contention that baseball should be a day game, but that wasn't in tune with the times. Night games are absolutely right. So many people can't attend day games. The story goes that when some people attended day games, they told their bosses they were going to their grandmother's funeral. And if the television cameras

Whether that fan went into hiding after that game, I don't know, but I do know that the Florida governor at the time, Jeb Bush, jokingly said he'd give the fan sanctuary in Florida.

I had been asked if there was anything in the Constitution to explain the history of the Cubs' failure to win a championship after so many years, and I can honestly report that I haven't bumped into it yet. But I plan to check.

I once had a brief conversation with President Obama about our Chicago backgrounds and him being a White Sox fan and me a Cubs fan. I think he found it curious that I was a South Sider, like him, but not a fan of the South Side White Sox and a supporter, instead, of the North Side Cubs. But when I was growing up and listening to the games on the radio, the Cubs had good teams and were in the first division all the time. The White Sox had poor teams. Since I followed the Cubs on the radio, geography did not make a difference.

When I was asked to throw out the first pitch for the game of September 14, 2005, in Wrigley Field, I had to really prepare. I was eighty-five years old and hadn't thrown a baseball in quite a while. I had played a little in my youth. I had played second base for a team called the Texaco Oilers during a summer job in Delavan, Wisconsin, while I was in college. But now the first time I tried to throw a ball in Washington, it went only about halfway to the plate. I couldn't believe it. Well, I had a law clerk who played baseball in college, and the two of us went to the Court's gymnasium and practiced throwing the baseball. I also practiced with my daughter Sue, who played on her high school team. I took it seriously.

When I went out to the mound at Wrigley Field, wearing a Cubs jersey with the name Stevens on the back, I pretended that I was an outfielder trying to prevent a runner on third from scoring after a long fly. When I made the pitch, it was a ball, not a strike, high and inside to a right-handed batter and high and outside to a left-handed batter, but it got to the plate.

I know Cubs fans are always wondering, can the Cubs win a National League pennant or the World Series in their lifetime? Can they do it in mine? I certainly think so. Whether they will or not is the question, of course. But I'm optimistic. I guess being a Cubs fan means you have to retain optimism. Next year is always going to be *the* year.

scanned the stands, they ducked down or covered their faces with their scorecards.

I was following the Cubs in 2003 when they got so close to winning the pennant, five outs away in the sixth game of the play-offs against the Florida Marlins. That's when Steve Bartman reached out to try for the foul ball to prevent Moisés Alou, the Cubs' left fielder, from catching the ball. And then the Marlins went on a hitting spree. The Cubs lost that game and the seventh game the next night. It was a real disappointment. I've always believed that that made the difference in the game: If Alou had caught that ball, the Cubs would have gone on to the World Series. I know Cubs fans were so upset that, after the season, that foul ball was blown up in a "ceremony" in Harry Caray's restaurant in Chicago.

INTRODUCTION
THE BOY, THE MAN, AND THE BALLPARK

One bright blue and gold summer morning in 1971, I stood behind the batting cage in Wrigley Field in Chicago in my official capacity as a thirty-one-year-old sportswriter while the Cubs in their home white uniforms took batting practice. I was wearing a sport coat and sunglasses and wielding a notebook and pen. It was all a disguise: I was faking it, for I was again eleven years old and I knew that at any moment one of those dreaded blue-uniformed ushers with epaulets and a cop's hat and scuffed black shoes would escort me out of there by the scruff of the collar.

That scene had played out numerous times during my childhood on the West and North sides of the city, when my friends and I would sneak into the ballpark (when workers' eyes were elsewhere, we'd slip through the vendors' gate, or slide down an ice-laden chute that stuck out like a long tongue from a beer truck through a ground-floor stadium window, or scale a turnstile, or blend angelically into a church group getting off a bus) and, once in, sneak down to the box seats at game time. We might be in those seats for an inning or so when—oh, oh, here he comes! "You kids got tickets for them there seats?"

That summer morning in 1971 was among my early experiences of being in Wrigley Field as a professional journalist, and one in which, gratefully, an usher didn't suddenly appear to check my nonexistent ticket stub. I had carefully tucked my baseball writers' pass in my pocket—I was then writing for Newspaper Enterprise Association, a feature syndicate based in New York, where I lived—and I was official. I stood there taking in the beautiful old ballpark, from the sweep of the double-decker stands, to the pennants of the major-league teams flying, like the flags at Camelot, on the rooftop circling the stands and on the great green and white, hand-operated scoreboard above the bleachers in center field, to the lush ivy-covered outfield walls to the striking redbrick low wall that separated the box

seats from the emerald ball field that, now, nearly sparkled in the sunlight.

Growing up, I was hardly aware of how special the park was—it was then just a place to try to see a major-league ball game for free. But it would eventually earn landmark status—any changes would have to be approved by the city council!—and would be widely known as one of the most extraordinary sports stadiums in the world, renowned by architects, landscapers, and laymen alike for its aesthetic design, its graceful symmetry, its pure beauty. "What I've always loved about Wrigley Field," said the noted Chicago architect Sheldon Schlegman, "is its intimacy. Anywhere you sit in the park—the bleachers, the grandstand, anywhere—you feel you're close to the field, which adheres to when it was built, when ballparks were constructed on a small scale. And it's nestled in a real neighborhood, in the middle of small homes and apartment buildings, not in some suburb with a sea of parking around it. It has retained its century-old charm; it's a magical place."

And while the Cubs, who have played in the ballpark continuously since 1916 (the park was built in 1914 for a Federal League team that became, like the league, defunct), had not played in a World Series since 1945 and had not *won* a World Series since 1908 ("Well," said the ebullient former Cubs broadcaster Jack

Brickhouse, "anyone can have a bad century"), I still followed them with unwavering, if often despairing, interest.

In fact, from 1947—the awakening of my baseball consciousness—to 1966, the Cubs established the unenviable record of finishing in the second division for twenty consecutive seasons (that is, in the bottom four of the eight-team National League from '47 to '61 and in the bottom five of the expanded ten-team league from '62 to '66) and generally finding themselves in the basement for many of those years.

One may wonder what harm following a team that invariably loses could do to the psyche, but in looking back I'd like to think it provided a dollop of reality, for as Shakespeare (perhaps a typical Cubs fan, if he were alive now) noted, "As flies to wanton boys are we to the gods; they kill us for their sport."

Of course, the mass of Cubs fans have not been done in, as far as I can tell, but they have had to deal with the incessant vagaries and vicissitudes of an unpredictable world. Even in later years, when the Cubs looked like they were going to triumph in

Batting practice, 2009.

A Cubs fan shows his support as the Cubs take on the Florida Marlins at Dolphin Stadium on September 27, 2007.

the play-offs, teetering on the verge of advancing to a World Series, some untoward bolt from the heavens seemed to ultimately stymie them. "Wait," cries the ever-optimistic Cubbie follower, "till next year." "Or," cries the ever-pessimistic Cubs fan, "the year after!"

When I was a boy in the 1940s, I knew that the Cubs had won sixteen pennants going back to 1876, their charter year in the National League. And I knew that the Yankees were making their move to top that record. When the Yankees won their fifteenth pennant in 1949, I hoped that would be the end of their string and that maybe the Cubs could add one or two in the coming years. That, of course, didn't happen. The Yankees won number sixteen in 1949 and seventeen in 1950. To add insult to injury, they went on to win in '51, '52, '53, '55, '56, '57, '58, '60, '61, '62, '63, and '64. Each of those early succeeding seasons was a twist of the knife in the Cubs fan's heart. After a while, one stopped paying attention. The cold fact is, however, that after the 2010 season, the number of Yankee pennants had risen to forty. And the ruthless—with or without Ruth—Yankees had captured their twenty-seventh World Series. The Cubs, meanwhile, were still stuck at just a pair of world championships.

George Will, the inveterate Cubs fan, Illinoisan, and conservative political Washington columnist, had written, "Liberals are temperamentally inclined to see the world as a harmonious carnival of sweetness and light, where goodwill prevails. . . . Conservatives (and Cubs fans) know better. Conservatives know that the world is a dark and forbidding place where most new

knowledge is false, most improvements are for the worse . . . and an unscrupulous Providence consigns innocents to suffer."

I read this in the early 1970s and quoted it in an article, and a Cubs fan living on Long Island disagreed with Will in a letter: "The central tenet of liberalism is the perfectibility of man . . . that society will be improved, that tomorrow will be better, that progress is inevitable. . . . Only if you believe that, can you be a Cubs fan."

Whichever side one comes down on, it is irrefutable that, win or lose, fans from all over the country travel to "the Friendly Confines"—as Ernie Banks, one of the greatest of Cubs ("Mr. Cub," as he came to be known), had called Wrigley Field—to watch and cheer. The now forty-one-thousand-plus seating capacity is almost always filled, with added standing-room-only adherents, many of whom from coast to coast had become fans when Chicago's WGN became the first television superstation, in 1978, and broadcast Cubs games via satellite. Until night arc lights were installed in the ballpark in 1988, Cubs games were sometimes the only form of sports entertainment on television during weekday afternoons from Maine to California. And since most of the Cubs games are still played during the daytime, many viewers around the nation remain or become Cubs fans.

The adage "No cheering in the press box" is, generally, firmly embraced by sportswriters. That is, you're a journalist first, a fan far, far second, if at all. If you're going to write fairly and objectively, as is the goal of most serious professionals, then you don't allow—or, surely, shouldn't allow—prejudices to cloud your observations. Covering a game should be like covering a fire, or an election, or a PTA meeting. Write what's there, not what you wish were there. And for all these years, while my heart said "Cubs," my head said, "Everyone gets their proper due." In the end, I hoped that what the great essayist E. B. White once wrote pertained to me: "All writing slants the way a writer leans, and no man is born perpendicular, although many men are born upright." Yet inevitably I kept a sly, if jaundiced, eye on the intrigues of the Cubs. How could I not?

While I was standing behind the batting cage that long-ago morning with the hitters going through their paces, jumping in and out of the cage to take their hacks, crack of the bat after crack of the bat echoing in the park, a ball that a hitter let pass from the batting-practice pitcher rolled under the netting of the cage and to my feet. I picked it up.

The ball was still white but stained brown and green in spots, from the several times it was slugged and had bounced in the dirt and hopped in the grass. The red stitching stood out almost sensually to my touch. For some unaccountable reason, I smelled it. Pungent to the core. There is a distinct muskiness to the tanned horsehide of a baseball. Smell being one of the greatest memory triggers, I was easily transported several yards into the milling stands and twenty years back to the moment when I obtained my first big-league baseball.

Strange how tight a grip baseball has on one's boyhood, or perhaps even girlhood, though I feel I can speak with more authority to the former. Even now, with basketball and soccer, particularly, growing in popularity for kids, baseball remains a powerful force of imagery and aspiration for young people. You can see them still flock to the ballparks, and there is no dearth of pitchers and catchers and shortstops in the youth leagues and high school teams. Posters of home-run hitters and strikeout aces still cover the bedroom walls of the starry-eyed.

Fans in the Wrigley Field bleachers, sometimes referred to—affectionately by the locals, less so by the opposition— as "The Bleacher Bums."

Cubs players Stan Hack (left), Billy Jurges (second from right), and Phil Cavarretta (far right) welcome former teammate and new manager of the Pittsburgh Pirates, Billy Herman, back to Wrigley Field in 1947.

In recent years, the influx of girls and women to baseball and softball has added millions to this panoply. Among the fans on a given day or night at Wrigley Field, the males might even be outnumbered by the females, dressed in bikini tops or furs, depending on the way the desultory wind is blowing from nearby Lake Michigan. From an upper-deck seat on a clear day—beyond the three-story apartment buildings with roof seating for games across from the park on Waveland and Sheffield avenues and, farther in the distance, the high-rise buildings along Lake Shore Drive—the great shimmering lake, plied by sailboats, may come into view.

Baseball fan and insightful humor writer James Thurber once allegedly declared that "the majority of American males put themselves to sleep by striking out the batting order of the New York Yankees." That wasn't one of my dreams—altogether. Growing up in Chicago, I had other notions, of hitting a baseball over the ivy-covered walls of Wrigley Field and onto the adjoining Waveland Avenue (or busting one into the right-center-field alley in the South Side Comiskey Park—but the more austere White Sox park never held for me the allure that "the Friendly Confines" did). Of course, I felt certain that if called upon I could perform double duty and stride in from the bull pen and strike out the batting order of the Yankees. (My dream included a Cubs-Yankees World Series, a very far-fetched idea, to be sure, yet the two teams actually played in the World Series in 1932 and again in 1938—the latter was the Cubs' second-to-last appearance in the so-called Fall Classic—with the vexatious Bronx Bombers winning both in forlorn four-game sweeps.)

I didn't become a major-league ballplayer, though I've spent close to half a century on major-league ball fields—*before* the game. I became a sportswriter and sports columnist, and when the batting cage was rolled away and the game began, I repaired to the press box. I had no problem with this, no lingering regrets. Major-league ball playing was for other people. They had their skills, and I, I'd like to believe, had mine.

Even before the conclusion of my North Side Sullivan High School baseball career, which had its ever-so-brief moments of actually muddling through, I had gone beyond, as the Bard wrote, "my salad days, when I was green in judgment." My judgment seemed to gradually improve as I advanced in age—trying to hit the darting curveball (as well as endeavoring to throw one) helped considerably in this regard. And it gave me added appreciation and respect for the special skills of those I would cover as a writer.

But on that summer day in 1971, I cradled the ball in my hand and recalled that other summer day, in 1951. The day before, my friends and I had fought in the autograph jungle under the cool stands as our Cubs paragons of those days—Andy Pafko, Hank Sauer, Phil Cavarretta, Roy Smalley, Dutch Leonard, Twig Terwilliger, Randy "Handsome Ransom" Jackson, and the ambidextrous Native American pitcher with the improbable name that we all memorized and loved to roll off our tongues, Calvin Coolidge Julius Caesar Tuskahoma McLish, nicknamed, unaccountably, "Buster"—emerged like gods from the clubhouse, big and self-assured and leathery-tanned, hair slicked and redolent of Wildroot Cream-Oil. It was a team that would wind up in eighth place that year, once again, but they were big leaguers, and our heroes. Last in the National League, but first in our hearts.

Roy Johnson, whom everyone called Hardrock, appeared. He was a tough-looking, craggy-faced coach, but pigeon-toed, which

gave away the humor under his gruff veneer. He was in a hurry, he said, and had no time to sign. I continued in hot pursuit. Maybe he'd change his mind. No, no, he persisted. In desperation he said, "Come to the park tomorrow, kid, and I'll give you a ball," slamming his car door a millimeter from my nose.

I believed him. My friends were much too sophisticated. "He was just givin' you the slip, dope." Hardly able to wait for the first crack of dawn through the window shade, I did not fall asleep easily that night.

Armed with my lunch—the usual soft fruit my mother packed carving a soggy hole in the bottom of a brown paper bag—I was off to Wrigley Field with my friends. They poked little jokes, even up to the time I left them in the grandstand (our stealthy assault on the box seats would come later). I ran down through the shadowy stands as the park began to fill, past vendors hawking peanuts, past the steamy hot dogs broiling succulently on portable grills.

I descended to the short, redbrick barrier along the first-base line. Straight out, maybe ten yards away, was No. 42, Hardrock

A quartet of Chicago Public League Sullivan High School outfielders, with sophomore Ira Berkow second from left (spring, 1955). "While the high school was located just some three miles north of Wrigley Field, the team demonstrated on more than one occasion that it was somewhat farther than that from the major leagues," reported the author.

Johnson, whacking fungoes into the bright blue sky. I watched a baseball drop through the clouds, momentarily obscuring part of the Baby Ruth billboard atop the building across the street, get lost momentarily in the white shirts in the sun-splashed bleachers, and finally disappear silently into the dark outstretched glove of a fielder in front of the flora on the outfield wall.

"Mr. Hardrock, sir," I called through cupped hands. No answer. I called again: "You promised me a ball yesterday, Mr. Hardrock, sir." *Whack* went another soaring fungo. "Just a dirty old ball, Mr. Hardrock," I pleaded. The few adults seated nearby tittered.

I'm not certain how long I kept this up, several minutes probably. Soon there was the predictable yank at the collar. I was explaining the situation to the grim usher when there arose this

great, throaty rumble: "Hey, kid!" I turned, and Hardrock Johnson tossed me a ball in a long, underhand motion. Up the stairs I flew.

My several pals all wanted to see the ball—slightly smudged but who cared!—and I showed my possession to them, one by one, with me holding the ball tightly. That finished, the ball created an uncomfortable but wholly welcome—and secure—bulge in the right front pocket of my jeans. Home, I fondled the hard ball with the bumpy seams. I inspected the dirt and grass stains closely, the Spalding trademark in a small drawn baseball, the stars etched alongside OFFICIAL BALL, NATIONAL LEAGUE, and the signature of Ford C. Frick, the league president. I smelled the intoxicating horsehide aroma of the ball—a scent that had not changed twenty years later, that has not changed in one hundred years.

My friends offered numerous suggestions on how to get the ball clean as new. The one that sold me was to put it in milk. I immersed the ball in a large bowl of milk for two days, periodically coming by and rolling it around with my finger to make sure no patch was left unmilked.

When I finally removed the ball, it had turned a sickly yellow. I mounted the ball on a shelf in my bedroom for a while. But eventually I took it out to play with it in nearby, narrow Independence Park. Soon, one end came unstitched and grew a flappy tongue, and in time, the whole cover came off and the ball was reduced to a sphere of string. I taped it up and we played with it a little while longer, until it seemed to just disintegrate into nothingness.

At the batting cage now, I felt the red ridges against the smooth, off-white horsehide. It was a ball that had been pretty well pummeled, a ball that I knew would have soon been discarded. But not by me. I slowly tossed the ball into the air a couple of times, smelled it again. Then I casually squeezed the ball into the pocket of my slacks, and went up to the press box. . . .

There is an addendum to this particular Wrigley Field story.

In early April 1986, I read a short obituary in *Sporting News* that Roy "Hardrock" Johnson, age ninety and living in a nursing home in Scottsdale, Arizona, had died. I admit it—this hardboiled sportswriter grew emotional as he read the news. And my thoughts inevitably returned to that summer morning when I was eleven years old and begged Hardrock Johnson to make good on his promise to give me a baseball—and he did!

The obituary related that, after his coaching career with the Cubs, Johnson had become a scout for the team in the Southwest. I called around and got the phone number of his wife, Fanetta.

She was eighty-six, and her voice sounded clear over the long-distance wires from Scottsdale to Manhattan.

"Some people called him Hardrock because he used to work the pitchers so hard as a coach," she said, "but most people called him Grumpy, including me and our daughter and even our grandchildren. But living with Roy was wonderful. We were always laughing. He had that grumpy look, and sometimes his temper was short, but usually it didn't mean anything."

The couple was from Haileyville, Oklahoma. To avoid becoming a coal miner like his father, Roy Johnson first became a prizefighter. It wasn't long before he understood that this was as tough a way to earn a living as digging coal, and turned to baseball, and pitching. He was a big leaguer for one season, with Connie Mack's last-place Philadelphia A's of 1918. *The Baseball Encyclopedia* attests that Johnson won one game and lost five.

Fanetta Johnson recalled how Roy would tell her about pitching to Babe Ruth, who was then still primarily a pitcher but making a reputation as a slugger with the Boston Red Sox. "Roy said that Mr. Mack told him, 'This guy can hit,'" recalled Mrs. Johnson. "He said, 'Don't give him anything. Make him bite. Or walk him if you have to.' Roy threw and the Babe hit the ball four hundred feet into the last row of the bleachers. Roy said, 'It might have cleared the Bunker Hill Monument, but at least I didn't walk him.'"

After 1918, Johnson spent many years in the minor leagues in a classic itinerant baseball life—playing, coaching, and then managing, in towns like Bisbee, Arizona; Bayard, New Mexico; and Ottumwa, Iowa. In 1935 he was promoted to be a coach with the Cubs.

"Roy loved to work," said Mrs. Johnson. "He was going out with his cane and sitting in a beach chair to scout high school and college games until just a year or so ago. And, you know, when he died he still had his teeth."

"Still had his teeth," I repeated. "That's nice, that's very nice." And I meant it.

ABOVE: The Cubs and the Los Angeles Dodgers line up at Wrigley Field before Game 1 of baseball's National League Division Series in Chicago, October 1, 2008.

FOLLOWING SPREAD: View of Wrigley Field from Murphy's Bleachers following a home run by Sammy Sosa, 2003.

PRESIDENT BARACK OBAMA AND THE CUBS

Barack Obama, then the Democratic nominee for president of the United States, in an ESPN interview, August 20, 2008:

INTERVIEWER: Who would you root for in a Cubs-Sox World Series?

OBAMA: Oh, that's easy. White Sox . . . You go to Wrigley Field, you have a beer, beautiful people up there. People aren't watching the game. It's not serious. White Sox, that's baseball. South Side.

(Obama has spent most of his adult life living on Chicago's South Side, still has his home there, and has been a Sox fan for many years. After the ESPN interview was aired and reprinted in newspapers, Cubs fans were irate, and blogs and letters and calls to talk shows tumbled forth.)

On June 18, 2010, Ira Berkow met President Obama at a baseball game in Nationals Park in Washington DC in which the Washington Nationals played host to the Chicago White Sox. Berkow and President Obama, wearing a White Sox cap, conversed on a range of matters.

Berkow asked, "Mr. President, I'd hate to pass up this opportunity, but I'm writing a book about Wrigley Field and wonder if you'd comment on it, and the Cubs."

President Obama, smiling, said politely, "I'm going to have to pass. If I comment on Wrigley Field and the Cubs, it'll only get me in trouble."

President Barack Obama throwing out
the first pitch at the All-Star Game held in
Busch Stadium, St. Louis, July 14, 2009.

1914–1929

TINKER to EVERS TO ALEXANDER THE GREAT

While a segment of the baseball world, and beyond, continues to consider the Cubs' turn-of-the-twentieth-century double-play combination of Tinker to Evers to Chance particularly wondrous, and the three—shortstop Joe Tinker, second baseman Johnny Evers, and first baseman Frank Chance—indeed all entered the Baseball Hall of Fame together in 1946, it is a curious piece of horsehide history that the three never played together and never turned a twin killing, as the sometime ballet at second base is called, in Wrigley Field, now home to the Chicago Cubs franchise for nearly one hundred years.

Wrigley Field, or Weeghman Park, as it was known then, wasn't built until 1914, and first it was home to the Chicago Whales in the upstart Federal League, a confederation that lasted just two seasons. The National League Cubs then moved into Weeghman Park, on the corner of Clark and Addison streets on the North Side of Chicago. The Tinker-to-Evers-to-Chance teams played in the old West Side Grounds, a wooden ballpark at Wood, Lincoln, and Taylor streets with a seating capacity of sixteen thousand. This was before outfield bleacher seating, but attendance was added by having fans stand and rim the outfield playing area.

The reason for the uncommon fame of the double-play combination is a melodic triplet written by Franklin P. Adams that first appeared in his column in the *New York Evening Mail* on July 10, 1910. Adams, who was from Chicago, was on his way to see a Cubs-Giants game in the Polo Grounds. The poem is seen through the eyes of a rueful Giants fan suffering because of the Cubs' magical double-play trio. It is titled "Baseball's Sad Lexicon":

> These are the saddest of possible words:
> "Tinker to Evers to Chance."
> Trio of bear cubs, and fleeter than birds,
> Tinker and Evers and Chance.
> Ruthlessly pricking our gonfalon bubble,
> Making a Giant hit into a double—
> Words that are heavy with nothing but trouble:
> "Tinker to Evers to Chance."

While that double-play combo never led the league in double plays in any of the eleven seasons the trio played together (1902–1912), and in only six of those seasons did they each play a full schedule, the three remain in popular culture to the present day, representing excellence, in one form or another, in togetherness. The Adams poem has apparently had a long-lived rhythmic resonance.

The rock band Rush, for instance, listed in the liner notes of their 1993 album *Counterparts* such counterparts as Larry, Curly, Moe—the Three Stooges—and lock, stock, barrel as well as Tinker to Evers to Chance. They've also been referenced on Broadway and in novels, sitcoms, and films, inspiring, among others, the 1949 Frank Sinatra–Gene Kelly film *Take Me Out to the Ball Game*, which included the song "O'Brien to Ryan to Goldberg."

A 1949 poem by Ogden Nash titled "Line-up for Yesterday" pays homage to the three Cubs infielders:

> E is for Evers
> His jaw in advance;
> Never afraid
> To Tinker with Chance.

Only Tinker, in the last year of his career, played for the Cubs in the ballpark that would later be renamed Wrigley Field. But that was in only seven games—four at his old stand of shortstop, two at third base, and one as a pinch hitter—since, at age thirty-six in 1916, it was getting tougher for him to ambulate in the infield. He managed the team that year, his first and only season as field leader for the National League Cubs. Evers also managed the Cubs, twice, both for one year, in 1913 (finishing third, fifteen games behind John McGraw's Giants) and 1921, when he was dismissed before season's end with the club in sixth place. In 1914 Evers was traded to Boston and played for them, and later the Phillies, for several more years, viewing Cubs Park (as Wrigley was named between 1920 and 1926) from a visitor's stance at second base. He did play one game on a Chicago home field again, but it was in Comiskey Park, when he managed the White Sox and at age forty-one put himself into the lineup at second base for one game and went hitless in three at bats. He was dismissed as manager after that season. As for Chance, he went to the Yankees as a player-manager in 1913 and never played in Cubs Park at all.

The Cubs were a dominant team in the first decade of the twentieth century, invariably in contention for the pennant, and won four pennants and two World Series in that time. Their player-manager was Frank Chance, a husky, no-nonsense individual who was nicknamed the Peerless Leader by Ring Lardner, then writing a column for the *Chicago Tribune* and soon to become a national literary figure for his short stories. His stories included semifictional accounts of the baseball players he covered, most famously in "You Know Me Al," which detailed the naïve pretensions of an anonymous, unlettered Cubs and/or White Sox player. But in covering the actual players for the paper, he wrote in the *Tribune* following a rainout in 1910, "Some of the boys went over to the racetrack to do a little donating. In the bunch were Manager Chance,

EVERS, CHICAGO NAT'L

PREVIOUS SPREAD: Cubs first baseman and manager Frank Chance, 1910.

ABOVE: Baseball card of Johnny Evers, Cubs second baseman, 1911.

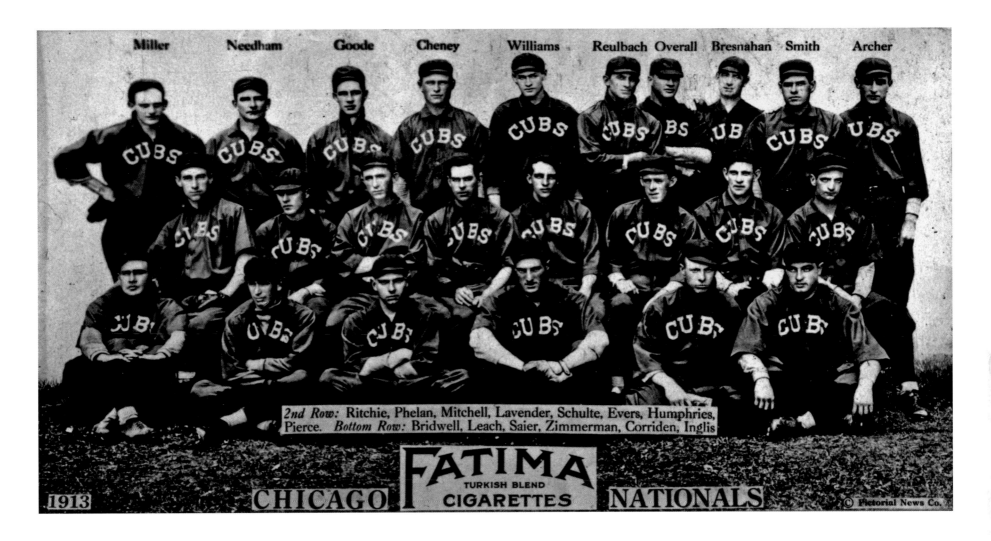

Miller Needham Goode Cheney Williams Reulbach Overall Bresnahan Smith Archer

2nd Row: Ritchie, Phelan, Mitchell, Lavender, Schulte, Evers, Humphries, Pierce. *Bottom Row:* Bridwell, Leach, Saier, Zimmerman, Corriden, Inglis

1913 CHICAGO FATIMA TURKISH BLEND CIGARETTES NATIONALS © Pictorial News Co.

Harry McIntire, King Cole, and 'Turkey' Richie. King didn't intend to donate, saying that he needed all his money to keep his kingdom going in Chicago. Of course there was a poker game."

(In fact, one of the criticisms of Lardner, written by a generally admiring friend, the novelist F. Scott Fitzgerald, was that "whatever Ring's achievement was, it fell short of the achievement he was capable of. . . . However deeply Ring might cut into it, his cake had exactly the diameter of Frank Chance's diamond." This narrow view was essentially refuted by the British novelist Virginia Woolf, who said that Lardner had acute insights into the human condition of America and "writes the best prose that has come our way.")

While Frank Chance was at one end of the storied double-play infield that Franklin P. Adams immortalized, at the other end, at third base in those glory years from 1905 to 1910, was Harry Steinfeldt. Steinfeldt is essentially lost to history, because

although he started several double plays, "Steinfeldt to Evers to Chance" apparently didn't have the ring for Franklin P. Adams that the Tinker-initiated double play did, and Steinfeldt may have missed out on election to the Baseball Hall of Fame because of it.

Steinfeldt, however, ranks well above Tinker in batting average, hitting a lifetime .268 to Tinker's .263, only somewhat below Evers' .278. Chance, at .296, had the most formidable bat in that infield, though only Steinfeldt ever led the league in any batting category, driving in eighty-three runs in 1906. Chance gets his due, having led the NL twice in stolen bases.

In an intriguing sidelight, Tinker and Evers had stopped speaking to each other because of a dispute in September 1905—some five years before the Adams poem. The pair had a fistfight on the field because Evers, who bore the nickname Crab in part because of his less-than-sunny disposition, had taken a cab and left his teammates behind in the hotel lobby. Tinker and Evers

ABOVE: Cubs team photo, 1913.

PAGE 32, LEFT: Frank Chance and his wife, c. 1910.

PAGE 32, RIGHT: Fred Merkle, 1918.

PAGE 33: Johnny Evers, 1913.

did not speak to each other again for thirty-three years, until they were asked to participate in a radio broadcast of the 1938 World Series—Cubs versus Yankees—where they were united in a tearful embrace. (Chance, being the manager during those standout playing years, spoke to the men together only when necessary.)

Evers was one of the smallest men to ever play major-league baseball—and one of the smartest. At five foot nine, Evers broke into baseball weighing about 100 pounds and never weighed more than 130. It was Evers, at second base, who sagaciously alerted the umpires to Fred Merkle's base-running gaffe on September 23 in the 1908 pennant race that ultimately cost the Giants the pennant. Merkle, a rookie and at age nineteen the youngest player in the National League, singled with two out in the bottom of the ninth inning of a 1–1 game. This put men on first and third. The next batter singled, apparently driving in the runner from third. The Giants fans in the Polo Grounds, under the impression that the game was over, poured onto the field to celebrate the victory over the Cubs.

Merkle, also believing the game was over, ran to the Giants' clubhouse and neglected to touch second base. Evers noticed this, retrieved a ball—perhaps the one that had been hit—touched second base, and appealed to umpire Hank O'Day. Since Merkle had not touched the base, the umpire called him out on a force play, rendering that the score from third did not count. The Cubs and Giants ended the season in a first-place tie and had a rematch a few weeks later, and the Cubs won, 4–2, to capture the National League pennant. Merkle eventually played first base for the Cubs,

from 1917 to 1920, finishing a sixteen-year career with a respectable .273 batting average. Normally considered a heads-up player, Merkle had to endure forever the nickname Bonehead for his nonplay in the 1908 game.

The new Chicago park, the one that would eventually become known as Wrigley Field, was constructed in a swift six weeks in 1914 by "Lucky Charlie" Weeghman, who was known as a lunchroom magnate because he owned restaurants and cafeterias. It was designed by Zachary Taylor Davis, who four years earlier had designed Comiskey Park for the White Sox, which had been hailed as a "baseball palace." It also incorporated the "fireproof" building codes that had recently been set into law. West Side Grounds had nearly burned to the ground in the late nineteenth century—ballplayers ran to the outfield fence, where the blaze had started, and beat the fire with their bats—and the devastating Chicago Fire of 1871 was still very much on people's minds.

Weeghman had owned the Federal League Dolphins. When that team, and that league, folded, he formed a syndicate to buy the Chicago Cubs from Charles P. Taft for five hundred thousand dollars. A member of the syndicate was William Wrigley Jr., who began his business career by selling first soap and then baking soda, which led to his manufacturing of chewing gum, which resulted in his great fortune and later to his becoming principal owner of the Cubs. (In selling the soap and soda, he handed out chewing gum as a small premium to his customers. When he discovered that the gum was more popular than the soap or baking soda, he switched gears.) Now, though, Weeghman was in charge, and he quickly moved the Cubs from the dilapidated West Side Grounds to Weeghman Park, and hired and then fired as manager the last vestige of the Cubs' double-play triumvirate, the paperhanger's son from Muscotah, Kansas, Joe Tinker. Tinker had managed the Whales for its two seasons of existence, but apparently the new owners wanted, as the euphemism has it, to go in a different direction.

The Cubs were looking forward to the kind of success they had enjoyed ever since they were one of the eight charter franchises of the National League, which was founded in 1876. From their inception to their entry into the new ballpark on the North Side (and under such names as, in the beginning, the White Stockings, then the Colts, the Orphans, and from 1902, because newspaper headlines noted the many young players on the team, the Cubs), they won ten pennants—in 1876, 1880, 1881, 1882, 1885, 1886,

three straight from 1906 to 1908, and 1910. They won the World Series in 1907 and 1908, but lost a disappointing and humiliating six-game series in 1906 to the Chicago White Sox—the only time the two teams met in a Subway Series.

The Cubs had captured the pennant in 1906 by winning 116 games in their 154-game regular-season schedule (a record number of wins that was tied only by the 2000 New York Yankees, in a 162-game schedule) and were twenty games ahead of John McGraw's second-place Giants. In that 1906 season the White

OPPOSITE: William Wrigley, owner of the Chicago Cubs, 1926.

TOP: James A. Gilmore, president of the Federal League with Cubs president Charles Weeghman, 1914.

BOTTOM: Game 2 of the 1907 World Series at West Side Grounds in Chicago. The Cubs defeated Detroit, 3–1.

ADRIAN C. ANSON.
ALLEN & GINTER'S
RICHMOND. Cigarettes. VIRGINIA

Sox were known as the Hitless Wonders for their anemic .228 team batting average (the Cubs as a team batted .262). But star Sox pitchers Ed Walsh, Nick Altrock, and Doc White proved too great an obstacle for the Cubs to surmount.

During their early years, the Chicago National League team had boasted some great players, including outfielders Mike "King" Kelly and Hugh Duffy; pitchers John Clarkson, Al Spalding, and Mordecai "Three Finger" Brown; as well as Adrian "Cap" Anson, first baseman and manager, who is widely regarded as the greatest player of the nineteenth century. Anson was by most accounts a hidebound man. Upon seeing Fleet Walker, an African American catcher for the Syracuse team of the International League, which Anson's club was facing in an exhibition game in 1888, Anson shouted to the umpires, "Get that nigger off the field!" From that point, and for nearly the next sixty years, until Jackie Robinson joined the Brooklyn Dodgers in 1947, there was erected an invisible and insidious color barrier in organized baseball.

In 1917, the Cubs were hoping—expecting—to climb back into the pennant race under new manager Fred Mitchell, the sixth Cubs manager in six years. One of the reasons for their optimism, besides center fielder Cy Williams, who the season before had led the NL in homers with twelve, was Jim "Hippo" Vaughn, a six-foot-four, 215-pound left-hander. Vaughn had led the pitching staff with seventeen wins in 1916 and was among the league's strikeout leaders.

Their optimism soon turned to pessimism. Williams hit only five home runs, and his teammates followed suit at bat. The Cubs finished in fifth place, twenty-four games behind the pennant-winning Giants. But left-hander Vaughn remained a stellar hurler, winning twenty-three games.

At once the brightest and most heartbreaking game for the Cubs that season came on May 2 in Wrigley Field, before a sparse crowd of some thirty-five hundred, when Vaughn and right-hander Fred Toney of the Reds hooked up for one of the most memorable pitching duels in baseball history. Each pitched a no-hitter for nine innings. Going into the Reds' tenth, it was 0–0. Vaughn weakened to the degree that, with one out, Larry Kopf slapped a soft roller between the second and first basemen into right field for the game's only hit. The next batter flied to center, but Williams couldn't hold on to the ball and

dropped it for an error. Now there were men on first and third. Then Jim Thorpe, the great gold-medal-winning decathlon athlete of the 1912 Olympics, came to bat. He tapped a pitch that bounced high in front of the plate. "Thorpe, who could run, if he couldn't hit major-league curveball pitching, was away like a flash," wrote Warren Brown in his book *The Chicago Cubs*. Vaughn lumbered in to retrieve the ball, looked to see if he could get Thorpe at first base, decided Thorpe was too fleet, and threw home instead to get the advancing Kopf. The throw caught catcher Art Wilson by surprise—he thought the play was to first—and the ball bounced off his chest. Kopf scored the only run of the game. Toney held the Cubs without a hit in the next inning. The Cubs lost, 1–0.

Unfortunately for the Cubs, they had had to play a tenth inning. There has never been another double no-hit game for nine innings in the history of major-league baseball.

"Once again," as Brown noted, "the Chicago Cubs, for better or for worse, had figured in baseball's enduring records."

But great hope sprung for the Cubs over the 1916–17 winter when they purchased the Phillies pitcher Grover Cleveland Alexander, whose hurling prowess had led to his nickname, Alexander the Great, conqueror of National League batters. Alexander, more commonly called Pete or Old Pete, came in the deal that included his battery mate Bill Killefer. In 1917, Alexander had led the NL in wins (thirty), earned run average (ERA), strikeouts, complete games, shutouts, fewest walks per nine innings, and innings pitched. In other words, there was no one like him. But the Phillies couldn't resist the huge bundle of sixty thousand dollars that the Cubs had laid before them.

Alexander opened the 1918 season by winning two of his first three games. For the season, however, there was one problem: Those three were his only games pitched. The United States had entered World War I, and Alexander was one of the numerous major leaguers who were called up for service.

Nonetheless, his departure didn't deter the Cubs' march to a pennant, their first in eight years, and they finished thirteen games ahead of McGraw's Giants. The Cubs' Vaughn led the league in wins with twenty-two and a 1.74 ERA, while shortstop Charlie Hollocher was a paradigm of offense with a .316 batting average.

It was an abbreviated season, because the "work or fight" governmental order halted all baseball right after Labor Day. In July,

secretary of war Newton D. Baker announced that baseball was not an essential occupation. The major leagues, however, were given permission to hold a World Series.

This was also the first time the Cubs would come face-to-face with the Red Sox's ace pitcher, who also happened to be their ace right fielder, though not simultaneously, to be sure. His name was George Herman "Babe" Ruth. Though primarily a pitcher when he came to the Red Sox in 1914—he averaged a 22–10 record for the next three seasons—his prowess with a bat had him moving to the outfield in games when his pitching stint was over.

In 1918, outfielder Ruth—trim and muscular, not the big-bellied player seen later in his career in film clips—tied for the American League lead in homers, with eleven, and led the league in slugging average, .555, while playing in only ninety-five games in the field. Pitcher Ruth also found time to win thirteen games

(losing seven). A Boston sportswriter named Burt Whitman wrote, "The more I see of Babe, the more he seems a figure out of mythology."

The Red Sox's manager, Ed Barrow, still hadn't decided whether Ruth should continue this double duty or resolve to play just one position. But for the Series, he opted for Ruth on the mound, and Barrow would confine Ruth there almost exclusively in these games. The Series opened in Chicago but not in Wrigley Field. The Cubs' management figured that Comiskey Park, with a seating capacity of 28,800—some 13,000 more than Wrigley Field—would make more money.

Game 1 opened with two left-handers on the mound, Ruth and Vaughn. Ruth allowed just six hits and outpitched Vaughn for a 1–0 victory. The Cubs won Game 2 behind Lefty Tyler but lost Game 3 to the submarine-style right-hander Carl Mays.

All three games were played in Chicago, in an effort to cut down on travel during the war. The crowds at Comiskey Park averaged some twenty thousand a game, more than could have fit into Wrigley Field but still disappointing to the owners—and the players, who would be splitting up slimmer Series shares than they might have in peacetime.

Now the Series moved to Boston. Ruth was on the mound again. The Babe tripled in two runs in the fourth and held the Cubs without a run until the eighth inning, when he gave up two runs to tie the game. In the bottom of the eighth inning, the Red Sox scored an unearned run to go ahead for good, 3–2. In the ninth, Ruth was switched to right field, and Joe Bush held the Cubs scoreless.

Ruth's sixteen scoreless innings against the Cubs, and the thirteen and two-thirds scoreless innings he pitched in the 1916 Series against the Brooklyn Robins (renamed the Dodgers in 1931), established a World Series pitching record of consecutive scoreless innings, exceeding by one the mark held by Christy Mathewson. (It wasn't until forty-three years later, in 1961, when Whitey Ford completed thirty-two consecutive innings pitched in World Series play, that Ruth's record of twenty-nine and two-thirds innings was eclipsed.)

The Cubs lost the Series to the Red Sox, four games to two. It would be eleven years before the Cubs played in another World Series.

Meanwhile, William Wrigley Jr. had purchased most of the Cubs' stock to become principal owner. He would aggressively resurrect the club's fortunes, but not immediately. The Cubs fell into third place in 1919 and into fifth place in 1920—and this despite Alexander returning from the military and winning sixteen games in '19 while leading the league in ERA, with 1.72, and in 1920 leading the league both in wins (twenty-seven) and ERA (1.91).

Disenchanted with the Cubs' play, Wrigley fired manager Mitchell and replaced him in 1921 with Johnny Evers, who himself was replaced after ninety-six games, with the team in sixth place. Bill Killefer became the new manager and witnessed the Cubs ending the season in seventh place. The Cubs moved up to fifth place in 1922 and enjoyed a peculiar highlight. On August 25, at Wrigley Field, with, it seemed, the wind blowing in every direction simultaneously—but mostly out—they beat the Phillies, 26–23. In one inning, the second, the Cubs managed to push

RIGHT: Red Sox slugger Babe Ruth, 1919.

OPPOSITE: Cubs second baseman Rogers Hornsby, 1930.

across ten runs. That, however, was paltry. In the fourth, they scored fourteen.

But wait—the game was hardly over. The Phillies scored eight runs in the top of the eighth and six more in the top of the ninth and had the bases loaded when the last out was made by the Cubs.

The records established that day still stand: most runs in a game (forty-nine), most hits in a game, two clubs (fifty-one: twenty-six for the Phillies and twenty-five for the Cubs). Remarkably, the Phillies used just two pitchers in the game, while the Cubs exploited their bull pen, as it were, and used five.

In 1923, Alexander, at age thirty-six, was still pitching effectively, with a 22–11 record for a team that finished in fourth place. In 1924, he dropped to 12–5 but still was among the league leaders in ERA (3.03), with now a fifth-place team. Despite a lackluster club, attendance rose by one hundred and fifty thousand to just over seven hundred thousand because management had installed bleachers in the outfield. Gabby Hartnett became the first-string catcher for the Cubs, and he would be a major factor for years to come. In 1925, as the Cubs went through three managers—Killefer, Rabbit Maranville, and George Gibson—Alexander won fifteen games, tops for the Cubs, who now plummeted to last place.

To the surprise of many, a manager for the Triple-A Louisville team who had neither played nor managed in the big leagues, Joe McCarthy, was hired by Wrigley to take over the Cubs. Bill Veeck Sr., who had begun his career as a journalist in Louisville and had developed a high opinion of McCarthy, convinced Wrigley to take a chance on him. Some of the Cubs players, scorning McCarthy, labeled him a "busher." McCarthy was undaunted.

Early in the season, McCarthy, who was a strict disciplinarian, had a problem to deal with: Pete Alexander. McCarthy had asked one thing of his players: Be ready to perform in the field. What they did after hours was up to them. Many, like Alexander, were hard drinkers. And Alexander, now thirty-nine, was no longer able to follow a long night with a substantive day. McCarthy called on him, and Alexander couldn't produce. He showed up drunk six days in a ten-day stretch in June. On the twenty-second of the month, with a 3–3 record, the Cubs placed Alexander on waivers, and the Cardinals claimed him. Apparently there was no rancor between manager and pitcher—Alexander was, in fact, heading for a pennant-contending team and, as it turned out, the World Series, where he would become a Cardinals hero.

As time went on, McCarthy would indulge listeners with tales about Alexander. One went like this:

As was customary, the Cubs pitchers had gathered before a series against an opponent that had a player who the Cubs had recently dealt to it. Alexander arrived to the meeting late, sat down, and fell fast asleep.

"We've got to change our battery signs," declared one of the Cubs. He said that when that traded player was on second, he'd be able to signal every pitch to the batter.

Alexander stirred.

"If he was *ever* going to get on second base, McCarthy wouldn't have let him go," said Alexander. Then Old Pete returned to his snooze.

Alexander's shining moment for the Cardinals came in the 1926 World Series, when, in relief, he struck out Tony Lazzeri of the Yankees with the bases loaded in the seventh inning of the seventh game and went on to preserve the win. The strikeout became the centerpiece of a Hollywood film about Alexander, *The Winning Team*, starring a future politician, one Ronald Reagan, as Ol' Pete.

McCarthy's experience with Louisville in the American Association helped him rebuild the Cubs. A castoff from the Giants, Hack Wilson was playing center field in Toledo. McCarthy thought Wilson would be a great addition to the Cubs and promoted him to Chicago. McCarthy also traded with the Indians for Riggs Stephenson, then in the minor leagues, and he and Wilson, along with right fielder Hazen "Kiki" Cuyler, traded from Pittsburgh before the 1928 season, would compose one of the best hitting outfields of all time. In 1926, Wilson led

Rogers Hornsby signing the contract that made him a member of the Chicago Cubs, November 13, 1938, in Chicago. With him are William Veeck (left), president of the Cubs, and William Wrigley Jr. (right), owner of the club.

the league in homers with twenty-one and Stephenson batted .338, as the Cubs managed to climb four notches from the previous season to fourth place.

In 1927, McCarthy plucked another American Association player for the Cubs, this one the shortstop Woody English, who became one of the best at his position. After a strong run at first place for much of the season, the Cubs faltered and finished fourth again. But with the excitement the team generated plus the grandstand being double-decked, 1,159,168 fans streamed into the park, making the Cubs the first National League team to draw more than one million customers.

Things were looking up as the Cubs and McCarthy climbed to third place in 1928, with Wilson again leading the league in homers, with thirty-one. The Cubs finished just four games behind the first-place Cardinals.

The following year, the Cubs made up those four games, and more. It was thought by management that the club needed one more player to give them true pennant possibilities. That one player turned out to be Rogers Hornsby, then player-manager of the Boston Braves, after a great career as player-manager for the Cardinals and the Giants.

Hornsby had won the league batting championship for six straight seasons, with averages from .370 to .424. He was—and, for many, still is—regarded as the best right-handed hitter in baseball history.

Ladies Day at Wrigley Field, 1934.

Wrigley, eager for a winner, opened his pocketbook and purchased Hornsby for one hundred and twenty thousand dollars and five journeyman players, the most ever paid for a player at that time. He didn't disappoint. The Rajah, as Hornsby was called, batted .380 in 1929.

The Cubs, who had begun broadcasting their games on radio in 1925 despite naysayers believing that people wouldn't come to the park when they could listen to the game at home, also instituted Ladies' Day, setting aside one afternoon a week to admit

RIGHT: Cubs fans following updates on the Playograph during the 1929 World Series in Chicago.

OPPOSITE: Cubs right fielder Kiki Cuyler hits a single in the Cubs Wrigley Field opener versus the Pittsburgh Pirates, 1929.

women for free. Both of these additions helped generate more interest in the Cubs. With a strong team that included Hornsby; fancy-fielding first baseman Charlie Grimm; the slugging outfield of Stephenson, Wilson, and Cuyler, each of whom batted in over one hundred runs (Wilson was tops with 159); and Pat Malone leading the league with twenty-two wins and Charlie Root second with nineteen, the Cubs again drew a record crowd, this time of nearly one and a half million.

The Cubs finished ten and a half games ahead of the second-place Pirates and found themselves about to meet the Philadelphia A's in the World Series. Managed by Connie Mack, the A's had run away with the American League pennant, ending up eighteen games ahead of the second-place Yankees. The A's boasted such stars as catcher Mickey Cochrane, first baseman Jimmie Foxx, third baseman Jimmy Dykes, outfielders Al

Simmons and Mule Haas, and pitchers George Earnshaw, Rube Walberg, and Lefty Grove.

Speculation centered on who would be the opening-game pitcher for the A's in Wrigley Field. It was assumed to be one of their three standouts. But Connie Mack stunned everyone. He chose the veteran Howard Ehmke, who at age thirty-five was in his thirteenth big-league season and had pitched a total of just fifty-four innings that year, though compiling a 7–2 record.

About two weeks before the end of the season, Mack called Ehmke into his office. "Howard," he said, "do you have one great game left in your arm?" Ehmke replied, "I think I do." He was right, remarkably so.

As 50,740 stunned fans looked on (Wrigley Field's seating capacity was increased by some 10,000 for the Series with the addition of extra bleachers built on Waveland and Sheffield avenues), Ehmke baffled the Cubs with tantalizing sidearm changes of speed and superb control, setting a new World Series record of thirteen strikeouts. He had a shutout until the ninth inning, when the Cubs pushed a run across. Ehmke gave up eight hits, but only one for an extra base, English's double. The Cubs' Root pitched well, giving up one run in seven innings before Guy Bush relieved and allowed a pair of runs. Final score: A's 3, Cubs 1. (Ehmke's Series strikeout record lasted until 1953, when Brooklyn's Carl Erskine struck out fourteen Yankees.)

The A's took Game 2, 9–3, with Earnshaw and Grove combining to strike out thirteen Cubs, *again*. The Cubs pulled themselves together and won Game 3, 3–1, Bush beating Earnshaw, who still posted ten strikeouts.

Game 4, in Shibe Park, would go down as one of the lamest innings in Cubs—and World Series—history. The Cubs led 8–0 going into the bottom half of the seventh. Cubs pitcher Jack Quinn was sailing along. Then disaster:

Al Simmons hit a home run to lead off the inning. OK, just 8–1.

Next, Foxx singled and Bing Miller hit a fly ball to center, in which Hack Wilson circled and circled and lost the ball in the sun for a base hit. Dykes singled. Foxx scored. OK, just 8–2.

Joe Boley singled, scoring Miller. Yes, just 8–3. George Burns batted for the pitcher Ed Rommel and popped out. One out. Max Bishop singled, scoring Dykes. Well, just 8–4. The slim left-hander Art Nehf now replaced Quinn on the mound for the Cubs. Haas greeted him with a fly ball to center that Wilson again lost in the sun, for a three-run inside-the-park homer. Oh no, now it's 8–7! Cochrane walked. Sheriff Blake replaced Nehf. Simmons singled. Foxx singled, scoring Cochrane with the tying run. And there was still only one out!

Starting pitcher Pat Malone was now hurried in from the bull pen to replace Blake, and the first thing he did was hit Miller with a pitch, loading the bases. Dykes doubled to the left-field wall, Simmons and Foxx scoring. Unbelievably, it was now 10–8, A's! Malone then got Boley to strike out, and Burns, up a second time as a pinch hitter in the inning, also struck out, to end one of the longest and most humiliating innings in Cubs history.

The Cubs went down in order in the top of the ninth, and the game—and essentially the 1929 World Series—was over. Well, not quite. Yes, there was a fifth game, two days later, on October 14, in Philadelphia. Ehmke was on the mound again for the A's in Game

5. He had lost much of his magic; in three and two-thirds innings he struck out no one, gave up six hits, and got the hook from Mack after the Cubs scored two runs. Walberg came in and shut out the Cubs the rest of the way. But Malone was pitching beautifully for the Cubs and had shut out the A's for eight innings. In the ninth, however, the A's put across three runs for a 3–2 win—ending the Series for the hapless Cubs.

Wrigley was incensed by, in his view, the humiliating way the Cubs lost the Series, especially to the "has-been" Ehmke in the first game and then by squandering their leads in the last two. And Wrigley was hardly the only one.

Fingers pointed and changes loomed well before the start of the 1930 season.

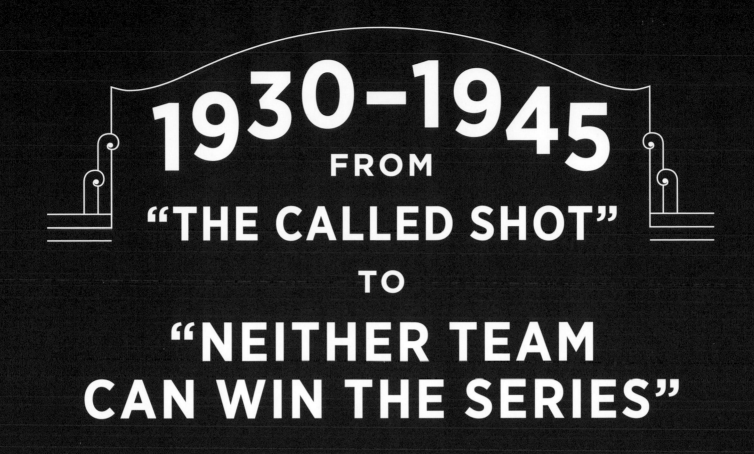

1930–1945

FROM

"THE CALLED SHOT"

TO

"NEITHER TEAM CAN WIN THE SERIES"

All through the winter of 1929 and the spring and summer of 1930, William Wrigley Jr. was seething. The owner of the Cubs believed that the team's manager, Joe McCarthy, had handed the World Series to the A's, four games to one, by making incompetent, if not to say ignorant, field decisions. Wrigley was not only a brilliant chewing gum magnate; he was also a premier second-guesser: How could McCarthy have not prepared better for Game 1, during which Ehmke, a supposedly has-been hurler, not only beat the Cubs but broke a World Series strikeout record? How in Game 4 could they

blow an 8–0 lead into the seventh inning and lose 10–8? How could McCarthy have allowed Hack Wilson to make *two* critical errors on fly balls that he said he lost in the sun in the A's cataclysmic ten-run seventh inning—didn't McCarthy have a better outfielder on the bench after the first error? And how come—? The list went on.

McCarthy knew his days were numbered. Even though the Cubs contended in 1930, with the Cardinals winning the pennant, he was looking around for managerial vacancies. The Yankees were also seeking a new manager—Bob Shawkey was considered just interim—and the Yankees' owners had an opinion of McCarthy that was evidently no longer shared by Wrigley. Nor, it seemed, by Bill Veeck Sr., the general manager, and a legion of muttering Cubs fans. With only about a week to go in the season, Wrigley accepted McCarthy's essentially forced resignation. "McCarthy lacks enough desire for a world championship," Wrigley stated, upon McCarthy's departure. The fact that McCarthy went on to win seven world championships with the Yankees contradicts Wrigley's impetuous analysis.

Rogers Hornsby, the acerbic, slugging, horse-playing second baseman, was named the Cubs' new manager. Hornsby had been player-manager of the Cardinals for two years, leading them to a pennant in his second season, 1926; the Giants for one year, 1927; and the Braves for one year, 1928.

In a surge that saw them win all four of their games behind Hornsby, the Cubs still finished two games behind the Cardinals, for second place.

Hornsby began the 1931 season critical of his players, as usual, and the sniping seemed to sap their energy, especially when they saw their thirty-five-year-old manager—then still considered the greatest right-handed batter of all time—playing one hundred games and hitting .331. The Cubs finished third that season, seventeen games behind the Cardinals. They seemed never in the race.

Warren Brown wrote:

As has been the case of many star ballplayers who have essayed managing, Hornsby was impatient with some of his material. His own playing standards were so high, and some things came so naturally and so easily to him that he was at a loss to understand why others were unable to grasp their lessons and remember them.

As a player and as a manager, Hornsby never failed to speak his mind. Many of the Cubs didn't like that, and while some of them openly resented it, others preferred to sulk and feel very unhappy about it.

One of the players who took a major share of Hornsby's opprobrium was Lewis Robert "Hack" Wilson, the five-foot-six, two-hundred-pound outfielder with an eighteen-inch neck who wore size five and a half shoes. He was built like a beer keg and was as powerful as an ox. In batting practice, he would pick up a handful of dirt and wipe the sides of his pants. "By the time the game started," wrote Bill Veeck Jr. in *The Hustler's Handbook*, "Hack would always look as if he had just delivered a ton of coal."

Though still derided by some fans as "Sunny Boy," for losing the ball in the sun twice in the fateful seventh-inning A's onslaught in the previous year's World Series, Wilson in 1930 had batted .356 and broke the National League record for single-season home runs, with 56—a record that stood for sixty-eight years, until Mark McGwire passed it in 1998—and runs batted in (RBI), with 190, a record that still stands.

In 1931, though he had led the National League in homers for four of the previous five seasons, and in the last two he had led in runs batted in, Wilson's output at the plate dropped with a thud, hitting just .261, with thirteen homers and sixty-one RBIs. What happened?

Over that winter, he recalled, "I drank more heavily than ever, and I argued with my manager"—Hornsby—"and with my teammates." Only thirty-one, Wilson had for years spent a great portion of his off-field activities behind a bottle. If you were looking for Wilson, you could find him either on a playing field or in a bar. And yet how he could hit!

While he would be inducted into the Baseball Hall of Fame, his twelve-year playing career was shortened by those extracurricular activities. When he died, in Baltimore, his hometown, on November 23, 1948, he was forty-eight years old and penniless.

In 1931, Wilson's salary was thirty-three thousand dollars, the highest in the National League. He is said to have made more than a quarter of a million dollars during his major-league career. Yet the funeral expenses were paid after some men in the bars Wilson frequented passed the hat. The gray suit he wore in his coffin was donated by the undertaker.

PAGE 46: Manager Rogers Hornsby receives birthday greetings from his team on April 27, 1932.

PAGE 48: Joe McCarthy, Cubs manager from 1926 to 1930.

PAGE 49: Manager Rogers Hornsby shakes hands with Cubs owner William Wrigley Jr., 1930.

THIS PAGE: Cubs centerfielder Hack Wilson, 1929 (left) and 1930 (right).

A week before his death, Wilson said that his life should serve as an example to youngsters of which road not to travel. "There are many kids in and out of baseball who think that just because they have some natural talent, they have the world by the tail," Wilson said on a *We, the People* radio program over the Columbia Broadcasting System (later called CBS). "It isn't so. In life you need many more things besides talent. Things like good advice and common sense."

In his last season, 1934, he played for Casey Stengel and the Brooklyn Dodgers. In a game against the Phillies in the compact Baker Bowl in Philadelphia, Stengel had come to the mound to remove pitcher Walter "Boom Boom" Beck. Wilson was in right field, his hands on his knees, his head down, exhausted from chasing baseballs hit off Beck. It was very hot, and perhaps Wilson had been out late the night before. Beck didn't want to leave the

game; he argued with Stengel and then flung the baseball, which cracked off the tin fence behind Wilson. Startled, Wilson leaped into action, raced to the fence, picked up the ball, and made a perfect throw to second base. "It was the best play Hack made all year," Stengel said. At season's end, Hack Wilson's days in the major-league sun were over, his batting numbers down to a .245 average, with six homers and thirty RBIs.

In later years, his radio remarks about throwing away talent were printed, framed, and hung in a prominent place on a wall in the Cubs' clubhouse in Wrigley Field, a reminder to the players of today just how far a star can fall.

With Hack having been traded away to St. Louis, Hornsby replaced as manager in August by the affable, banjo-playing first baseman Charlie Grimm, and the excellent Billy Herman installed at second base, in 1932 the Cubs went from second place to first and won the pennant. It began with a fourteen-game winning streak in August under Grimm, whose easy demeanor earned him the nickname Jolly Cholly. Grimm's persona was the reverse of Hornsby's hornets' nest deportment.

The outstanding pitching, led by Lon Warneke (twenty-two wins), Guy Bush (nineteen wins), and Charlie Root and Pat Malone (fifteen each), along with a scintillating double-play combination of the spry, handsome twenty-three-year-old shortstop Billy Jurges and Billy Herman, sparked the Cubs. Jurges, however, missed three weeks in midseason, having been shot by a rejected lady friend.

Jurges was staying in a hotel in Chicago and the woman, Violet Popovich, an attractive young brunette who had dated numerous other baseball players—including Cubs outfielder Kiki Cuyler—and was known as a Baseball Annie, called Jurges from his hotel lobby on the morning of July 6, 1932, and said she wanted to see him.

"I said, 'C'mon up,'" Jurges related years later.

When she came to my room I told her, "I'm not going to go out on any more dates. We've got a chance to win the pennant. I've got to get my rest."

And she pulled a gun out of her purse and started shooting. I was hit three times. In the right chest, once in the back on the right side. Then I grabbed the gun and it went off a third time. A bullet went through the palm of my hand. Then she ran out.

Jurges got help and was taken to a hospital where, he said, "I was bleeding like a pig." He recovered in time to help the Cubs reach the World Series two months later. He also went on to enjoy fifteen more solid seasons in the big leagues. His assailant, who did no jail time when Jurges didn't press charges, soon after the shooting signed a twenty-two-week contract to sing and dance in city nightspots, billed as "Violet (I Did It for Love) Valli—the Most Talked Of Girl in Chicago." There would be a similar incident involving a Cubs player seventeen years later, when Eddie Waitkus took a bullet from a deranged female fan, an obsessed stranger, and it nearly cost him his life.

In 1932, the Cubs went into the World Series against the Yankees, managed now by Joe McCarthy, just two seasons gone from managing the Cubs. The first two games were played in Yankee Stadium, the New Yorkers winning them both, followed by the historic, controversial, and still widely discussed Game 3 in Wrigley Field on Saturday, October 1, played before a crowd of 49,986 (some 10,000 seats had been added—as was the case in the 1929 Series and would be again in the 1935 Series—when temporary bleachers were installed on the streets of Waveland and Sheffield).

There was fierce bench jockeying, particularly by the Yankees. Their focal point was Mark Koenig, who had played shortstop for six years for the Yankees but had been shipped to the minor leagues. In August, the Cubs called him up from the San Francisco Mission Reds to help when Jurges was forced out of the lineup due to his bullet holes.

Koenig was sensational. In thirty-three games he batted .353 and was instrumental with hits that made the difference in late-inning wins for the Cubs. In parceling out Series shares, Cubs players voted Koenig a half share. The Yankees considered this cheap, especially since he had contributed so much to the Cubs' pennant drive. Babe Ruth led the verbal barrage. The fans had learned from the newspapers about the give-and-take of the two teams, and they joined the Cubs in taunting Ruth—"fat man" was probably as nice a sally as the Cubs' dugout mustered in their remarks to the great slugger. In Game 3, Ruth hit a three-run

Ticket for Game 3 of the 1932 World Series game at Wrigley Field, won by the New York Yankees, 7–5.

homer in the first inning off starting pitcher Charlie Root but still didn't silence the Cubs revilers. With the game tied at 4–4 in the fifth inning, Ruth came to the plate again.

Root wound up and threw. Called strike one. Ruth held up one finger. Root wound up and fired again. Called strike two. The Cubs' bench was howling at Ruth. Again Ruth held up a finger.

Warren Brown covered that game for the *Chicago Herald-Examiner* and wrote some fourteen years later:

There are those who will always contend that what the Babe did this third time was point out toward the center field corner, as Root prepared to pitch.

They will contend further that as the pitch came up to him (and in this cannot be contradicted), that Ruth whaled away at it, and the last glimpse anyone in the park had of that baseball was when it dropped over the fence just beyond where the Babe pointed.

That's the legend, and there are those who can add all sorts of flourishes to it.

Whether Ruth pointed at Root, pointed at the fence, or whether he remembered his manners and didn't point at all, but merely indicated that there were two strikes on him and he still had the big one left, is something that will not be debated here. Indeed, it will not be examined any more closely than the claims of *seven* separate persons, outside Wrigley Field after the game, each one exhibiting the baseball which he insisted was the one Ruth hit.

However it be told, or whatever its facts, it was and is a good story. So was the home run.

Charlie Root—whose nickname was Chinski in homage to his tendency to throw close to hitters to discourage them from getting too comfortable in the batter's box—forever disputed Ruth's so-called home-run indication:

Ruth did not point at the fence before he swung. If he had made a gesture like that, well, anybody who knows me knows that Ruth would have ended up on his ass. The legend didn't start until later. I fed him a changeup curve. It wasn't a foot off the ground and it was three or four inches outside, certainly not a good pitch to hit. But that was the one he smacked. He told me the next day that if I'd have thrown him a fastball, he would have struck out. "I was guessing with you," he said.

It has come down in legend as "the called shot." There are paintings now, drawn by people who were not at the game, with Ruth pointing toward center field. There is a film clip of the game in which Ruth makes some kind of hand gesture, but it is murky.

The esteemed sportswriter Red Smith was in the press box

OPPOSITE: Team photo, 1932.

BELOW: Babe Ruth of the New York Yankees hits a home run in the third game of the 1932 World Series against the Cubs at Wrigley Field, October 1, 1932. It was during this game that Ruth gestured with his bat before hitting a home run, giving birth to the legend of the "Called Shot."

that afternoon, covering the Series for the *St. Louis Star-Times*. His paper did not have a Sunday edition, so he wrote a wrap-up for the Monday paper, following Game 4. In his twenty-fourth paragraph, Smith wrote of Ruth's ongoing clashes with the Chicago fans and players. Before the game, fans in left field "pelted him with lemons. But at the plate he still clowned, signaling balls and strikes in mock gestures until he found a pitch that he liked.

Twice he found what he wanted, and twice he smashed the longest drives ever seen in Wrigley Field."

Smith said later that no one in the press box made much of
a stir about a "called shot," and it wasn't until the next day that
some of the New York writers wrote that it had happened. "Ruth
did make a deliberate set of gestures—not a quick, convulsive
one—but it did not occur to me that he was calling his shot," Smith
wrote years later. "Some myths," said Smith, "won't die."

In his biography of Babe Ruth, *Babe: The Legend Comes to
Life*, Robert Creamer wrote that Ford Frick, a sportswriter at
the time—later the commissioner of baseball for Major League
Baseball—who did not attend that game and was a friend and
biographer of Ruth's, some years later asked Ruth about "the
called shot":

———————————

"Did you really point to the bleachers?" Frick asked.

Ruth, always honest, shrugged. "It's in the papers, isn't it?"

**"Yeah," Frick said. "It's in the papers. But did you really
point to the stands?"**

**"Why don't you read the papers? It's all right there in the
papers."**

**Which, Frick said, means he never said he did and he
never said he didn't.**

———————————

Except that in the spring following the '32 Series, as reported
in Jerome Holtzman and George Vass's book *Baseball, Chicago
Style*, Ruth was interviewed by Hal Totten, a pioneer broadcaster in Chicago, and responded differently to a question about
whether he had called the home run.

"Hell, no!" Ruth replied. "Naw, keed, you know damn well I
wasn't pointing anywhere. Only a damned fool would have done
a thing like that. If I'd have done that, Root would have stuck the
ball right in my ear. I never knew anybody who could tell you
ahead of time where he was going to hit a baseball. When I get to
be that kind of fool they'll put me in the booby hatch."

Lost in the haze of the Ruth tale is that the Yankees beat the
Cubs in Game 3, 7–5, and the next day, despite the Cubs building
a 4–1 lead in the first inning and raising fans' hopes for a miracle
comeback in the Series, the Yankees walloped them again, 13–6,
to sweep the Series, four games to none. (For the record, Ruth had

Members of the Cubs and New
York Yankees carry a large
American flag onto the field
during 1932 World Series pregame
ceremonies at Wrigley Field.

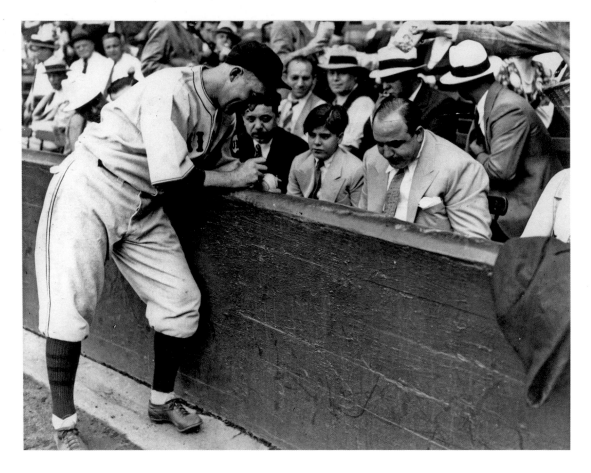

ABOVE: Gabby Harnett of the Cubs autographs a ball for Chicago crime boss Al Capone, right, and his twelve-year-old son, Al Jr., 1931.

OPPOSITE: Fans lined up outside Wrigley Field the day before tickets go on sale for the 1935 World Series between their hometown Chicago Cubs and the Detroit Tigers.

of the nation was searching for, especially law-enforcement officials. In fact, the FBI posted signs in all the post offices offering the then-munificent sum of fifteen thousand dollars for the notorious bank robber John Herbert Dillinger caught dead or alive. He had undergone plastic surgery to disguise himself. According to the Web site Celebrity Cubs Fans, a man named Robert Vogel claimed to have sat two seats away from Dillinger in the grandstand when the Cubs played the Dodgers on June 26. Vogel said that the man looked vaguely familiar, and he wondered if in fact it was Dillinger. (Other accounts, such as the one in Peter Golenbock's *Wrigleyville*, have it that Dillinger was dressed in a mailman's uniform when he attended games and sat in the bleachers.)

The bank robber and killer had actually been a good baseball player in his youth. An infielder on his town team in Martinsville, Indiana (a 1924 team photo shows Dillinger in uniform), he remained a lifelong baseball—and, presumably, Cubs—fan. Some three weeks later, on July 22, the FBI shot and killed Dillinger as he left the Biograph Theater on Lincoln Avenue after seeing the movie *Manhattan Melodrama* with his lady friend, now widely known in murder lore as "the Woman in Red." Vogel supposedly said that when he saw a photograph of the corpse in the newspaper he knew that his suspicions had been correct.

Whether the Vogel (and Celebrity Cubs Fans) story is true or not, it is undisputed that Dillinger appeared in public when he was Public Enemy No. 1, having, after all, gone to a movie theater on the last night of his life. It is doubtful that Dillinger at any time sat near crime boss Al Capone in Wrigley Field, but Scarface Al went to games at the Cubs' park even though his office was on the South Side and he may have favored the White Sox. The North Side was run by Bugs Moran. Capone sent a squadron of his men armed with machine guns to a North Side warehouse to eliminate Moran and his henchmen, resulting in the infamous 1929 Valentine's Day Massacre. Moran, however, escaped and still held on, tenuously, to his territory. There is a photograph of the stout, balding Capone and his son in the front row of the box seats in Wrigley Field with catcher Gabby Hartnett, smiling and autographing a baseball for Sonny Capone.

When baseball commissioner Judge Kenesaw Mountain Landis saw the photograph, he reprimanded Hartnett for associating with a known hoodlum. Bad for baseball's image, Landis admonished.

apparently exceeded his quota of miracles. He grounded weakly into a double play in his last at bat in Game 3 and had one single and struck out twice in Game 4.)

The Cubs fell to third place in 1933, six games behind the pennant-winning Giants. The combination of a disappointing season and the crushing Great Depression brought the Wrigley Field attendance down to 590,000, some 300,000 below the 1932 mark and well below the 1,085,422 in the stands in 1931.

In 1934, the Cubs finished third again, trading away, among a host of strange moves, first baseman Dolph Camilli, a promising young power hitter and excellent fielder, even though Charlie Grimm was slowing down at first base. In exchange for Camilli, the Cubs obtained first baseman Don Hurst, a six-year major-league veteran. Camilli went on to become one of the premier sluggers in the National League and, playing for Brooklyn, was the league MVP in 1941. Hurst played fifty-one games for the Cubs, batted .199, and never played in the majors again.

Among the seven hundred thousand–plus fans who attended games in Wrigley Field in 1934, it was said, was a man who much

"Judge," said Hartnett, "if you don't want anybody talking to the Big Guy, *you* tell him."

In the closing weeks of the 1935 season, the Cubs proved to be pretty substantial guys themselves—until it came time for the Fall Classic. "The consistency the Cubs had been showing in losing World Series as rapidly as they got into them," wrote Brown, "was now being matched by their faculty for gaining a National League pennant. They had won in 1929, paused until 1932, and won again. Now in 1935 they came roaring through the stretch in September putting together an incredible string of twenty-one straight victories, many of them with sensational finishes."

The Giants and Cardinals had been fighting it out for first place, with the Cubs a short distance away. Then came the hot streak. The Cubs went into St. Louis needing to take two games out of the five-game series to win the pennant. In the eighth inning of the opener, Phil Cavarretta batted with the score 0–0. The nineteen-year-old first baseman had been awarded the regular first-base job by manager—and now second-string first baseman—Charlie Grimm. Cavarretta had played high school baseball just two years earlier at Lane Tech, a mile-and-a-half ride on the streetcar down Addison Street to Wrigley Field. Now he had a chance to be a hero, and he didn't disappoint. The left-handed-batting Cavarretta powered a home run over the right-field fence, and Lon Warneke held the Cardinals for the next two innings, for a 1–0 win. The Cubs clinched the following day when Bill Lee beat Dizzy Dean, 6–2. The Cubs ended the regular season four games ahead of second-place St. Louis.

"You ever go seventy-five miles an hour on the highway while everybody else is doing fifty?" recalled Cavarretta, in Donald Honig's *The Chicago Cubs: An Illustrated History*. "That's how we felt. We passed the Giants and caught up with the Cardinals right at the end of the season."

The Cubs met the Detroit Tigers in the World Series. "The meeting of the Cubs and Tigers posed a problem for all forecasters," wrote Brown. "The Tigers had been in four previous World Series and had lost them all. The Cubs were making their fifth try after blowing four in a row."

The Cardinals had beaten the Tigers the year before in a seven-game Series, and in their view, the brazen bench jockeying they inflicted on the Tigers had unnerved the Detroit players, which led to the Series win. The Tigers tried the same tactic with the Cubs.

Some of the Cubs' bench jockeying in return was so profane and antagonistic that plate umpire George Moriarty strode to the Cubs' dugout to warn them to stop; he especially cited the razzing toward Hank Greenberg, the Tigers' star slugging first baseman. In his autobiography, *Hank Greenberg: The Story of My Life*, Greenberg recalled that the Cubs players were "calling me Jew this and Jew that."

Years later, Tuck Stainback, who had been a rookie outfielder for the Cubs then, recalled that his teammates "got on Hank's back. . . . I remember Jurges hollering, 'Throw him a pork chop, he'll never hit it!'"

Years later, Jurges spoke about that element of the '35 Series: "It's just ribbing each other. What the hell!" Recalled Cavarretta: "I was Italian and they'd call me 'dirty dago,' that was pretty heavy, but what the Cubs called Greenberg, well, some of those words shouldn't be printed."

None of it helped. The Tigers beat the Cubs, four games to two, despite Greenberg missing two of the games. Ignoring the razzing, Greenberg hit a two-run homer in the first inning of Game 2, but in the eighth inning he slid into home and Hartnett tagged him out but fell on Greenberg, who twisted awkwardly and broke his left wrist. He did not play again until the following year.

The Cubs couldn't repeat in 1936, or '37, finishing second both seasons. Philip Knight Wrigley, who had become owner of the club upon the death of his father, William Jr., in January 1932, wanted both a championship team, like his father, and also wanted to keep Wrigley Field "parklike," as opposed to cathedral-like, in the model of, among others, crosstown Comiskey Park. To beautify the ballpark, Wrigley had his general manager Bill Veeck Jr. install hundreds of ivy and bittersweet plants on the outfield walls in the 1937–38 off-season. The plants were part of the renovations that also added the massive steel scoreboard and expanded the bleachers.

Another part of the "renovation," it was hoped, was Jay Hanna "Dizzy" Dean, of all people. The Cubs paid the Cardinals the lordly sum of one hundred and eighty-five thousand dollars plus two pitchers and an outfielder to take Dean off their hands. Dean had been a thirty-game winner four years earlier and had remained one of baseball's great stars and characters, but in the 1937 All-Star Game, he was hit by a line drive on the big toe of his right foot. When Dean was told the toe was fractured, he said, "Fractured hell, it's broken." Either way, he came back too soon from the injury to

Left to right: Cubs sluggers Kiki Cuyler, outfielder; Gabby Hartnett, catcher; Riggs Stephenson, outfielder; and Charlie Grimm, manager and first baseman, 1932.

ABOVE: Cubs catcher Gabby Hartnet is greeted at home plate by Chicago's bat boy after his homer in the second inning of Game 4 of the 1935 World Series versus the Detroit Tigers.

RIGHT: Fans seeking tickets for a 1935 World Series game between the Cubs and the Detroit Tigers at Wrigley Field.

On September 27, the first-place Pirates came into Wrigley Field for a season-ending three-game series, leading the Cubs by one and a half games. Dean beat them in the first game, 2–1. The Cubs were now half a game behind Pittsburgh.

The second game was tied 5–5 going into the ninth inning. It was getting dark, and there were no lights to illuminate the field. The Pirates went down in order, and the Cubs were told that the game would be halted after their at bats. Mace Brown, the Pirates' top reliever, retired the first two Cubs batters. Then Hartnett came up. Brown got two strikes on him.

"Brown wound up and let fly," recalled Hartnett. "I swung with everything I had and then I got that feeling—the kind of feeling you get when the blood rushes out of your head and you get dizzy."

The ball soared over the left-field wall, and the Cubs were in first place by half a game, and, as it happened, in first to stay. The blow has come down in history as "the Homer in the Gloamin'." While the fans erupted with frenzied delight, the manager was mobbed at home plate by his Cubs underlings.

The Cubs met the Yankees again in the World Series, this time without Babe Ruth, who had retired, but still with Lou Gehrig. In reality, little had changed, as the Cubs absorbed another melancholy Series loss by the Yankees. This was the Cubs' sixth straight World Series defeat—and, as in 1932 against New York, they were swept again, four games to none.

Cavarretta, who was being platooned in right field with Frank

continue pitching. And when he could pitch again, it became clear that changing his motion because of his ailing toe had changed him as a pitcher. Yet the Cubs hoped he still had some magic left—and, it happened, he indeed would prove to have just enough.

The Charlie Grimm–led Cubs, despite a winning record halfway through the first half of the '38 season, needed a lift to contend, and it was hoped that a new manager could provide it. The Cubs didn't have to go far to find that man. He was behind the plate, in the form of Gabby Hartnett.

Dean came through with a 7–1 record and a 1.81 earned run average but admitted, "I never had nothin'. I couldn't break a pane of glass and I knew it." Dean, who had four times led the league in strikeouts with 190 or more each season, now recorded just 22 of them. But he was a wily pitcher, throwing slow curves and even slower changeups with such great control that he walked only eight batters in seventy-four innings.

"I ain't what I used to be," he said. "But who the hell is?"

Hartnett, besides leading the team as manager with a great second-half surge, also provided the push that would send the Cubs back into the World Series.

TOP: Cubs pitcher Dizzy Dean and manager Gabby Hartnett talk things over prior to the start of Game 2 of the 1938 World Series versus the New York Yankees. The Yanks won 6–3 and went on to sweep the Series.

BOTTOM: Dizzy Dean pitches to the Cardinals' Don Padgett in Dean's Cubs debut, April 31, 1944. St. Louis beat Chicago 5–4.

OPPOSITE: Game 1 of the 1938 World Series between the Cubs and New York Yankees. George Selkirk's bouncer to Cubs second baseman Billy Herman scored Yankees Hall of Famer Lou Gehrig after Herman fumbled the grounder. The Yanks won 3–1.

Demaree after the Cubs had traded for first baseman Rip Collins, batted .462 in the Series, with six hits in thirteen at bats. He hit even better than the Yankees' young star center fielder, Joe DiMaggio, who batted .267.

In an interview with this author, Cavarretta said that he had been "thrilled" to be playing the Yankees, "but I can't say I was overawed." He continued: "I mean, we had a lot of respect for the Yankees, sure, but we were pros too, and we were league champions. We weren't nervous; we were confident. But as it turned out, we were overmatched. They beat our brains out."

One of his vivid memories was of Gehrig, who had been called the Iron Horse for his record-breaking streak of consecutive games played, over fourteen seasons. "I saw Gehrig when I was a small boy and he played in Wrigley Field for a high school team in New York against Lane Tech, the high school in Chicago I eventually went to," said Cavarretta. "I was sitting way up in the upper deck, in the boondocks, but remember thinking how big and strong he was. He hit a home run into the right-field bleachers in that game. And now I saw him playing first base against us, and he looked sick, getting kind of thin. It looked like an effort for him to move around the bag, and he had no power swinging the bat. Of course, we had no idea that he was so ill." (Gehrig batted .286 in the Series; his only hits were four singles. He was diagnosed the next season with amyotrophic lateral sclerosis, or ALS—now known as Lou Gehrig's disease—and died in 1941, at age 38.)

The Cubs broke their string of reaching the World Series every three years, with six lean years from 1939 to 1944.

After an assortment of bad trades, they slipped to fourth place in 1939 and fifth in 1940. Hartnett was fired as manager, and Jimmie Wilson was hired. In 1941, Wrigley named Jimmy Gallagher, a sportswriter who had been critical of the team, general manager. It didn't help: The Cubs foundered to sixth place that year as well as the year after.

When World War II broke out for America after the Japanese attacked Pearl Harbor on December 7, 1941, the Cubs, like all other teams, scrambled to find decent players, with so many of the good ones serving in the military. The Cubs even moved up a notch in the standings, to fifth place, in 1943. Grimm had returned as manager, and the Cubs retained some of the players from their last World Series, including Cavarretta and third baseman Stan Hack. Center fielder Andy Pafko emerged as a new star and, along

with right fielder Bill "Swish" Nicholson, provided much-needed power at bat. And the Cubs had added two fine pitchers, Claude Passeau and Hank Wyse. The Cubs moved up another place in the standings, to fourth, in 1944.

Then, in 1945, with the acquisition from the Yankees in mid-season of pitcher Hank Borowy, the Cubs took off. Borowy finished the season at 11–2 for the Cubs. Cavarretta led the league in hitting with .355 and was named the league's MVP.

The Cubs edged the Cardinals by three games to win the pennant. They again played the Tigers in the World Series. Hank Greenberg had returned from four and a half years of military service and was again providing home-run and RBI power for Detroit. (He would hit two homers in the Series, to lead the Tigers in that category, while Pafko hit the lone homer for the Cubs.) Other standouts for the Tigers were slugger Rudy York and twenty-five-game-winning left-hander Hal Newhouser.

OPPOSITE: Cover of the 1938 World Series program.

ABOVE: The Cubs' 1938 infield. From left to right: Rip Collins, first base; Billy Herman, second base; Bill Jurges, shortstop; and Stan Hack, third base.

ABOVE: Chicago Cubs old-timers at Wrigley Field on July 9, 1944, for a war bond drive. From left to right: Mickey Doolan, Rogers Hornsby, Mordecai Brown, Jimmy Vaughn, Jimmy Archer, and Freddy Lindstrom.

OPPOSITE: A packed house for a 1938 Cubs game versus Boston.

Though the war ended in August with the unconditional surrender of the Japanese, many of baseball's stars were still unavailable to compete at the end of the 1945 season. So the Cubs-Tigers World Series was hardly expected to be a classic. "It was the fat men against the tall men in a game of picnic baseball," surmised New York sportswriter Frank Graham. And columnist Warren Brown noted, "Neither team can win the Series."

Brown's forecast proved incorrect, however, though it was close. The Series went seven games, with the Tigers winning Game 7, 9–3. The Tigers more or less ended matters in the first inning when they scored five runs off Borowy, who had won Game 5 and had been called upon with one day's rest. It was a failed gamble for manager Grimm.

The Cubs in 1945 were now 2–8 in World Series competition, and this was their seventh straight World Series loss.

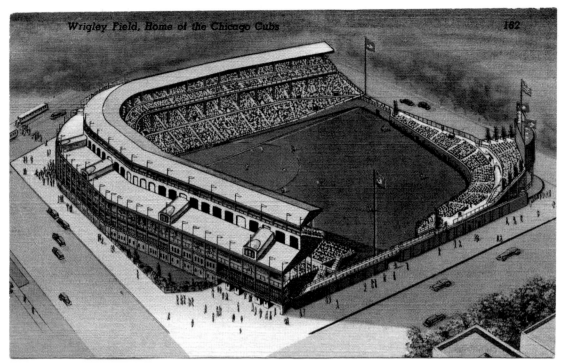

Although in the following years first Billy Sianis and then his nephew and new tavern proprietor, Sam Sianis, have attempted to "lift" the curse—even after Cubs officials have allowed Billy Goat Tavern billy goats, successors to Murphy, to come onto the field in anticurse rites—success has eluded the Cubs ever since.

But at least they had been playing regularly in Fall Classics through 1945.

Then came the drought.

OPPOSITE: Detroit Tigers second baseman Eddie Mayo slides safely across home plate in the eighth inning of the final World Series game at Wrigley Field on October 10, 1945, as Cubs catcher Mickey Livingston (11) vainly attempts to snag the throw and tag Mayo. The Tigers won the game (9–3) and the 1945 World Series.

LEFT: Sam Sianis, proprietor of the famous Billy Goat Tavern in Chicago, appears at Wrigley Field with his goat in 1984.

RIGHT: Postcard of Wrigley Field, 1945.

Before Game 4, an incident occurred that, to the superstitious, delivered the Cubs to a terrible fate for that Series and for decades to come. The owner of the Billy Goat Tavern in Chicago, a die-hard Cubs fan named Billy Sianis, had bought two tickets for that game and decided to bring as his companion his pet billy goat, Murphy. Apparently the creature disturbed enough of the crowd in the grandstand—it smelled and did not sit on its seat and so obscured the view of those seated behind it—to prompt officials (some reports had it that the directive came from P. K. Wrigley himself) to throw Sianis and his pet out of the park. Sianis then leveled his now famous curse at the Cubs, saying, "The Cubs will never win a World Series so long as the goat is not allowed in Wrigley Field." After the Cubs lost the Series to the Tigers, Sianis said, "Who stinks now?"

1946–1965

COULD YOU LOSE
A FLY BALL
IN THE MOON?

Some Cubs fans compared it to being dropped down a bottomless elevator shaft; others said it was more like sitting through a long horror movie. Another imaginative crowd gloomily viewed it as a return to the Dark Ages. However one describes the team's purgatory, it lasted for twenty consecutive seasons, though it seemed interminable to avid Cubs fans.

Following the Cubs' loss in seven games to the Tigers in the 1945 World Series—a valiant but inevitably melancholy undertaking for them—the Cubs began a descent into the lower realms of the standings. In 1946 they finished third, but in 1947 they dropped to sixth to begin two decades of finishing in the second half of the eight-team (and later ten-team) National League. In 1948 they crashed to last. They didn't climb back into the first division until 1967.

I started following the team in 1947, when I was seven years old. Jack Brickhouse began announcing Cubs games on WGN-TV the following year, and I tuned in when I could. (Brickhouse stayed in the broadcast booth for the next thirty years, and upon his retirement, his signature response to a positive Cubs play, "Hey, hey," became hugely popular, so popular, in fact, that "Hey, hey" would hang from flags on both foul poles at Wrigley Field.)

In 1948, I especially started rooting for first baseman Eddie Waitkus. He did a little midair hop when catching a throw and toeing first base, all in one motion. It was an elegant if funny kind of dance step, and it tickled me. Waitkus succeeded in making the National League All-Star team that year (he walked in one pinch-hit appearance) and batted .295 for the season. Then, as often happened with standout players for the Cubs, he was traded. Over the winter, in an unfathomable deal from my boyhood lights, the Cubs dealt Waitkus to the Phillies for two pitchers, Monk Dubiel and Dutch Leonard, who were anything but all-stars.

Turned out, I was hardly the only fan of Waitkus. Ruth Ann Steinhagen, a nineteen-year-old woman living on the North Side, was another. She had fallen in love with the smooth-fielding first baseman now with the Phillies. She missed him desperately, dreamed about him, had built a shrine for him in her bedroom. In a report later prepared by the chief of the Cook County behavioral clinic—in response to an order from the felony court, which found her deranged—she admitted, "As time went on, I just became nuttier and nuttier about the guy. I knew I would never get to know him in a

normal way.... And if I can't have him, nobody else can. And then I decided I would kill him."

She purchased a secondhand rifle and then checked into a room at the Edgewater Beach Hotel, where Waitkus and the Phillies were staying. After the game on June 14 and dinner with a teammate, Waitkus returned to his hotel room. He was surely in a good mood, having again been selected as a player in the upcoming National League All-Star Game. Steinhagen sent Waitkus a note saying that she had to see him and it was "important." She wrote that she was in room 1297.

This was near midnight. Waitkus, a twenty-nine-year-old bachelor, went up to see what this mystery was all about. Ruth Steinhagen opened the door, and Waitkus entered the room and said, "Well, babe, what's happening?"

Then she went into a closet, took out a .22 rifle, and shot him.

Even though Waitkus was hit in the chest and lungs, doctors had to operate from his back to extract the deeply imbedded bullets.

The rifle shot that exploded in the room that night exploded

PREVIOUS SPREAD: Phil Cavarretta, new manager of the Cubs, yells encouragement to his team during a game with Philadelphia Phillies in Philadelphia, 1951.

TOP: Longtime Cubs broadcaster Jack Brickhouse.

BOTTOM: Philadelphia Phillies first baseman Eddie Waitkus sits in a wheelchair in a Chicago felony court, June 30, 1949, during a hearing for Ruth Steinhagen (left), who was alleged to have shot him in a Chicago hotel. Steinhagen was judged insane and committed to Kankakee State Hospital.

the next day onto the front pages of newspapers across the country. I read it with shock and sadness. Waitkus eventually recovered, returned to the Phillies, played the full 1959 season at first base, and made a major contribution to the pennant-winning "Whiz Kids." The Associated Press named Waitkus, who batted .284, the comeback player of the year.

Three years later, Steinhagen was pronounced sane and released from the psychiatric ward. Waitkus died of cancer in 1972, at age fifty-three. Some doctors have expressed the theory that the stress of the shooting, combined with his four surgeries, allowed the cancer to take hold. "So I think Ruth Ann Steinhagen was more successful than she thought," Eddie Waitkus Jr. wrote in a letter to me.

An episode in Bernard Malamud's novel *The Natural*, and the subsequent movie of the same name, was based on the shooting of Waitkus.

On a pure baseball front, the Cubs had begun the '49 season the way they had ended 1948, in last place. Wrigley again changed managers, shifting Charlie Grimm to a vice president's office and installing Frankie Frisch, who had managed the world-champion "Gashouse Gang" Cardinals of 1934. But fifteen years had passed, and the Cubs had no great Dean brothers pitching, no great Ducky Medwick in right field, and no great Frankie "Fordham Flash" Frisch himself playing second base.

And so: last again, thirty-six full games behind the league-leading Dodgers.

But there were two particular bright spots in 1949. After fifty games, the Cubs made one of the best trades in their history, dealing outfielders Peanuts Lowrey and Harry "the Hat" Walker to the Reds for two other outfielders, speedster Frankie Baumholtz and slugger Hank Sauer.

Sauer finished the season with thirty-one homers (twenty-seven for the Cubs), third in the league. He would improve those numbers and became a fan favorite, nicknamed the Mayor of Wrigley Field. His cheek invariably bulged from his chaw of tobacco. Fans would toss packets of chew to him, which he stuffed into his pockets or tucked into the ivy wall behind him in left field, to be retrieved at a later date.

Andy Pafko had another good season, in 1950, hitting .281. The problem was the pitching staff and a few of the other regulars as well as the benchwarmers, and surely, the issues extended up the line.

For the Cubs, 1950 was like déjà vu all over again, to quote a certain stubby Yankees catcher: They finished the season last in fielding and in hitting and next to last in pitching and in the NL standings.

Following the season, the Cubs made a trade with the Dodgers for a six-foot-five first baseman who had played just one game for

Manager Frankie Frisch (left) talks with Cubs captain Phil Cavaretta, 1949.

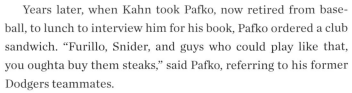

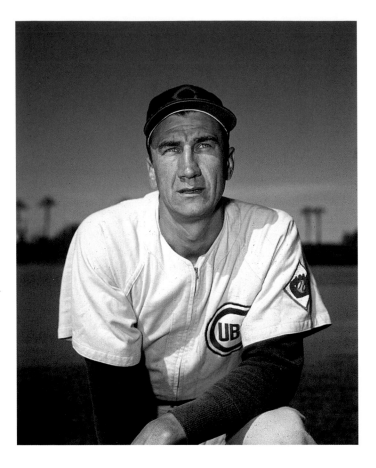

Brooklyn in his lone appearance in the major leagues. He played sixty-six games for the Cubs in 1951. He batted .239, with two homers, and then was gone from baseball. He had also briefly played professional basketball with the Boston Celtics. Chuck Connors's greatest success, however, came when he moved to television and starred in the *Rifleman* series.

In 1951, the Cubs finished at rock bottom in the standings again, the third time in four seasons. In mid-June they again traded away one of my favorite players, Andy Pafko, who had an odd, squat batting stance that looked perfect for milking cows. In 1950 he had led the Cubs with a .304 batting average and thirty-six homers and made the All-Star team for the fourth consecutive year. So what did the Cubs then do with Andy Pafko? Trade him, naturally. In an eight-player deal, Pafko went to the Dodgers. He played left field for them and was one of "the Boys of Summer" memorialized in Roger Kahn's book of that name and a solid contributor to pennant-winning teams, with the Dodgers and, in the last half of the fifties, the Milwaukee Braves.

Years later, when Kahn took Pafko, now retired from baseball, to lunch to interview him for his book, Pafko ordered a club sandwich. "Furillo, Snider, and guys who could play like that, you oughta buy them steaks," said Pafko, referring to his former Dodgers teammates.

A Cubs fan reading this would cry aloud, "Say it ain't so, Andy!" Nonetheless, that was the Cubs complex—the club sandwich complex.

There were two moments in the Cubs careers of Pafko and Cavarretta that are emblematic of the good and the perverse.

In a game in 1949 against the Cardinals in Wrigley Field, Pafko, playing center field, caught what he contended was a blooper off the bat of Rocky Nelson. At the time, there was a runner on first base with two outs in the top of the ninth inning, with the Cubs leading 3–2. The second-base umpire, Al Barlick, signaled that the ball had been trapped, not caught, and the game was not ended—not at all. Pafko ran into the infield to argue with Barlick and neglected to call time-out. When Pafko finally realized that time hadn't been called, the base runner had scored, and Nelson was heading for home, Pafko rifled the ball to the plate. Unfortunately, the throw bounced off Nelson as he slid home, giving the Cardinals a 4–3 lead, and eventually and ruefully, the score held up. The Cubs lost. It is said that Nelson hit the only "inside the glove" home run in baseball history.

For many baseball fans around the country, 1951 will be remembered for Bobby Thomson hitting the home run that has been called "the shot heard round the world." It was struck with two men on and one out and the Giants trailing the Dodgers 4–2 in the bottom of the ninth inning of the third and final play-off game for the National League pennant. The person with the single best view in the world was the Dodgers' left fielder, Andy Pafko, who observed the ball flying over his head into the left-field stands. But the home run that was most important that year to this Cubs fan—and to many others—was one walloped by Phil Cavarretta. I didn't see Thomson's home run, but I did see the one by Cavarretta, on television.

It was the afternoon of Sunday, July 29, 1951. As usual, the Cubs were in a dogfight for last place, this time with the Pirates. The Cubs were playing a doubleheader against the Phillies, the defending league champions who were battling the Dodgers for first place. Cavarretta was a week into the job as player-manager. But he had relinquished his starting first-base job to Dee Fondy

to the plate. He had a strange habit of wiping his bat between his thighs before stepping into the batter's box. I didn't know why—and of course it didn't affect his swing. (Years later he explained to me that he'd spit while in the on-deck circle or taking warm-up swings and try to hit the flying saliva with his bat to work on his timing. Whatever works, right?)

Roberts wound up and threw. And the dark-complexioned, left-handed Cavarretta swung and pounded Roberts's first pitch into the right-field bleachers for a grand-slam homer! Jack Brickhouse, the Cubs announcer, went bananas. So did I.

When I interviewed Cavarretta long after he had retired, he told me he wasn't nervous about calling upon himself in that situation. "I always loved a challenge," he said. "And if I struck out? Well, they'd have to say I at least had the guts to try. That was anything but defeatist, wouldn't you say?"

I'd say so. But by "defeatist," Cavarretta was referring to something else:

During the spring training of 1954, manager Cavarretta told owner P. K. Wrigley that since the Cubs had finished in seventh place the year before, they needed particular help at catching, and in the infield, and in the outfield, and, oh yes, with pitching too. Perhaps Cavarretta knew what he was talking about, since he had played for three Cubs pennant-winning teams, in 1935, '38, and '45.

"Defeatist attitude," Wrigley told Cavarretta—and Cavarretta was abruptly Cubs history.

"I'd never had a defeatist attitude in my life," Cavarretta said later. "Mr. Wrigley was wrong."

The firing established a Cubs record of sorts. No baseball manager in history had ever been fired in spring training!

Actually, the Cubs had had raised hopes with Cavarretta as manager. The team finished at a rare .500 in 1952, good for fifth place.

Hank Sauer got credit for the Cubs' rise in the standings. He had his best season in 1952, when he homered in the All-Star Game, tied Ralph Kiner for the league lead in homers (thirty-seven), and was named league MVP. Frankie Baumholtz, meanwhile, who had come over in the trade with the Reds that included Sauer, played a fine center field in 1952 and hit .325, second in the league.

Inevitably, the Cubs' fortunes took a poor turn, and they finished seventh in 1953. Then came Cavarretta's spring appraisal of '54 and his dismissal.

and was sitting on the bench. In the second game, the Cubs rallied for two runs to tie the score, 4–4, in the seventh inning. There were now two outs, and the bases were loaded. The Phillies brought in their ace, right-hander Robin Roberts, who rarely relieved. At this point, fledgling manager Cavarretta looked down his bench for a pinch hitter for the pitcher Dutch Leonard.

He looked and looked and decided that, yes, the manager was the best available hitter. Then a venerable Cubs hero in his eighteenth season with the team, Cavarretta grabbed a bat and strode

ABOVE: Ralph Kiner in his first at bat as a Chicago Cub, June 4, 1953.

OPPOSITE: The enormous scoreboard towers above the centerfield bleachers in Wrigley Field.

it.'" Sometimes, it seemed, Baumholtz barely had the energy to run back to the dugout after an inning.

During a night game in Boston, Sauer was in pursuit of a fly ball, and this time *he* shouted, "I got it!" Alas, the ball landed twenty feet in front of him. Sauer returned to the bench and, with a smile, explained to manager Frisch, "I lost it in the moon."

The most significant development for the Cubs in 1954, as it turned out, came on September 17, when the Cubs' first black player appeared in their lineup. Ernie Banks, a lithe, six-foot-one, 160-pound, twenty-two-year-old shortstop, had been purchased for twenty-five thousand dollars from the Kansas City Monarchs of the Negro American League. Three days later, with a whip-quick, wristy, unexpectedly powerful swing, Banks hit the first of his 512 career home runs off Gerry Staley of the Cardinals.

Banks came up to the Cubs with another African American player, Gene Baker, a second baseman. Baker had excelled in the minor leagues, and many considered him a superior prospect to Banks.

The Cubs were relative latecomers to bringing up black players, and management was surely responsible. As *Tribune* columnist Mike Royko wrote on March 21, 1997, in what would be his last column before dying of a brain aneurism, "The only other baseball feat [P. K. Wrigley] was known for was running the worst franchise in baseball. . . . And a big part of that can be blamed on racism. If not Wrigley's, then that of the stiffs he hired to run his baseball operation."

Baker was the one first assigned to the club. As reported by Jerome Holtzman and George Vass, when general manager Wid Matthews mentioned to Wrigley that they had brought up yet another black player, the owner asked, "Who?"

Matthews answered, "Fellow named Ernie Banks."

"Gee whiz!" exclaimed Wrigley. "We are already bringing up a Negro player this year. Why did you go out and get another one?"

"Well," Matthews replied, "we had to have a roommate for the one we've got."

In that 1997 column, Royko added, "By the time Cubs management got over their racial fears, the black league was getting ready to fold. Fewer players were available and better teams competed for them. Other sports, college and pro, began going after black athletes."

In fairness, nine of the sixteen major-league teams still did

OPPOSITE: Cubs Hall of Famer Ernie Banks, 1968.

LEFT: Cubs second baseman Gene Baker, c. 1955.

Perhaps the portent of things to come in the 1954 season happened in spring training, shortly after Stan Hack was named manager of the Cubs, replacing Cavarretta. The story is told that a rookie right-handed pitcher named Bob Zick introduced himself to Hack. "I'm Zick," he said. "I'm not feeling too well myself," Hack supposedly replied. Zick went on to compile a 0-0 record, giving up 15 runs in 16.1 innings in his lone season in the major leagues.

Early in that season, Ralph Kiner, the league's home-run leader for the previous seven seasons, was traded to the Cubs from the Pirates. He played right field, and Sauer played left. Both were notoriously slow-footed. Swift center fielder Baumholtz exhausted himself chasing down fly balls all over the outfield. As Kiner later recalled, "All I ever heard from Baumholtz was 'I got

Brooklyn Dodgers legend Jackie
Robinson (left), boxer Ezzard
Charles, and the Cubs' Andy Pafko,
1951.

not have a black player at the end of the 1953 season (five teams in the National League and four in the American League, including the Yankees). By the time the Cubs had called up their first black player, however, the Dodgers had a half dozen or more, including Jackie Robinson, who broke the color barrier in the major leagues in 1947.

On the afternoon of May 18 of that year, a crowd of 46,572 paying customers established the Cubs' all-time single-game record. It was Jackie Robinson's first game in the Cubs' home park.

One of those in the stands was fourteen-year-old Mike Royko.

In a column on October 25, 1972, on the day that Jackie Robinson died, Royko wrote,

———————————————

I had to see Jackie Robinson. . . .

Usually, we could get [to the park] just at noon, find a seat in the grandstand, and watch some batting practice. But not that Sunday. . . .

By noon, Wrigley Field was almost filled. . . .

I had never seen anything like it. . . . But this was

twenty-five years ago, and in 1947 few blacks were seen in the Loop, much less up on the white North Side at a Cubs game.

That day, they came by the thousands, pouring off the northbound Ls and out of their cars.

They didn't wear baseball-game clothes. They had on church clothes and funeral clothes—suits, white shirts, ties, gleaming shoes, and straw hats. I've never seen so many straw hats.

As big as it was, the crowd was orderly. Almost unnaturally so. People didn't jostle each other.

The whites tried to look as if nothing unusual was happening, while the blacks tried to look casual and dignified. So everybody looked slightly ill at ease.

For most, it was probably the first time they had been that close to each other in such great numbers.

We managed to get in, scramble up a ramp, and find a place to stand behind the last row of grandstand seats. Then they shut the gates. No place remained to stand.

Robinson came up in the first inning. I remember the sound. It wasn't the shrill, teenage cry you now hear, or an excited gut roar. They applauded, long, rolling applause. A tall, middle-aged black man stood next to me, a smile of almost painful joy on his face, beating his palms together so hard they must have hurt.

When Robinson stepped into the batter's box, it was as if someone had flicked a switch. The place went silent.

He swung at the first pitch and they erupted as if he had knocked it over the wall. But it was only a high foul that dropped into the box seats. I remember thinking it was strange that a foul could make that many people happy. When he struck out, the low moan was genuine.

I've forgotten most of the details of the game, other than that the Dodgers won and Robinson didn't get a hit or do anything special, although he was cheered on every swing and every routine play.

––––––––––––––––

There was one play, Royko wrote, that he'd "never forget":

––––––––––––––––

... Robinson played first, and early in the game a Cub star hit a grounder and it was a close play.

Just before the Cub reached first, he swerved to his left. And as he got to the bag, he seemed to slam his foot down hard at Robinson's foot.

It was obvious to everyone that he was trying to run into him or spike him. Robinson took the throw and got clear at the last instant.

I was shocked. That Cub, a hometown boy, was my biggest hero. It was not only an unheroic stunt, but it seemed a rude thing to do in front of people who would cheer for a foul ball. I didn't understand why he had done it. It wasn't at all big league.

I didn't know that while the white fans were relatively polite, the Cubs and most other teams kept up a steady stream of racial abuse from the dugout. I thought that all they did down there was talk about how good Wheaties are.

––––––––––––––––

Robinson went on that season to bat .297, hit twelve homers, lead the league in stolen bases with twenty-nine, be named rookie of the year (at the relatively advanced baseball age of twenty-eight), and lead the Dodgers to the pennant—on the way to a Hall of Fame career. Banks and Baker went on to form an excellent double-play combination for three seasons, 1954–1956, before Baker was traded to the Pirates in May 1957.

Wrigley hired former star Cubs third baseman Stan Hack to take over for Cavarretta at the Cubs' spring training camp in Mesa, Arizona. The Cubs proved Cavarretta a prophet—the team indeed needed help at most positions—and finished in seventh place, thirty-three games behind Leo Durocher's first-place New York Giants.

A footnote to the 1954 season: The Cubs sold right-handed pitcher Dave Cole to the Phillies. Cole had finished with a record of 3–8 for the Cubs. Upon learning of the sale, Cole was upset. "Oh, no," he said. "The Phillies are the only team I can beat."

In 1955 the Cubs moved up a sorry notch to sixth. Banks exploded for forty-four homers, the most ever hit by a big-league shortstop, and Samuel "Toothpick Sam" Jones pitched a no-hitter to provide one of the rare bright spots. The Cubs then retreated back to the cellar in '56 and '57. Well, in '57 they only tied for the cellar, or, charitably, seventh place, with the Pirates; the Cubs actually had to beat the Cardinals on the final day of the season, and did, to achieve that dubious distinction.

Sam Jones baseball card, 1956.

The 1957 season was a special one for me. I grew up playing Little League, PONY, and high school baseball against pitcher–third baseman Jim Woods. He became a huge pitching and hitting star and led his team to the Illinois state championship in 1956. In June 1957, I played against Woods in a Chicago public league high school game, he for Lane Tech, me for Sullivan, both seniors. Three weeks later, at age seventeen, six feet tall, and 175 pounds—about *my* height and weight—the redheaded Woods was signed by the Cubs, and went directly to Wrigley Field! Jim Woods was a major leaguer! This was phenomenal. (That summer, while dreaming of being in the big leagues like Woods, I had to settle for working as a laborer going from Chicago alley to Chicago alley on a city garbage truck, a job my father, a midlevel politician, helped me get.)

"When I first joined the Cubs, I was amazed when I walked into the big-league clubhouse," Woods recalled to me years later. "You never had to do anything for yourself. People did everything for you. And I saw the center fielder Jim Bolger smoking in the clubhouse. I thought athletes didn't smoke. Unbelievable. And in the dugout, that was amazing too. Bob Scheffing"—the Cubs manager between '57 and '59—"swore at the umpires. I always thought you were supposed to be polite to the umpires."

Woods remembered standing in awe at the power and bat speed of Stan Musial and Hank Aaron and Ernie Banks during batting practice. "It was," recalled Woods, "like a magic show." As for his new teammate Ernie Banks, Woods recalled, "A great guy. He'd try to build my confidence by telling me that I would get a good shot one day. He'd holler on the bench to Scheffing, 'C'mon, put the kid in.'"

Woods got into only two games for the Cubs that year, both as a pinch runner. He was traded to the Phillies and played third base and pinch-hit for them in thirty-four games in 1960 and '61, in one game crushing a double off Sandy Koufax. And then his big-league career was over. That showed me just how difficult it was to play, let alone excel, in the major leagues. Woods, after all, had been a schoolboy phenom.

The Cubs finished fifth in both 1958 and '59 and might well have not finished at all, seemingly, except for Ernie Banks, who in '58 hit 47 homers and drove in 129 runs and in '59 hit 45 homers with 143 RBIs. He was named most valuable player in the National League in both of those seasons.

Scheffing was fired after the 1959 season. In 1960 Charlie Grimm was back running the Cubs from the dugout. But after a

OPPOSITE: Ernie Banks signs autographs for his fans at a Cubs game.

ABOVE: Infielder Jim Woods at spring training, 1958.

6–11, eighth-place start, Wrigley committed another of his odd-ball moves, moving Lou Boudreau from the broadcast booth—he was then the Cubs' radio analyst—to the dugout to manage the Cubs and sending Grimm upstairs to take Boudreau's place behind the microphone.

Nothing much else changed: seventh place for the Cubs.

And then came historic, if not preposterous, 1961.

Instead of one manager, Wrigley decided that handfuls of them would be more effective! A screwball scheme? Sure, but nothing else had seemed to work.

So on January 19, 1961, Wrigley announced his so-called College of Coaches. The Cubs would platoon several men, sending one to manage the team for days or weeks, or perhaps months, and then sending him away to the minor leagues and bringing up someone else to pilot the club.

Ron Santo, among others, found it confusing. "One day you're told you're a running team," he said. "The next day you're told that you're a slugging team."

It was a merry-go-round of skippers, and Wrigley adhered to it for the 1961 and '62 seasons. Vedie Himsl, Harry Craft, Elvin Tappe, Lou Klein, and Charlie Metro became interchangeable managerial parts, with Bobby Adams, Dick Cole, Rip Collins, Charlie Grimm, Goldie Holt, Fred Martin, and Verlon Walker on deck if needed. In the first year, Tappe had the longest managerial stretch, for seventy-eight games, while Himsl's rein was the shortest after posting an 0–3 record in his third managerial stint during this stunt. In 1962, Metro, with a marathon 112 games, was the longest-serving manager, while Tappe, with 20 games, was the briefest.

"Managers are expendable," explained Wrigley. "I believe there should be relief managers, just like relief pitchers, so you can keep rotating them."

Turned out, Cubs relief pitchers did about as well as the relief managers—that is, not terribly well. The Cubs finished seventh in 1961, and with two expansion teams added to the now ten-team league, they finished ninth, behind the new Houston team in eighth and ahead of the woeful tenth-place Mets.

"Do you think the other coaches wanted Vedie to win nine straight?" veteran infielder Don Zimmer said years later. "They were jealous of each other."

In 1963 Wrigley hired Bob Kennedy as "permanent head coach," Wrigley said, but told reporters, "You can call him

'manager' if you wish." That year, Wrigley also hired a man with no baseball experience, Robert Whitlow, a retired air force colonel, to run the team as general manager. Wrigley called him the athletic director. The result: seventh place once again. Whitlow was soon moved to a front-office position that essentially rendered him invisible.

Before the 1964 season, two incidents occurred that would mar the team's hopes for the year. The first was the tragic death of Ken Hubbs, their starting second baseman for the past two seasons and the first rookie to ever win a Gold Glove Award. Hubbs died in an airplane crash just before spring training.

OPPOSITE: Wrigley Field, 1959.

ABOVE: Cubs coach Elvin Tappe (left) with Houston Colts manager Harry Craft, 1962.

LEFT: Lou Brock, 1963.

RIGHT: Cubs pitcher Ernie Broglio, 1964.

The other event was a six-deal trade with the Cardinals in June. The key figures in the deal were Cubs outfielder Lou Brock and Cardinals pitcher Ernie Broglio.

At this point Brock hardly had Hall of Fame written all over him, a designation that would change by the time he retired in 1979. As the Cubs' left fielder, he batted .263 in 1962 and .258 in 1963, hitting nine homers in each season, and was a decent if average base stealer, not among the top five in the league. He was batting .251 in fifty-one games when he was traded.

In St. Louis, suddenly and to the utter chagrin of the Cubs, Brock emerged as a force. He finished the 1964 season hitting .348 as the leadoff hitter for the Cardinals, cracking twelve homers and stealing forty-three bases, second in the league to Maury Wills. He also batted .300 in the World Series as the Cardinals beat the Yankees in seven games. The Cubs, for their part, finished eighth once again.

Right-hander Broglio, who had been a twenty-one-game winner in 1960 and had an 18–8 record in 1963, was 3–5 at the time of the trade and 4–7 for the Cubs the rest of the season. Pitching with a sore arm that had developed in St. Louis, Broglio won a total of three more games while losing twelve for the Cubs over the next two seasons. He never played major-league baseball again.

Cubs fans watched painfully as Brock played thirteen more seasons for the Cardinals, two of which saw him in the World Series, hitting a lifetime average of .293 and leading the league in stolen bases eight out of his first nine full seasons in St. Louis. In 1974, he set the major-league single-season record with 118 stolen bases.

"I think the Cardinals got the benefit of my maturing at that point," Brock said, "and the Cubs gave up on me too soon."

As for Broglio, the pitcher would say, "It doesn't bother me anymore that I'll always be remembered as the other guy in the Lou Brock deal. . . . I didn't make the trade."

While the College of Coaches was technically still extant, it was yet left to Bob Kennedy to be the one and only "head coach," or manager, of the Cubs in 1963 and 1964. The best he could do was finish in seventh and eighth place. In the middle of 1965, another season in which the Cubs were again headed to baseball oblivion, Kennedy was fired and Lou Klein was hired to replace him. All that the Cubs got for this change was another eighth-place finish.

But Wrigley had another ace, or knave, up his sleeve, and his announcement of the new manager for 1966 would stun the baseball world and once again provide a glimmer of hope for the ever-buffeted Cubs fan.

LEFT: A 1963 game between the Cubs and the St. Louis Cardinals at Wrigley Field.

ABOVE: Cardinals outfielder Stan Musial (6) stands at first base with Cubs first baseman Steve Boros (17) during a 1963 game.

1966–1983

LEO THE LIP, SWEET BILLY, AND THE GREAT BASEBALL RANT

After two years of a glut of "head coaches" roaming to and from the Wrigley Field dugout to parts unknown, Cubs owner Phil Wrigley decided, once again, to do the unpredictable, if not the implausible, and hired of all people Leo Durocher, the erratic, often irascible "Leo the Lip," to lead the Cubs on the field for the 1966 season.

"Philip K. Wrigley's capacity for astounding Cubs fans and the baseball world in general with unexpected moves was inexhaustible," Jerome Holtzman and George Vass wrote in *Baseball, Chicago Style.*

At age sixty—and after forty years in the game—Durocher had spent a lifetime antagonizing great swathes of people, on and off the field. He seemed the opposite of the retiring, genteel owner of the team. Durocher was not only abrasive, but he could twist a fact so that it was unrecognizable as truth. Yet he had played with and managed winning teams, from his stint as a light-hitting shortstop in the late 1920s New York Yankees (and a teammate of Babe Ruth's, who once accused Durocher of stealing his wristwatch from his locker), to playing with the Dizzy Dean–led "Gashouse Gang" world-champion St. Louis Cardinals in the mid-1930s, to managing the Dodgers to one pennant, in 1941, and the Giants to two pennants, in 1951 and 1954, winning the World Series in '54.

Durocher had been suspended by baseball commissioner Albert "Happy" Chandler for one year, 1947, after allegedly consorting with gamblers and gangsters. Around that time Durocher also had an affair with the actress Laraine Day that was made public and criticized by Brooklyn's influential Catholic Youth Organization. Durocher and Day married soon after.

Durocher has become identified with the phrase "Nice guys finish last" and has even been cited in *Bartlett's Familiar Quotations*. Supposedly, as manager of the Dodgers in July 1946, with his team in first place and about to play the New York Giants, he said, "The nice guys are all over there, in seventh place, not in this dugout." By which he meant that there is no correlation between being a team of "nice guys" and winning. Factors such as player talent had more to do with it—as did, apparently, managerial skills.

So when Durocher inherited a team that had had rotating head coaches but no manager for the previous seasons, he asserted himself. At the press conference organized to introduce him to the local writers, he stated, "If no announcement has been made about what my title is, I'm making it here and now. I'm the manager. I'm not a head coach. You can't have two or three coaches running a ball club. One man has to be in complete authority. There can be only one boss."

After noting where the Cubs had finished in the National League standings the season before, he asserted that "this is definitely not an eighth-place team."

And, now, famously and ironically, he was correct. Under Durocher in 1966, the Cubs finished in tenth and last place.

But change was coming.

Wrigley said that he hired Durocher to manage the Cubs because "I needed somebody to wake them up." And indeed, the following season the Cubs rose from their slumber.

In 1967, a handful of young and talented players had arrived on the scene in trades—catcher Randy Hundley and pitcher Bill Hands from the San Francisco Giants; pitcher Fergie Jenkins and outfielder Adolfo Phillips from the Phillies. Second-year left-hander Ken Holtzman, a University of Illinois product, looked like a true find. Those players, plus the Cubs' stars, first baseman Ernie Banks, outfielder Billy Williams, third baseman Ron Santo, and second baseman Glenn Beckert in the field, and starting pitcher Dick Ellsworth and rookies Rich Nye and Joe Niekro in the bull pen, provided a spark not seen in Wrigley Field for two decades.

The Cubs stunned the baseball world with a summer surge that landed them in first place. From mid-June to early July, they won seventeen of nineteen games and found themselves in the odd and heady position of first place in the NL standings, though soon to be overtaken by the pennant-winning St. Louis Cardinals. The Cubs, though fourteen games behind the Cardinals, finished third, with a stunning 87–74 record, the team's best record since the 1945 pennant. Jenkins led the pitching staff by winning twenty games (and losing thirteen), for the first of his six straight twenty-win seasons for the Cubs. With a little luck he would have won more—he lost five 1–0 games, frustratingly tying a major-league record for most 1–0 losses in a season.

The 1968 season arrived with great expectations. The city was excited about pennant possibilities. Attendance soared to 1,043,409, surpassing a million for the first time since 1952. Alas, the team's fortunes did not match the fans' enthusiasm. The Cubs ended up third again, with a slightly inferior record to the previous season, 84–78.

Still, the Cubs were figured to contend in 1969, the first season in which the leagues were split into two divisions, with five teams in each division. Indeed, the Cubs appeared to be headed for a championship season. Shortstop Don Kessinger joined Banks, Beckert, Santo, and Hundley to compose the largest contingent of players from any National League team. The Cubs held first place for 155 straight days, as they broke another attendance record with 1,674,993 and led the NL East, and the New York Mets, by eight and a half games as late as August 14. And then, and then—

But let's back up for a moment. It is June 26, and in the third

inning of a game against the Los Angeles Dodgers, Durocher complains of a stomachache and leaves the ballpark. He doesn't go home or to a hospital or even to a pharmacy. Instead, he hops on a chartered plane and flies to Camp Ojibwa in Eagle River, Wisconsin, four hundred miles away, to see his stepson (he was remarried by this time, to the former Lynne Walker Goldblatt, a Chicago socialite). When the trip is discovered, he is blasted for "deserting" the team. Wrigley says that Durocher owes the players an apology.

Meanwhile, Durocher was irritating the players in another way. He was often critical of Banks, who suffered from bad knees—some thought Durocher envied the popular "Mr. Cub"—and he was quick to berate a player, like the sensitive new center fielder Don Young, upon making a miscue. Santo struck out, and Durocher embarrassed his star third baseman in front of the rest of the team.

And so the Cubs began to falter just as the Mets went on a hot streak. Chicago led by five and a half games on September 2 and within a week were two and a half ahead. Then they lost two straight to the Mets. Now the Cubs' lead was down to just half a game. Shortly after, the Mets beat Montreal in a doubleheader, the Cubs lost, and the Mets took over first place—for good.

New York Mets outfielder Cleon Jones leaps for a fly ball near the ivy-covered outfield wall in Wrigley Field, 1969.

New York Mets pitcher Tom Seaver working on a no-hitter versus the Cubs in the eighth inning at Shea Stadium in New York, July 10, 1969. At bat is Cubs third baseman Ron Santo.

The Mets, in only the eighth year of their existence and having never finished higher than ninth, were aflame. They had won thirty-nine of their last fifty games, with the powerful twenty-four-year-old right-hander Tom Seaver winning twenty-five games (and, eventually, the Cy Young Award for the best pitcher in the league, en route to the Hall of Fame). The Cubs had played just over .500 ball since early August—simply too paltry in contrast to the surging Mets.

Now it was the night of September 24. Barry Holt, a North Sider who had followed the Cubs since boyhood and who described himself as a "true Cubs fan," who disdained the raucous, beery "Bleacher Bums" in Wrigley Field as nonserious baseball observers, hoped vainly for a miracle.

A thirty-one-year-old attorney with a wife and two daughters, Holt, on this night, alone in the den of his home, slowly reached over and turned off the radio because he did not care to listen to the description of the Mets' division-winning celebration, of how the Mets fans poured onto the field of Shea Stadium, of how the champagne poured over the players' heads in the clubhouse.

Holt took the end of the Cubs' phenomenal fade with grace, but with a hand that shook just a bit, to be sure, and with a blink that brought the curtain down on a single, slippery tear.

Holt got station KMOX out of St. Louis and listened to Harry Caray describe the Cardinals game against the Mets in the last week of the season. He recalled:

——————————

To the very end, I thought that maybe the impossible was possible. That the Mets could lose to the Cardinals—St. Louis was starting its ace, Steve Carlton—and then lose to Philadelphia, and then the Cubs would win all their games and would be two games down with the two last games of the season left against the Mets in Chicago.

I didn't want to turn the radio on until I figured it was about the sixth inning. I mean, I couldn't listen to it if the Mets jumped off to a big lead. So I thought I'd wait and then hope that when I put it on, the Cardinals would be ahead.

——————————

During that season, Holt said, he would kill himself to listen to the game on the radio or watch it on television, despite the long hours at his law office. At one time, he would kill himself to get out to Wrigley Field. Not this year. When once he would watch seventy or so games in person, this year he saw only twenty. "It was a different kind of summer out there," said Holt.

A lot of longtime Cubs fans went to fewer games that year, he contended, because Wrigley Field was so crowded with people who had never been out there before.

"The real Bleacher Bums used to sit in right center field. They'd do a lot of betting. This year you'd see them out there sometimes, but they'd be scattered. You'd find one sitting quietly between two guys in crash helmets piling up beer cans. It was a less knowledgeable crowd, but tremendously loyal, anyway. But I spent more time listening to the games on radio than ever before."

When Holt turned on his radio that late September evening, it happened to be the sixth inning. He heard that a rookie, someone named Campisi, was pitching for St. Louis.

——————————

Obviously Carlton had been knocked out. But I hoped that he had come down with a sore arm and was taken out. Then Harry Caray told the score, 6–0, and I knew the Cardinals would not touch Gary Gentry.

But then in the ninth inning the Cardinals got men on second and third with no outs. And I felt like I was watching a horse race and I had money on the horse that ran dead last, but I didn't tear up my ticket because I hoped the tote board would flash that the other eleven horses had been disqualified.

Then Vada Pinson struck out. And Joe Torre hit a bouncer to Bud Harrelson at short, who threw to Al Weis, who threw to Donn Clendenon for the double play.

And it was like the old days, when you thought that Bob Rush would soon realize his potential and be better than Don Newcombe, and Roy Smalley was better than Marty Marion. Those were the days when you asked someone how the Cubs did, and they said the Cubs lost and you knew the Cubs didn't lose but that the game ended before they could catch up.

——————————

"Those three weeks," third baseman Ron Santo recalled, "were a nightmare."

The Cubs finished second, eight games behind the Mets. It was one of the great flops in baseball history. The 155 straight games in which they remained atop the standings was the longest period any team has ever held first place without winning the pennant.

Who was to blame? Many critics accused Durocher, who was said to have played his regulars into exhaustion.

Phil Wrigley said that the Cubs players had received too much attention. "Chicago players aren't used to being celebrities," he said. "They didn't know how to handle it. They got overconfident."

In June 1970, I was with several other sportswriters in the Cubs' manager's office, before the Cubs were to play the Mets in Shea Stadium. His baseball cap lying on his desk, his mostly bald pate shiny under the ceiling bulbs, Durocher mentioned that he didn't read the sports sections of newspapers because, he said, "I don't read fiction." He was asked if he'd read the recent article in *Look* magazine entitled "How Durocher Blew the Pennant," by William Barry Furlong. In it, he was called "the most unprincipled man in sports."

"Nah," he said, "I didn't read it. But a lot of my friends told me what was in it. A lot of guys write things about me and I never see 'em. I wouldn't know 'em if I tripped over 'em. But this guy who

wrote it, they tell me he's got buckteeth and dirty fingernails. You gotta hate this guy right away. Right? I mean, buckteeth and dirty fingernails."

The last time I'd seen Bill Furlong, he had neither buckteeth nor dirty fingernails. But Leo the Lip had his views, and he held firmly to them.

The Cubs, again in first place on that afternoon in June 1970, went out and lost to the Mets again, and again relinquished first place. Despite making deals that landed veteran outfielder Johnny Callison, starting pitcher Milt Pappas, and reliever Hoyt Wilhelm, the Cubs wound up in second place again, five games behind the championship-winning Pittsburgh Pirates.

The season held a few bright spots for the Cubs, but none more glowing than the one on May 12. Ernie Banks, now thirty-nine, in his eighteenth season with the Cubs and stationed part-time at first base by Durocher, swatted the five-hundredth home run of his major-league career. Banks hit only twelve in all during the season, his lowest output since he first came up to the big leagues in 1953.

In 1971, Banks hit 3 homers in thirty-nine games for a total of 512, one of the few players to hit more than 500 homers in a career, and was just 9 behind Ted Williams. But Banks had slowed down perceptibly—his knees and back ached—and perhaps the greatest Cub of all retired at season's end.

Banks had been replaced at first base in 1970 by Jim Hickman, who had an outstanding season, batting .315 with 32 homers and 115 runs batted in, and made the National League All-Star team, driving in the winning run with a single to center in a 5–4, twelve-inning game.

He was Cinderella on spikes. In a nine-year career to that point, he had never hit higher than .257 and never had more than seventeen homers or fifty-seven runs batted in.

In the early part of the 1971 season, though, Hickman was having a tough time both on the field and off. He had developed bronchitis, which he had trouble shaking. Indeed, with his coughing and spitting up, his teammates jokingly moved away from him on the dugout bench. He would wind up with a .256 batting average, nineteen homers and sixty RBIs, a typical journeyman season for him.

"Last season was a real pleasure," he said, with sincere brown eyes, as he sat in his uniform and shower shoes in front of his locker in the Cubs' clubhouse in 1971. He said that 1970 was not only an unbelievable season for him but one he freely admitted he knew he could never duplicate.

———————————

Now, you can see how guys like Aaron and Mays and Banks are always saying that they love baseball, they love baseball. But if you go through seven or eight years playing the way I did, you might say something different.

I mean, you struggle along for years hitting two hundred and it gets to be a drag. Aaron and Mays and Banks come to the park every day and wonder how *far* they're going to hit the ball. I'd come to the park every day and wonder if I'm going to *hit* the ball. But you get a little success, and you can really enjoy the game.

———————————

Hickman, then thirty-two and in his tenth big-league season, said he planned to play two more years (it turned out to be three) and retire to his hometown of Henning, Tennessee, population five hundred, about a forty-minute drive from Memphis. He owned a very small row-crop farm, growing cotton and beans.

"I'd like to stay in Henning," he said.

———————————

I'd have to buy a larger farm to make a decent living. But there is not much land available around Henning, and not too many people at home want to turn loose their land. So that's out.

I still don't know anything except playing baseball. But I do have some money saved up now. I'm not rich by any means, and if I quit baseball today, I'd have to get a job tomorrow.

I gave away my education to play baseball. I had a scholarship to college, but I wanted to be a big-league ballplayer right away. I don't even know if I wouldn't do it all over again.

Who knows, maybe if I'd have gone to college I might have had to go to the Salvation Army for my meals. Heck, I'm just glad I'm in the big leagues. I believe that things turn out for the best. Maybe I can stay in baseball as a scout or something when I'm through.

But for my four boys, I'd want them to get their education, so they can be more prepared than me to meet life.

———————————

Ernie Banks, in the twilight of his career, 1969.

On August 23 of that 1971 season, a player rebellion against Durocher broke out in the clubhouse. When Durocher harshly criticized Cubs right-hander Milt Pappas after a defeat, players came to the pitcher's defense. One was Santo. Durocher then accused Santo of, as Holtzman and Vass wrote, "malingering and front-office politics, saying, 'Ron, the only reason we're having a "Ron Santo Day" is because Billy [Williams] and Ernie [Banks] had one and you asked John Holland for one.'" Holland was the Cubs' general manager. "Santo had to be restrained from attacking Durocher. Player discontent festered."

Wrigley continued to support Durocher, while the Cubs seemed spiritless and finished in a third-place tie in the division.

Wrigley's patience was finally exhausted, and on July 24, 1972, he announced that he'd dismissed Durocher, with the team's record at a lackluster 46–44. The new manager, Whitey Lockman, a former player for Durocher with the Giants, got along with the team and improved the Cubs' record by leading them to a 39–26 finish, good enough for second place but eleven games behind the Pirates.

Down the stretch, a remarkable thing occurred in a game against the San Diego Padres. On September 2, Pappas had a perfect game going into the ninth inning. "A pitcher is aware of what's going on, and by the time you get to the seventh or eighth inning, the bench knows what's going on," Pappas recalled in *Cubs Forever* by Bob Vorwald. He had the perfect game into the ninth and an 8–0 lead. The first two batters to face him made out. He had a 1–2 count on pinch hitter Larry Stahl.

———————————————

I'm one pitch from the greatest thing a pitcher can do. Next pitch was a slider on the outside corner, ball two. Next pitch, another slider on the corner, ball three. All these pitches were right there, and I'm saying, "C'mon Froemming, they're all right there." [Bruce Froemming was the plate umpire.] Now comes the 3–2 pitch, again on the outside corner, ball four. I went crazy. I called Bruce Froemming every name I could think of. I knew he didn't have the guts to throw me out because I still had a no-hitter. The next guy, Garry Jestadt, popped to Carmen Fanzone, and I got the no-hitter, which was great. But those balls should have been called strikes.

———————————————

Randy Hundley, the Cubs catcher, said, "There were a couple of pitches that were questionable, but I think if Bruce Froemming had called those pitches strikes, nobody would have ever said a word about it."

At a later date, when Pappas questioned those called balls, Froemming said, "If I had called a pitch like that a strike, I wouldn't be able to sleep nights."

Pappas replied, "Then how in the hell do you sleep all those other nights when you blow calls?" (From *The Cubbies: Quotations on the Chicago Cubs*, by Bob Chieger.)

That Pappas game was recalled years later, on June 2, 2010, when Armando Galarraga of the Detroit Tigers had a perfect game with two outs in the ninth inning until Jason Donald hit a ground ball and was called safe at first. Replays showed the umpire, Jim Joyce, was wrong that Donald had beaten the throw. Thus arose the Pappas-Froemming incident of thirty-eight years earlier. When Tyler Kepner of the *New York Times* called Froemming, he said, "The [last] pitch was outside. I didn't miss the pitch; Pappas missed the pitch. You can look at the tape. Pappas, the next day, said 'I know the pitch was outside, but you could have given it to me.' That pitch has gotten better over the years. The pitch is right down the middle now."

In a 2007 interview with ESPN, Pappas said, "I still to this day don't understand what Bruce Froemming was going through in his mind. . . . The score is 8–0 in favor of the Cubs. What does he have to lose by not calling the last pitch a strike to call a perfect game?"

Kepner wrote, "What Froemming would have lost is integrity, even if only he knew. Umpires can show no bias, to a team or to a situation. Froemming never worked the plate for a perfect game, but he never manufactured one either."

Though the Cubs finished second in 1972, their fortunes for the next decade began to founder. From 1973 to 1983, they would never finish higher than third and generally either ended up in last place or barely escaped the cellar. They reached .500 in only one of those seasons (and that was an 81–81 record for fourth place in 1977, under manager Herman Franks). Managers came and went. So did general managers. Some of the best players in the past seemed to wilt, and the brightest new stars did not feel altogether embraced.

In 1973, twenty-nine-year-old Fergie Jenkins, the ace of the

Cubs pitcher Milt Pappas following his two-hundredth career win, September 21, 1972.

pitching staff, slipped from six straight twenty-game-win seasons to an 8–9 record by the All-Star break. The six-foot-five, 205-pound Jenkins had given up the huge total of twenty-five homers and, though he had had an impressive record of completing games, was being pulled from games by the seventh inning. "I started looking over my shoulder to the bull pen in the late innings," he said. "I never did that before." He was being booed, and that hurt.

At one point, the normally even-tempered Jenkins became so disgruntled at being taken out of a game that he took bats from the Cubs' rack and flung them onto the field. The Cubs' management thought that Jenkins's problem might be in his head and recommended a psychiatrist. Despite the stigma among athletes about seeking psychological help, Jenkins agreed to see a doctor. He remembered walking through the campus of the University of Illinois at Chicago for his first visit to the therapist. He remembered being embarrassed at the many people who recognized him and greeted him with "Hi, Fergie"; "Keep in there, Fergie, it'll come back." However, they did not know why he was on campus. And when Jenkins entered the building of the psychiatrist, he remembered thinking, "What am I doing here, anyway? I'm not off my rocker."

"I saw the doctor eight or ten times," recalled Jenkins. "He was a couch analyst, but I sat in a leather chair. We went back into my life, and talked.

"It seemed I could talk to him about things that I couldn't talk to anyone else about, including my wife." He spoke of baseball anxieties, but also about personal and family problems.

"When the doctor and I talked," he recalled, "I began to see myself clearer. And when I left his office, I was feeling lighter. It was literally a load off my mind."

After the All-Star break, Jenkins's record was six wins and seven losses—not much different from the first half of the season, but he gave up only seven homers. "I was pitching much better," he recalled. Jenkins finished the season at 14–16 (tied for most wins on the club, with Burt Hooton and Rick Reuschel) and a 3.89 earned run average, but completed just seven games. By season's end, Jenkins decided that he had resolved his problems and no longer needed the psychiatrist's help.

Meanwhile, the Cubs decided they no longer needed Jenkins's help. They traded him to the Texas Rangers, where, in 1974, he promptly won twenty-five games, tying Catfish Hunter of

rebuilding year. Glenn Beckert went to San Diego, Randy Hundley to Minnesota, and Ron Santo to the White Sox.

The mid-1970s might best be summed up with a ditty composed by some Wrigley Field fans, about relief pitcher Oscar Zamora:

When the pitch is so fat
That the ball hits the bat—
That's Zamora.

One of the so-called new building blocks of that period, third baseman Bill Madlock, obtained from Texas in the Jenkins trade, actually did become a star. In 1974, although he batted .313, along with outfielders Rick Monday and José Cardenal both hitting close to .300 and Reuschel with a club best of thirteen wins against twelve losses, he couldn't prevent the Cubs from plummeting to a last-place finish.

The season did include one extraordinary feat. Pitcher Bill Bonham struck out the side in the second inning of a game against the Expos, struck out all *four* batters, in fact. When a Cubs pitcher strikes out the side, it may set a record, or at least tie one. In that second inning of the first game of the doubleheader on July 31 at Wrigley Field, Cubs catcher Rick Stelmaszek dropped the third strike on the second batter, which allowed him to reach first safely. Bonham struck out the next two batters in the inning, thus entering the record books, along with a handful of other pitchers. Whether this is a record for Cubs fans to be proud of is squarely in the eyes of the beholder.

The last-place Cubs did not give Bonham a lot of support overall in the season. He was 11–22, the twenty-two losses tying him for the unfortunate league lead. He managed a 3.85 earned run average, however, which on a better team might well have reversed that record, as it did for Jack Billingham of Cincinnati's Big Red Machine (second place in the 1974 NL West), who had a 19–11 record with a 3.95 ERA.

In 1974, Billy Williams, who Philadelphia sportswriter Stan Hochman once described "as quiet as an empty church, steady as the sunrise," was thirty-six years old and in his sixteenth season with the Cubs. He had been relegated to part-time duty but still batted .280 (two years earlier he had led the National League

Hall of Fame outfielder Billy Williams, 1969.

Oakland for the most wins in the major leagues, and completed twenty-nine games, which led the major leagues. He had several more winning seasons and was elected to the Baseball Hall of Fame.

Jenkins wasn't the only onetime Cubs star to be sent packing after the 1973 season, which was seen as yet another so-called

with a .333 average). Yet, at season's end, Williams was traded to Oakland for Manny Trillo, whom the Cubs hoped would solve their second-base problems after a handful of aspirants at that position had been found wanting.

Sweet-swinging Williams had been one of the Cubs' most popular players from the time he came up to the major leagues in 1959. (Rogers Hornsby, then a Cubs minor-league coach, called a Cubs official with a scouting report on Williams, then with Triple-A Houston. Hornsby: "I suggest you bring up Williams. Best hitter on team." The Cubs official responded, "He's better than anyone else down there, huh?" Hornsby: "He's better than anyone up there.") Williams was personable, he was hardworking, and he could hit like few others. He was also philosophical. When traded, he said, "In baseball, a player knows just two things: today and yesterday. There's never a tomorrow in a player's career until it gets here. I guess maybe it's better that way."

The fans protested Williams's departure, but general manager John Holland defended his position by extolling the virtues of Trillo, then twenty-three and a virtual unknown: He had played only a handful of games in the major leagues, for Oakland, in the previous two seasons. Holland's move seemed to work, as Trillo played adequately if not spectacularly at second for the next four seasons, before being traded in 1979 to Philadelphia.

The enactment of free agency in the mid-1970s disturbed Wrigley, as players' salaries escalated. Wrigley said that one day baseball might have to be subsidized, "like grand opera."

Bill Madlock became the centerpiece of Wrigley's (a) folly, (b) parsimony, or (c) shortsightedness? One or all might be the correct answer. After leading the league in batting with a .354 average in 1975 and .339 the following season, Madlock sought a raise.

"No ballplayer is worth one hundred thousand dollars a year," said Wrigley. "Three years ago, I signed Billy Williams for one hundred and fifty thousand. I asked him if he realized he was getting three times my salary as Wrigley Company chairman. Know what he said? 'So what?'"

Madlock sought a long-term, million-dollar contract, more than even Banks had ever earned but at least commensurate with what other players of Madlock's caliber, and below, were reaping. Wrigley refused to pay it. He also said that Madlock's stocky build wouldn't hold up under continuing major-league pressure and that he would be gone from the major leagues "in a year or two."

"We'll trade Madlock if another team is foolish enough to have him," said Wrigley. The Giants were just that foolish and swapped center fielder Bobby Murcer and third baseman Steve Ontiveros for Madlock. Oddly, Murcer received about the same salary that Madlock had sought. Madlock went on to win two more batting titles and finished a fifteen-year career with an imposing .305 lifetime average.

Three years earlier, in July 1973, I had the rare opportunity for an exclusive with Wrigley in his office on the top floor of the ornate Wrigley Building on bustling Michigan Avenue.

"I'm loose," he said, greeting me, with distinctive pouches under his friendly eyes. He stood at the door in white shirtsleeves, a little smaller in build than one might have expected from this genuine mystery man—he admitted to having paid his own way into games in the ballpark he owns by wearing a hat and sunglasses, sitting in the bleachers in supposed incognito. But he was invariably discovered, by fans and photographers, and had quit going to games ten years earlier. Now, he appeared a little hunched from his seventy-nine years of cowering from the public glare. He had never appeared on television or radio. He had made only two speeches that anybody knew about. Both came when he received awards. He said, "Thank you," the first time. The second time, he burst wide open. He said, "Thank you very much."

While he was called the Howard Hughes of baseball, he did not see himself in the mold of that famous Hollywood eccentric.

Then he told me a story that occurred to him.

A fella had a flat tire in front of an insane asylum. Several of the inmates came to the bars and watched him take off the bad tire and start to put on the spare. But he accidentally kicked all the nuts [Wrigley surely meant "lugs"] down an open manhole. He didn't know what to do.

One of the inmates called out, "Why don't you take another nut from each of the other wheels and put them on the fourth and then fix it up as soon as you get to the nearest service station?"

The driver looked with amazement that such an intelligent idea should come from the inmate.

"I may be crazy," said the guy behind the bars, "but I'm not dumb."

Wrigley seemed to identify in some way with the man behind the bars. Some people indeed thought he was sometimes frayed in the noodle. Yet he ran a highly successful gum company (making the then-monumental sum of ten thousand dollars a day), if not an entirely successful baseball team.

Wrigley held out against installing lights in Wrigley Field—the Cubs were the lone team in the major leagues not to have night games—because he thought baseball should be played in the daytime. He was the first owner to televise home games. Other owners resisted this, feeling that it would induce fans to sit at home rather than go through the ballpark's turnstiles. Conversely, Wrigley believed TV would whet fans' appetites and make them want to see games in person. He was also the first owner to suggest allowing children into games at half price. He believed kids were the fans of the future and that they should be persuaded to attend games, but he also felt that if kids got in free, "we'd be raising a generation of deadbeats. If they paid, say half price, they would have more respect for themselves. But this was heresy at the time." And, to a great degree, it remains heresy today.

But all of his ideas, from those above to his College of Coaches, to his hiring an "athletic director" with no baseball experience to run the team, to his switching his manager, Charlie Grimm, with his radio color commentator, Lou Boudreau, and his assorted other unusual moves, came to an end on April 12, 1977. P. K. Wrigley, who had ran the team for the previous thirty-four years, died, at age eighty-two. His son, Bill Wrigley, who did not have nearly the interest in the Cubs that his father did, took over the team, which continued for the next several years to be National League East doormats.

One of the few prideworthy Cubs spots in the late 1970s was relief pitcher Bruce Sutter, who developed a split-finger fastball that was sometimes unhittable, coming in as a fastball and suddenly dropping at the plate like deadweight. In 1979, his Cy Young Award–winning year and one of the six years in which he was named to the National League All-Star team, Sutter saved thirty-seven games for the Cubs, tying the then NL league record. At one point, Hank Greenwald, the play-by-play announcer for the San Francisco Giants, exclaimed, "Three more saves and Sutter ties John the Baptist." None of which prevented the Cubs from trading him, however, in 1980, to the St. Louis Cardinals, where he continued to be one of the best pitchers in baseball—returning several times to Wrigley Field to customarily stifle the bats of his former mates. Sutter is now enshrined in the Hall of Fame.

On May 17, 1979, the Cubs played another game that would enhance their history of improbability. The Cubs fell behind the Phillies, 17–6, in the fourth inning but managed to tie them, 22–22, in the eighth inning. Inevitably, it seemed, all went for naught. The Cubs lost, 23–22, on Mike Schmidt's home run in the tenth inning. It also spoiled a special day for first baseman Dave Kingman (called Dave Ding Dong for his sometimes eccentric or even antisocial behavior, or "King Kong Kingman" for, assumedly, the same reasons, plus his power), who hit three of the eleven homers in the game. (One of his home runs in Wrigley Field—not in that game—is said to be the longest homer ever hit out of that park. It carried beyond the left-center-field wall and bounced on the street at 3700 N. Kenmore, some six hundred feet from home plate. All of the "fan fielders" who regularly gather with their baseball gloves on Waveland Avenue, just beyond the left-field wall in hopes of catching a home-run ball, gave chase down Kenmore, the street that forms a T at Waveland.)

The Cubs finished fifth out of six teams in 1979 and sixth—and last in the division—the following year.

In June 1981, plagued with problems from inheritance taxes after his father and mother died just a few months apart, Bill Wrigley sold the last-place Cubs to the Tribune Company, which

also owned the WGN radio and television stations that aired the team. It was the end of a sixty-year era in which the Cubs were owned by three generations of the Wrigley family. Total price: $21.5 million, including the ballpark and the land.

The new owners brought in brash, six-foot-five Dallas Green, manager of the Phillies' 1980 world champions, to become general manager. Green said that he was going to start "a new tradition," even though the Cubs had had a significant one for over a century. Giving him the benefit of the doubt, Green might well have meant the "tradition" of the previous four decades.

Green brought in Lee Elia, who had been his coach with the

OPPOSITE: Relief specialist Bruce Sutter demonstrating his oft-unhittable split-finger fastball, 1979.

ABOVE: Outfielder Dave Kingman sends a two-run homer toward the fence at Wrigley Field, May 17, 1979. Kingman hit three homers in the game and accounted for six runs as the Cubs lost to the Philadelphia Phillies, 23–22.

Phillies and his college roommate at the University of Delaware. The team also brought back Fergie Jenkins, at age thirty-nine and near the end of his nineteen-year career. Somehow Jenkins led the team with fourteen wins (against fifteen losses). And Green made one of the best deals in the history of the club, sending Iván DeJesús to the Phillies for shortstop Larry Bowa and a minor-league infielder named Ryne Sandberg. Bowa became a Cubs starting shortstop for three seasons, and Sandberg emerged as one of the best players of his era, a future Hall of Famer.

In 1982, the Cubs again finished with a dismal (73–89) record, for fifth place. The following season, they were 5–13 when, on April 29, the Cubs suffered a one-run home loss to the Dodgers and Elia made some notorious postgame remarks, recorded by Les Grobstein, one of the reporters present. His rant became not only one of the most popular tirades in baseball history, but possibly the most listened to—it is replayed continually on the Internet to this day. Elia took issue with the fans in the ballpark in which only day games were still played and who routinely derided the team's and Elia's, well, skill levels.

Elia's rant, somewhat expurgated:

I'll tell you one f—n' thing—I hope we get f—n' hotter than s— just to stuff it up them three thousand f—n' people that show up every f—n' day. Because if they're the real Chicago f—n' fans, they can kiss my f—n' a—, write that down and print it! They're really, really behind you around here, my f—n' a—. What—what the f— am I supposed to do, go out there and let my f—n' players get destroyed every day and be quiet about it? For the f—n' nickel-dime people that show up? The m——s don't even work! That's why they're out at the f—n' game! They oughta go out and get a f—n' job and find out what it's like to go out and earn a f—n' living. Eighty-five percent of the f—n' world's working. The other fifteen come out here! A f—n' playground for the f—s. Rip them f—n' c———s, like the f—n' players! We've got guys bustin' their f—n' a— and them f—n' people boo—and that's the Cubs? My f—n' ass! They talk about the great f—n' support that the players get around here—I haven't seen it this f—n' year. . . .

Perhaps from exhaustion, or laryngitis, Elia eventually ended his philosophical oration. Four months later, in August, with the Cubs' record at fifty-four wins and sixty-nine losses, and in fifth place, where they eventually wound up, Elia and his colorful vocabulary were dismissed. Charlie Fox was handed the assignment of mop-up interim manager.

While Elia's speechifying was surely a remarkable moment in the Cubs' otherwise dreary 1983 season, truly much better things were—and, it being the Cubs, were not—on the horizon for the 1984 campaign.

Iván DeJesús after being picked off at first base, May 5, 1977.

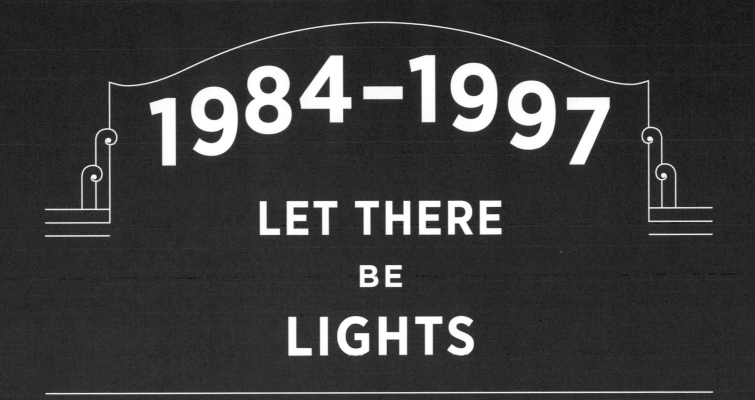

1984–1997

LET THERE BE LIGHTS

Before the 1984 season, Jim Frey, in tinted spectacles and with a quiet demeanor and a build that one might expect more in an accounting professor than in a ballplayer or a hard-bitten baseball manager, had indeed been named the new field leader of the Cubs. Frey had been a fourteen-year minor-league outfielder, a good player with a .302 lifetime batting average, but never good enough to crack the major leagues. Except, that is, as a hitting coach for the previous twelve years, with the Baltimore Orioles and the New York Mets, then as manager of the American League pennant-winning Kansas City Royals in 1980. Now, in one of his most daunting assignments as the Cubs' tenth managerial change in twelve years, Frey assumed command of a

Cubs manager Jim Frey argues with plate umpire Lee Weyer as Bob Dernier looks on, 1985.

ABOVE: Ryne Sandberg slugs a triple during a 1984 game against the Cincinnati Reds.

OPPOSITE: Ryne Sandberg after the Cubs clinched the 1984 National League East pennant.

team that had finished close to last in its division the season before.

Real estate advice to Cubs managers looking for housing must have been "Rent, don't buy." But one underestimated Jim Frey at one's own peril. He had a savvy and experienced baseball mind, an ability to get the confidence of a ballplayer, and a sometimes ironic wit.

Our conversation in the dugout one day turned to his having awakened at four that morning in his North Side apartment. He

said he rose and padded over to the window, eager to see what the weather was like that game day.

"What did you see?" I asked him.

"Nothing," he said. "In my neighborhood, it's dark at that time of day."

To an objective observer, he seemed the right man for his dubious job with the Cubs. He had chosen the right kind of neighborhood to live in.

His wisdom went beyond this. Frey gave some critical advice

to Ryne Sandberg, his twenty-four-year-old second baseman with great potential. Frey suggested that Sandberg change from a spray hitter settling for singles (he had hit only seven and eight homers, respectively, in his previous two years in the major leagues) to being more aggressive at the plate. Sandberg, at six foot one and 175 pounds, was big enough, thought Frey, that he could rattle fences. Accepting Frey's advice, Sandberg responded with nineteen homers, thirty-six doubles, a league-leading nineteen triples, and a .314 batting average. In the field, he also managed to lead the league with 550 assists. And Frey had a subtle way of paying a compliment, which players like Sandberg would appreciate. Following that season, Frey said of Sandberg, "They say he made six errors in 1984, but I can't remember any of them."

Sandberg, who became one of baseball's best fielding second basemen, once said, "I know that being active in sports as a youngster gave me a lot of the ability that I have today. Not that catching toads helps me catch balls, but who knows?" Well, whatever works, surely.

Few ballplayers have ever had as great a day as Sandberg had on June 23, 1984, against the Cardinals at Wrigley Field. With the Cubs behind 9–8 in the bottom of the ninth, Sandberg homered to tie the game. In the tenth, he blasted another home run to tie the game again. The Cubs won 12–11 in eleven innings, with Sandberg driving in seven runs.

General manager Dallas Green had acquired some very helpful players for the 1984 season, including Bob Dernier in center field and Gary "Sarge" Matthews in left field, but especially the six-foot-seven right-hander Rick Sutcliffe—nicknamed the Red Baron for his red hair and his sometimes haughty demeanor on the mound. On June 13, two days before the trading deadline, Green brought Sutcliffe to the Cubs in a seven-player deal with Cleveland. Sutcliffe seemed a risk: He had undergone surgery and that season had only a 4–9 record with the Indians.

Sutcliffe won his first two Cubs starts, lost to the Dodgers, and then won fourteen straight games, for a 16-1 record overall for the regular season.

"He's deliberate; he almost leers at the hitter," wrote Michael K. Herbert in *Inside Sports* magazine. "Crowd the plate, and he's not reluctant to play some chin music. At the end of each inning he doesn't walk off the mound—no, Rick Sutcliffe struts."

The Cubs started slowly in 1984, but by the All-Star break they were half a game out of first place. On August 1, they took the lead

The Cubs' Leon Durham (left) is congratulated at home plate by teammates Jody Davis (center) and Bob Dernier after slamming a two-run homer in the first inning of Game 5 of the National League Championship Series against the San Diego Padres, in San Diego, October 7, 1984. San Diego won the game, 6–3, clinching the National League pennant.

in the NL East. And that's where they were on September 15, when they faced the Mets in Wrigley Field, leading them by seven and a half games with fifteen games to go in the season. It was hardly lost on Cubs fans that the Mets had crushed their pennant hopes fifteen years earlier. They now hoped—they now worried.

Before the game, Frey spoke to a circle of reporters in the Cubs' dugout. He was talking about taking over the team in spring training and trying to divest it of "negativeness." Wrigley Field is the only ballpark in the major leagues without lights, he said.

"A lot of people, including some players, believed that the Cubs could never win playing in the hot summer afternoons and heat of Chicago and with that tough wind day after day," said Frey. "I told 'em: 'We have to make positives out of negatives. We're used to these handicaps. Other clubs are not.'"

Frey said he had to overcome the memory of the Great Flop of '69. "I was asked about the June Swoon so much that I'd lie in bed and think, 'What did I do wrong in 1969?'" he said. "And I was a scout for the Orioles then!"

It was getting close to game time, and the fans had now packed the stands and the roofs on the streets across from the ballpark. Sutcliffe was pitching for the Cubs, and pitching well. In the sixth inning, ahead 2–0, the Cubs loaded the bases. They scored once, reloaded the bases, and their young catcher, Jody Davis, hit the first pitch to him into the center-field bleachers. Davis disappeared into the dugout, but the fans kept cheering, pleading for a curtain call, to which, like Sarah Bernhardt, he graciously assented. After the Cubs ended the inning and he rattled out to home plate in his catcher's paraphernalia, he was greeted by yet another ovation.

The score now stood at 7–0, and the Mets were finished, for the game and, as it happened, the season. It was not going to be a swoon of any sort for the Cubs, at least on the way to the NL East title. The vendors had hawked T-shirts that read BELIEVE IT OR NOT—IT'S TRUE! THE CUBS!

At game's end, the scoreboard flashed THE MAGIC NUMBER IS 7. The fans gave that a standing ovation too. Seven Cubs wins or Mets losses and the Cubs were in.

Now, as the ground crew rolled out the tarpaulin onto the field—there was a light drizzle—many fans stood around. A vendor was still selling beer a half hour after the game. It seemed that the fans, for so long denied championship realities from the team they'd thrown their emotions into, did not want to let go.

A fan in a Cubs cap and a red Windbreaker stood in an aisle down the left-field line. What, he was asked, is everyone looking at?

"Damned if I know," he replied.

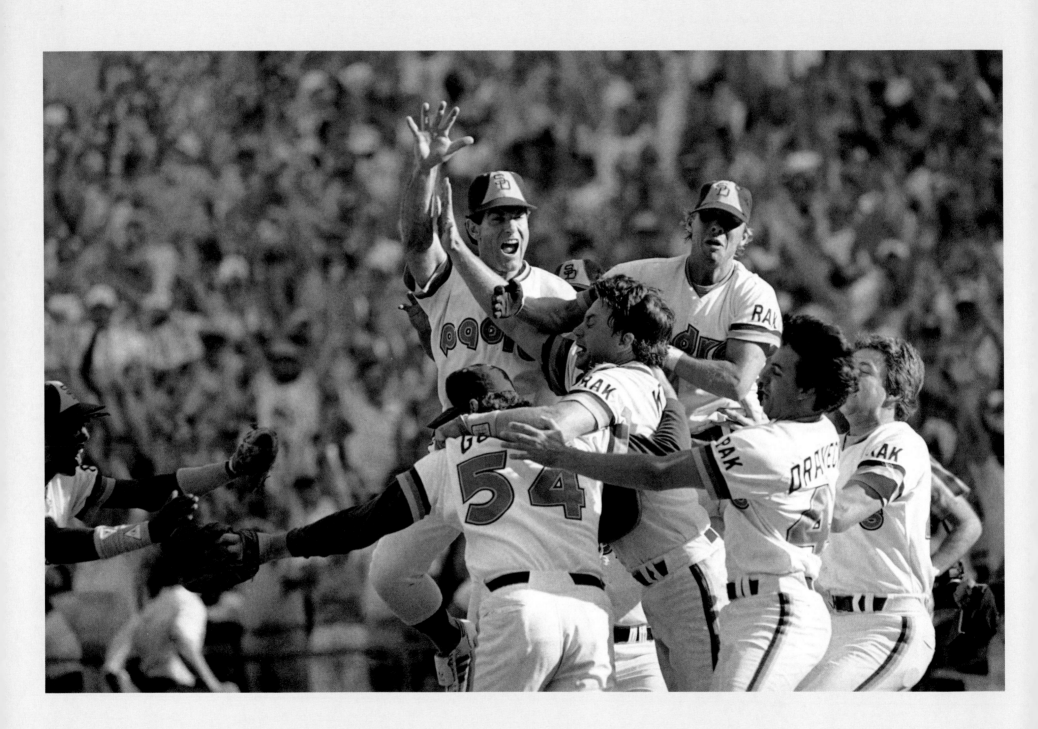

The Cubs ended the regular season at ninety-six wins and sixty-five losses, and six and a half games in front of the second-place Mets. It was the first season that Cubs attendance soared past two million, to 2,107,655. Jubilation reigned in the Windy City.

The Cubs now met the San Diego Padres, winners of the NL West, in a best-of-five series for the right to go to the World Series. Behind Sutcliffe, the Cubs took the opener in Wrigley Field, 13–0, clubbing six homers, including one by Sutcliffe.

Giddy might not be overstating the fans' reaction.

"All of a sudden, it hit me," wrote the ardent Cubs fan and *Chicago Tribune* columnist Mike Royko. "These are the Cubs—the Chicago Cubs—beating the hell out of people. Bullies, that's what we've become. Big, bad, mean bullies. And, oh boy, does it feel great. Why didn't we think of this years ago?"

The next day in Wrigley Field, Steve "Rainbow" Trout beat the Padres, 4–2, giving up just five hits in eight and one-third innings, with the reliable reliever Lee Smith taking care of the last two outs. The Cubs now needed just one more win to find themselves in the World Series for the first time in thirty-nine years—one more game out of three, if need be, a seemingly easy task after these last two convincing victories.

I had covered those two games, done a lot of traveling, and decided not to fly to San Diego for what appeared to be a one-game clinching of the pennant. I planned to cover the Cubs in the World Series instead, which would open in Detroit with the Tigers. Now, as previously stated, there was "no cheering in the press box," but there are boyhood allegiances that simply cannot be snuffed out in adulthood, though journalistic professionalism does require one to truly seek balanced reporting. So I returned to New York and, like much of the nation, watched the game in San Diego on television.

The Padres took Game 3, 7–1. The Padres won—or should I write the Cubs lost—Game 4, 7–5, with Steve Garvey, the San Diego first baseman, walloping a game-winning, ninth-inning home run off the now less-than-reliable Lee Smith. It was now all even at two games apiece.

The Cubs' menacing hurler Sutcliffe took the mound for the fifth and final game. With one out in the seventh inning and the Cubs ahead 3–2, first baseman Leon "Bull" Durham bent down his large frame to glove Tim Flannery's ground ball, but he didn't bend far enough. The ball rolled through his legs, Carmelo

Martínez scoring to tie the game. The Padres scored three more runs, with Tony Gwynn driving in two runs with a double and that no-goodnik Garvey driving in another with a single, to win the game, 6–3. It was as if a circus tent, or worse, had collapsed on Cubs fans.

At the game's conclusion, the phone rang in my home. My wife, Dolly, answered. It was our sympathetic friend and neighbor David Fox, who knew of my passion and what my disposition at that moment might be.

He told Dolly, "Ginny and I would like to take you and Ira out and get Ira drunk."

"David," Dolly replied, "he's already drunk."

Not quite true, though I had poured myself a shot of vodka.

The loss in that play-off series was a terrible blow to Cubs players, Cubs executives, and Cubs fans. There was the haunting question of whether Frey should have removed Sutcliffe, who, to some, seemed to have been tiring earlier in that seventh inning. "He had good stuff, he was the best pitcher in the league the last three months, and he wasn't being hit hard," Frey said after the game. "I thought he'd pitch out of the inning."

Dallas Green remained in seclusion in his office, or home, or, perhaps, rehab center, for the next three days.

"I just cried," recalled Barbara Snower, who had Cubs season tickets. "Friends called, and we consoled each other. There was one fortunate aspect: I had arranged my son Jeffrey's Bar Mitzvah for October 14, which was a World Series day. I hadn't realized it when I organized the affair. And I would've been distracted at the Bar Mitzvah if the Cubs had been in it. My husband, Jerry, knew I was still grieving for the Cubs, and he introduced me that afternoon and said, 'And now, my guiding light, No. 14....'"

She laughed recalling it. Fourteen was the number Ernie Banks had worn with the Cubs.

And what of Ernie, who had been retired from the Cubs and baseball for thirteen years? I had visited him the year before. Ernie Banks smiled. It was perhaps the most famous smile in sports.

Once, he would greet someone with, "It's a beautiful day today for a ballgame, let's play two." That was a different life. Banks, now fifty-two, his hair thinning, wore steel-rimmed spectacles for reading his business papers. He sported a dark tie and a blue suit vest as he sat in his office at Equitable Life Assurance on Michigan Avenue. He had been named to the Hall of Fame in 1977, had

San Diego Padre Steve Garvey (upper left) leaps onto teammates Rich Gossage (54), Terry Kennedy (center), Dave Dravecky (lower right), and Tim Flannery in celebration of their 6–3 NLCS victory over the Chicago Cubs, October 7, 1984, in San Diego.

served part-time in the promotions department for the Cubs but was let go when he missed appointments.

Banks had not had a particularly easy time of it since he retired. He tried the banking business, going to work for the Ravenswood Bank of Chicago.

"They put me through an entire program starting with the teller," said Banks. The vision of the great slugger behind a cashier's window might seem odd, if not unfortunate. Not for sunny Ernie.

And I enjoyed it. I love people, love being around them, and I could have even been a teller for the rest of my life. But I hoped to rise in finance, and took courses at several colleges. But sports always seemed to take me away from it.

They always thought of me as Ernie Banks, the ballplayer. It was hard to make a new identity. There was always the company softball team, and racquetball with the bank president, and functions to attend.

I think I had a fear of failure in doing something outside of sports, like a lot of athletes do. And people don't help, because they keep talking about your past. They are trying to be nice, but they don't understand the problems an athlete has in adjusting to a new career.

Wherever I go in Chicago, people are always coming up to me—just like a woman this morning in the drugstore—saying, "Ernie, I'm still a big fan of yours. I want to thank you for all the pleasure your playing ball gave me." I think that's great, that they still remember me and wish me well after all these years. But, you know, that doesn't put money in my pocket.

Banks played before free agency and never made more than sixty-five thousand in one season. While he was able to save a substantial sum, most of it was now gone.

"But I spent it the best way you can," he said. "I put my three kids through the best private schools and then helped them each in college.

"The bank had a social psychologist, and employees go to see her. I told her my problem about people always putting me back in the past, and she said, 'You can't change what you were, and you can't change the way people look at you. So why don't you

just enjoy it?' And that's what I try to do now." His smile now was wan.

After the Cubs nose-dived in the '84 play-offs, they seemed to carry over their despondence to the following season—that and a rash of injuries had the Cubs tumbling to fourth place, seven games under .500 at 77–84 and twenty-three and a half games behind the first-place Cardinals.

One brief period of excitement at Wrigley occurred in 1985 when an opposition team, and its player-manager, arrived in Wrigley Field amid a great hullabaloo, a train of reporters and camera crews. It was the Cincinnati Reds and Pete Rose, who was two hits shy of tying Ty Cobb's career record for base hits, 4,191. That mark had lasted for fifty-seven years, since Cobb retired in 1928. It was a record—like Lou Gehrig's 2,130 consecutive games and Cy Young's 511 career victories—that until the last two years or so had seemed unassailable. But Rose, at forty-four years old, still played with the enthusiasm that had earned him the nickname Charlie Hustle.

Now, on a hot afternoon, September 8, 1985, Rose came to bat in the first inning. He eased into his distinctive crouch from the left side of the plate, wrapping his white-gloved hands around the handle of his poised black bat. He looked like a mongoose about to lurch after a snake, the snake being the white spheroid thrown by the Cubs' pitcher, Reggie Patterson.

It was a meaningless game for the Cubs, who were eighteen and a half games behind the NL East–leading Cardinals, while the Reds were eight and a half games behind the Dodgers in the NL West but still clinging to pennant hopes.

Cubs fans were now actually cheering for Rose, a player they had enjoyed jeering over the years for his take-no-prisoners style of play. A display of true sportsmanship and appreciation for athletic achievement seemed to take hold in the stands.

Rose responded with a single in the first inning. The scoreboard filled in the details: COBB 4,191 ROSE 4,190. Rose singled again in the fifth, to tie Cobb, and received a standing ovation. After the game, the ever-ebullient Rose recalled when he signed his first professional contract with the Reds' organization, right out of Western Hills High School in Cincinnati, and took a plane and bus to play for the minor-league Geneva, New York, team. "I couldn't believe somebody was actually going to pay me to play baseball, something I woulda done for free," he said. "I thought somebody didn't know what he was doing."

CUBS

ERNIE BANKS 1st base

ABOVE: Ernie Banks baseball card, 1964

OPPOSITE: The Cincinnati Reds' Pete Rose tips his hat to the crowd from first base after tying Ty Cobb's hitting record with a line drive to right field against the Cubs, Sunday, September 8, 1985.

Rose broke the record in Cincinnati four days later, and retired two years after with 4,256 base hits, a record that still stands.

For their part, the Cubs bounced around in the lower part of the standings for the next few years of the 1980s while continuing to play musical chairs with an assortment of managers, Jim Frey among them, who was replaced in midseason 1986 by Gene Michael. There were two particular upbeat spots for the Cubs, however.

In an act that, once proved, would cost millions of dollars in penalties, the owners in 1987 illegally colluded to keep salaries down and turned their backs on expensive free agents. But one of those free agents, Andre Dawson, the thirty-three-year-old star outfielder with Montreal, wanted to play for the Cubs and wanted to play in Wrigley Field. The eleven-year veteran with ailing knees—he would eventually endure twelve surgeries—wanted to get away from the artificial turf of the Expos' Olympic Stadium and play on natural grass, like that in Wrigley Field. Dawson and his agent, Dick Moss, contacted Dallas Green and said that Dawson would sign a contract even with a blank space for the dollar figure. Green responded by offering Dawson five hundred thousand dollars, twice below his market value—and half his Expos salary—but with two hundred and fifty thousand dollars in incentives if Dawson made the All-Star team, started in the All-Star Game, and was named most valuable player in the league.

The lanky Dawson—nicknamed Hawk not for the name the locals call the stiff wind in Chicago but for his superb fielding skills—did all three to get his incentives bonus, and led the league in home runs, with 49, and runs batted in, with 137. He also covered the outfield as ubiquitously as the crabgrass (the length of which the zealous Wrigley Field groundskeepers kept at pure minimum). When he was named the most valuable player in the National League, some critics carped that the member of a cellar-dwelling club should not receive such an honor. I believe it shouldn't have mattered, and didn't, that he won the award with a team that finished sixth in the six-team NL East division, just as it shouldn't have mattered and didn't when Ernie Banks won the MVP Award in 1958 and 1959 when the Cubs finished fifth both seasons. Without Banks or Dawson, the Cubs might have finished in Lake Michigan.

Earlier in that 1987 season, on May 19, there was a moving scene in the ballpark that many will long remember. For nearly

two months, the faithful at Wrigley Field had risen for the seventh-inning stretch, turned west to an empty window in the broadcasting booth, and sang "Take Me Out to the Ball Game." At Wrigley Field, the baseball pious often sway to the tune.

For the last several years, a tradition had been built with Harry Caray, the effervescent broadcaster. He leaned out of that window, holding a long silver microphone like a baton, and urged the virtual congregation, "Now let's hear ya! A one, a two, a three: Take me out to the ball game, take me out with the crowd. . . . " But for almost two months, there had been no Harry Caray in that window. The fans had no live lead but a recording of Caray crooning that baseball staple.

At age seventy, Caray had suffered a stroke in February. But on this day, for the first time since his illness, he was back, being cheered like mad, and warbling as of old.

"No," he said later, "I didn't practice singing. I don't wanna get on-key."

Caray returned to Wrigley Field from his home in Palm Springs, California, to work a game. "The new Harry Caray," as he described himself. He had lost forty-one pounds during his illness and rehabilitation. He ate less and drank a great deal less, dropping from 229 pounds to 188. No more late-night drinking bouts, he said, no more late-night eating binges.

Since moving from the White Sox games to the Cubs in 1982, Caray had established himself as one of the most popular and beloved figures in the city. His love of life in all its forms, his love of baseball—and now his love of the Cubs—proved infectious.

At the ballpark now, a vendor yelled out, "We missed ya, Harry, the whole town missed ya." Indeed, there were billboards on the expressways in Chicago that stated the prevailing sentiment: HURRY BACK, HARRY.

When Caray walked onto the field, the ballplayers greeted him.

"How ya doin', Ryno?" said Caray.

"Good," said Ryne Sandberg, "but heck with how I'm doin'. How you doin'?"

Harry was doing fine, it appeared, and he was back in the booth, and off-key as of old.

The 1988 season, meanwhile, another bleak one for the Cubs, saw them finish fourth, with a 77–85 record, and saw the departure of general manager Dallas Green. Green had fought to have lights installed in Wrigley Field—the last major-league ballpark to install lights after Detroit's Briggs Stadium (renamed Tiger Stadium in 1961), forty years earlier. And finally it happened in Wrigley Field too.

On Sunday, the last day game before the first night game, the Cubs played the Phillies. After the game, as is customary at Wrigley, a flag was flown atop the scoreboard to inform passersby, including riders on the nearby rumbling elevated train, how the Cubs had fared. A blue flag with a white *L* signals a loss, while a white flag with a blue *W* means a win. In the late afternoon, the flag that flew was blue with a white *L*. The Cubs went out with the old in typical style.

Perhaps they would go in with the new differently. At 6:09 Chicago time, on the humid, ninety-degree Monday night of August 8, 1988, 540 floodlights were turned on in the old ballpark, and the whole historic place glowed.

The game began and the Cubs took an early 3–1 lead over the Phillies. In the third inning a dust storm swirled in the infield and

play was halted briefly. Play resumed, and before long thunder and lightning boomed in the night sky, bringing *ooh*s from the standing-room-only crowd of more than forty thousand. One wondered, might the gods have been made angry about night lights glowing in hallowed Wrigley Field?

"What's next," someone in the press box wondered, "a plague of locusts?"

No, but there did come a downpour, with fans and players running for shelter. And the game was called in the fourth inning. The first full night game at Wrigley Field ensued the following evening, and the Cubs beat the Mets, 6–4. By agreement with the city council, night baseball would be limited to only eighteen dates, out of eighty-one Wrigley Field home games.

So a Wrigley Field tradition had ended, and maybe it was not altogether for the best. Wrigley Field had been independent—unique in at least one widely known respect. It didn't follow the crowd, and all because of its former owner. The late P. K. Wrigley believed that baseball should be played in the sun, on natural grass, and that the team ought to be a considerate neighbor in its residential community. It is true that just before World War II he was about to install lights because of a decrease in attendance. But he gave up the lights and cables and steel to the war effort, and later thought better of bulbing up his ballpark.

While the Cubs had done poorly in the standings for most of the previous four decades, they nonetheless had remarkable success at the box office, breaking the two-million mark in three of the previous four seasons in a relatively small park holding little more than forty thousand people. A midseason, midweek game against another noncontending team might draw thirty thousand fans. Cubs fans are so crazy, according to some of their South Side critics, that if their team wins two straight games, it elicits pennant fever.

Some said that big-league baseball would never be quite the same with lights in Wrigley Field. Fact is, little remains the same. Dinosaurs came and went, men's plumed hats came and went, and even the Hula-Hoop craze came and went.

Change, though, is often difficult. And those who wish to retain a link to the past, to clutch something that once was static on a swiftly spinning planet, can take solace in the fact that the lights in Wrigley Field aren't miserably obtrusive from an aesthetic viewpoint. The light structures lie low on the roof and seem a part of the parkscape, and there are no lights above the outfield bleachers.

With its natural grass and sloping symmetry and ivy-and-redbrick outfield walls and quirky hand-operated scoreboard and the cozy closeness of the seats to the field and the congenial visual sense of the stands and bleachers, Wrigley Field remained the peachiest of ballparks.

Some wondered if night games at home would make the Cubs players feel like other major leaguers. Or like major leaguers, period, since it was no longer news that the Cubs, for the most part, had had considerable problems winning a pennant or world championship in the previous seventy years.

I wondered, "Maybe the Cubs will play better in the dark."

There was another change in the 1988 season, and it was at shortstop.

The player was Shawon Dunston, a first-pick overall whom the Cubs took in the amateur baseball draft of 1982. Dunston was a senior at Thomas Jefferson High School in Brooklyn. Three years later, the Cubs brought up the loose-limbed, six-foot-one Dunston, and he played with the unsteadiness of a man on a sea-tossed ship. After one 0-for-5 day at the plate, he lay awake all night wondering what it took to get a hit in the big leagues.

His manager, the longtime baseball operative Don Zimmer, observed, "He doesn't know how to conduct himself on a baseball field." Zimmer saw Dunston chase foul balls "that he had no chance for, that were forty feet into the stands." At bat, "he would swing and miss so hard he'd wind up in the other team's dugout."

Not a nut, the manager concluded, but a young man with immense raw talent who simply didn't have it under control.

"He was like a colt running in the field," Zimmer, a horseplayer, noted. "He seemed to be looking for his legs."

In attempting to get the double-play pivot at second base down, Zimmer observed of Dunston, "He was so fast, so eager, that he'd get to the base before the ball. Then when he got the ball, his legs were so crossed up, he couldn't throw it properly." In 1986, Dunston led all National League shortstops in homers, with seventeen, but also led major league shortstops in errors, with thirty-two.

"One day he'd play like King Kong," said Jim Frey, then the Cubs' general manager. "The next game you'd watch and say, 'Who's wearing Dunston's shirt?'"

One day in May 1988, Dunston was on first base with a hit. "And I see him chatting with Leon Durham," said Zimmer. Durham, the former Cubs first baseman, had been dealt to the Cincinnati Reds.

ABOVE AND RIGHT: Aerial views of Wrigley Field during the first night game in Wrigley Field history, August 8, 1988.

"I was hot. I called Shawon into my office after the game and said, 'It's tough enough to play this game without clowning out there. I'm not putting up with it.' I benched him the next day. I don't know if that was the reason, but from then on he became a changed ballplayer."

In the six weeks after that, Dunston went from a batting average of .232 to close to .300. He hit homers, drove in clutch runs, stole bases, and played the field like Lothario with a mitt.

"He has become one of the best and most consistent players in the league," said Zimmer.

And in July, Cardinals manager Whitey Herzog completed his National League roster for the All-Star Game. One of the players chosen was Shawon Dunston.

The Cubs made the play-offs in 1989, under Zimmer, who seemed to press the right buttons, and behind an outstanding young pitcher, Greg Maddux (with a 19–12 record and uncanny control), a revived Rick Sutcliffe (16–11), and Dunston hitting a respectable .278 and with a cannon for an arm in the field.

Vin Scully, the renowned play-by-play announcer for the Los Angeles Dodgers, was behind the NBC microphone for this play-off series. Scully, who had an affection for Wrigley Field, opened his broadcast with a description of the ballpark:

She stands alone on the corner of Clark and Addison, this dowager queen, dressed in basic black and pearls, seventy-five years old, proud head held high and not a hair out of place, awaiting yet another date with destiny, another time for Mr. Right.

She dreams as old ladies will of men gone long ago, Joe Tinker, Johnny Evers, Frank Chance. And of those of recent vintage like her man Ernie. And the Lion [Leo Durocher]. And Sweet Billy Williams.

And she thinks wistfully of what might have been [shots of the 1984 play-offs on the screen], and the pain is still fresh and new, and her eyes fill, her lips tremble, and she shakes her head ever so slightly. And then she sighs, pulls her shawl tightly around her frail shoulders, and thinks, "This time, this time it will be better."

It wasn't. The Cubs lost that first game 11–3, Greg Maddux being chased in the fourth inning. The Cubs won the next game, but then lost the last three by one run, two runs, and one run, to lose the Series four games to one.

The Cubs foundered anew, and Zimmer was replaced within two years. In 1994, two unusual events occurred—unusual even for the Cubs and Wrigley Field. One was the appearance of one of Chicago's icons in a baseball uniform, Michael Jordan. The other was the sudden discarding of a baseball uniform, at age thirty-four and still a force on the diamond, by Ryne Sandberg.

On the chilly but sunny afternoon of April 7, Jordan, the thirty-one-year-old, six-foot-six rookie right fielder for the White Sox, spoke with a few reporters before the exhibition game against the Cubs.

"What if I got a hit today?" he said. "You guys would fall over, wouldn't you?"

The reporters smiled but courteously withheld comment. Well, he was considered by many the greatest athlete in the world, the man who had recently led the town's Bulls to three National Basketball Association championships in the past three seasons, the man known as Air Jordan for his ability to fly through the air without the aid of a cape or propeller. The previous October, Jordan had shocked the sports world by deciding to give up basketball and try his hand at baseball. He had spent the previous two months before the Wrigley Field exhibition game playing for the White Sox's minor-league affiliate, the Double-A Birmingham Barons. He had trouble batting over .200. But the

called. The game ended in a tie. Jordan went back to the minor leagues and, with his baseball career at a standstill, returned to the Bulls the following year and helped them win three more consecutive titles.

Two months after Jordan's appearance, Sandberg made his disappearance. He shockingly quit baseball on June 13, after thirteen big-league seasons and in only the second year of his four-year $30.5 million contract, citing family problems and intimating displeasure at the Cubs' inability to build winning teams (he was also hitting just .238 at the time, but had hit .309 the season before and had again made the All-Star team). And the Cubs again finished in last place. In 1996 Sandberg returned to play for the Cubs, and the Cubs finished a dispiriting fourth, though Sandberg played solidly, hitting twenty-five homers and driving in eighty-five runs. They were last in 1997, but something was brewing for the next season, and some of the most memorable moments in Cubs—and baseball—history were just offstage.

OPPOSITE: Cubs pitcher Greg Maddux hangs his head after giving up a home run to San Francisco's Will Clark in Game 1 of the 1989 NLCS, won by the Giants, 11–3.

LEFT: NBA legend turned Chicago White Sox player Michael Jordan rips a sixth-inning RBI double against the Cubs, April 7, 1994.

Sox decided to bring him to Chicago for this annual City Series game against the Cubs.

When the right fielder trotted out to his position to start the game for the White Sox, the fans in the bleachers bowed and cheered. Jordan was treated as royalty, which, as far as Chicagoans were concerned, he was.

When he came to bat for the first time, hitting in the sixth position, he popped up to first base. But in the sixth inning, he hit a high chopper that bounced off the top of the glove of the leaping third baseman for a run-scoring single. The crowd gave him, lo the opposition, a standing ovation. In the very next inning, there was reason for the reporters to fall over. He cracked a game-tying double down the third-base line. The crowd erupted again.

But not all went so well. He made a baserunning mistake, misplayed a single in right field, allowing the runner to get to second, and in the ninth inning, with the score tied and a chance to put his team ahead, he struck out on three pitches, the last one

1998–2002

THE
HOME-RUN CHASE
HEARD
ROUND THE WORLD

The year 1998 saw continued fighting in Kosovo, a peace accord in Northern Ireland, and President Clinton accused in a White House sex scandal. Amid all the news, a rare but thrilling baseball event captivated millions. It occurred in the summer and early-fall months on baseball diamonds in the States, with particular emphasis on the old, ivy-walled Wrigley Field in Chicago and the newer Busch Stadium in St. Louis.

Sammy Sosa, an effusive twenty-nine-year-old Dominican right fielder for the Cubs, who would do a pogo-stick double hop at the plate after belting a ball that was heading to clear the fence, and thirty-four-year-old Mark McGwire, a redheaded, goateed, muscular-as-Paul-Bunyan first baseman for the St. Louis Cardinals, were engaged in a riveting pursuit of the major-league, single-season home-run record of sixty-one set by the Yankees' Roger Maris in 1961. It was perhaps the most hallowed record in American sports. The episode resembled a great horse race, with two powerful steeds barreling neck and neck down the stretch, first one pulling ahead and then the other as they neared the finish line.

And this took place just four years after a season that had been shortened by a strike by the major-league players, and for the first time since 1904, no postseason play-offs or World Series were held. Many fans had become disenchanted with what they perceived as the greed of either the players or the owners, or both, and threatened to turn their backs on baseball. But the McGwire-Sosa home-run explosion brought fans across the

nation back to the ballparks in droves—and to the edge of their seats. For the Cubs, the attendance that year, 2,623,000, was just some 30,000 short of the Wrigley Field record set the year before the 1994 players' strike.

"It's amazing," McGwire said, sitting in front of his locker in the Cardinals' clubhouse in Wrigley Field while the homers had been adding up. "I've seen editorials and the front-page stories about what this means to people. Just today I got a letter from the prime minister of Japan, and one from Bob Dole." (Dole was the 1996 Republican candidate for president who lost to Bill Clinton.)

It all began on Opening Day in April with a bases-loaded home run by McGwire. He homered in the next three games. Sosa got his first four games into the season. By May 19, McGwire had reached twenty homers faster than anyone in any season ever, then became the fastest to reach thirty homers, and then the fastest to reach forty.

Meanwhile, Sosa kept pace, especially with his spectacular twenty homers in June—a major-league record for hitting home runs in a calendar month. Earlier in his career, Sosa was the kind of Mad Hatter batter who swung so violently and so indiscriminately that, it was said, he would attack even a white paper cup if it came floating toward home plate. Slowly, he developed patience at the plate, waiting for a pitch in his strike zone and not that of Wilt Chamberlain's. Home runs continued to boom off his bat, but he remained one, two, or three homers behind McGwire. Metaphors for what was transpiring spilled off writers' keyboards. Perhaps the most appropriate was the game of home-run cat and mouse, McGwire playing Tom to Sosa's Jerry. By July 10, Sosa had pulled into the lead with two homers over McGwire, 37–35.

What made the rivalry even more intriguing was that McGwire and Sosa came essentially from two different worlds. McGwire, the son of a Southern California dentist, had lived a rather privileged life, while Sosa grew up in an impoverished home, if admittedly in the Dominican Republic's baseball hotbed of San Pedro de Macoris, where his first baseball glove was a used cereal box and where he shined shoes and picked oranges to help his widowed mother put food on the table. "I'm happy to go do my job and everybody go crazy," Sosa had said. "I love it. Oh, what a country!"

McGwire had been a strapping, six-foot-five, 245-pound ballplayer since he broke into the major leagues in 1986 and was a home-run slugger from the start, whacking forty-nine home runs

PREVIOUS SPREAD: Fans watch the start of a game between the Atlanta Braves and the Cubs at Wrigley Field, July 6, 2009.

BELOW: Mark McGwire and Sammy Sosa share a moment together as they both pursue the 1998 National League home-run championship—and single-season home run record.

in his rookie year, tying Andre Dawson of the Cubs for the major-league lead.

Sosa, on the other hand, had been a skinny, six-foot, 165-pound twenty-year-old when he broke in with the Texas Rangers in 1989. He was traded that year to the Chicago White Sox by the Rangers' managing partner, one George W. Bush, the same W. who later lived for eight years in Washington DC.

Growing more muscular, Sosa began hitting home runs in his fourth full season in the major leagues—thirty-three of them, when he had hit just eight the season before. Bush, who had once desired to become commissioner of baseball, said that one of his biggest mistakes (some thought he said "only" mistake) was to trade Sammy Sosa. The two remained friends, and Sosa excused Bush, telling me, "I was young and raw, and I probably would have traded me too."

In the two previous seasons, Sosa had hit forty and thirty-six homers, respectively; McGwire fifty-two and fifty-eight. There was natural speculation that McGwire indeed could soon break Maris's record. Sosa was an afterthought in that regard, if he was thought of at all.

When the Cubs and Cardinals met for a two-game series at Wrigley Field, beginning the night of Tuesday, August 18, 1998, Sosa and McGwire, each with forty-seven homers for the season, surprisingly and outwardly expressed the seeming joy they were sharing publicly with each other in their competition. After Sosa took batting practice, he looked to the Cardinals' side of the field and saw the team doing stretching exercises. Suddenly, he made a beeline for McGwire, who was on the ground twisting his ample body. A phalanx of reporters and cameramen followed Sosa.

"Get away! Get away!" McGwire shouted, laughing. Then he got up, and he and Sosa hugged. And then they parted. It seemed that neither had time to whisper sweet nothings in the other's ear.

Neither player hit a home run that night, each going hitless and striking out a total of six times. Sosa wondered if he was trying too hard. When a Cardinals pitcher walked Sosa, the crowd booed. When the Cubs hurler walked McGwire, the crowd booed. They wanted fireworks, and under these circumstances, from either side of the aisle.

The next afternoon, the chase to surpass the record took a dramatic turn—three dramatic turns, in fact, as Sosa grabbed the major-league home-run lead from McGwire only to see McGwire grab it back.

Sammy Sosa responding to cheers after hitting another homer in 1998.

When Sosa lined a home run into the left-field bleachers in the fifth inning, it gave him forty-eight for the season, one more than McGwire.

Sosa was ahead in the race for the first time all season. As he ran past McGwire, who was standing impassively by first base, and completed his home-run trot, many in the sellout crowd of 39,689 launched into a roaring chant: "Sammy! Sammy!"

What was McGwire thinking as Sosa cruised by him?

"Not much, really," he said after the game. "Just that Sammy's an awesome player."

As, of course, was McGwire, who over the next five innings answered in home-run fashion not once but twice. He sent one baseball clear out of Wrigley Field in the eighth inning to tie the game, and another into the center-field bleachers in the tenth to reclaim the homer lead with forty-nine and, for good measure, bring his team to an 8–6 victory.

At this point, McGwire was on pace to hit sixty-four homers—he had thirty-eight games left in the season—and Sosa sixty-two, with thirty-six games remaining.

On Tuesday, August 25, McGwire returned to Busch Stadium after a nine-game road trip and having taken a giant step toward reaching the record. He had departed with forty-seven homers and came back with fifty-three, two in front of Sosa and eight short of Maris's sixty-one.

On Friday, August 28, in the top of the fifth inning in Busch Stadium, a small, unobtrusive numerical figure in a corner of the center-field scoreboard that a moment earlier had read MCGWIRE 54/SOSA 52 now read SOSA 53.

Then it was 55 to 54. In Denver on August 30, Sosa belted his fifty-fourth—a five-hundred-foot shot that tied McGwire—but a few hours later in Busch Stadium McGwire answered that with his number fifty-five.

On September 1, McGwire, still slightly ahead of Sosa, propelled home run number fifty-six to tie the National League record set by the Cubs' Hack Wilson in 1930. Six days later, the Cubs came into Busch Stadium with McGwire at sixty and Sosa at fifty-eight. McGwire hit number sixty-one on September 7 and number sixty-two the day after, breaking the record while Sosa watched from his position in right field. And what was Sosa thinking? After the game, he said, "I was thinking, 'He's the man!'" Sosa remained at fifty-eight.

But neither McGwire nor Sosa stopped there. Sosa took the home-run lead when he hit his sixty-sixth, with about a week to go in the season. Just forty-five minutes later in Montreal, "Big Mac"—the reason for the prodigious hamburger appellation was obvious—tied Sosa at sixty-six and quickly took the lead in the following days, hitting a pair in each of two back-to-back games at season's end.

McGwire finished with seventy to Sosa's sixty-six, ending a breathlessly delightful summer in baseball. McGwire's team failed to make the play-offs, while Sosa's did, barely, with pitchers Kevin Tapani (nineteen wins), Steve Trachsel (fifteen wins), and rookie strikeout ace Kerry Wood, along with first baseman Mark Grace (.309 batting average) having provided added spark during the season. But it took a 5–3 win behind Trachsel in a one-game Wild Card tiebreaker in Wrigley Field over the Giants, with whom they had finished second in the NL Central division, for the Cubs to enjoy their first postseason appearance in nine years. The joy was short-lived. The Cubs were swiftly eliminated by the Atlanta Braves in a three-game sweep. Sosa hit no homers in the series, going 2 for 11 with one double and four strikeouts.

LEFT: The scoreboard at Busch Stadium in St. Louis shows home-run totals for Cardinals slugger Mark McGwire and the Cubs' Sammy Sosa, September 27, 1998.

In addition to his 66 home runs for the regular season, Sosa also batted .308 and led the league with 158 runs batted in and 134 runs scored, which earned him the Most Valuable Player Award in the National League. He received thirty first-place votes to McGwire's two.

The record, however, was soon broken. Just three years later, the Giants' Barry Bonds passed McGwire by hitting seventy-three homers.

But in the following seasons, the reputations of all three sluggers, McGwire, Sosa, and Bonds, would be tarnished. All three would be accused or suspected of taking illegal anabolic steroids or human growth hormones. Before a 2005 Congressional hearing in Washington on steroid use in the major leagues, McGwire refused to talk about any drug use he might or might not have indulged in. "I'm not going to go into the past or talk about my past," he told a congressman. "I'm here to make a positive influence on this." He added, "My lawyers have advised me that I cannot answer these questions without jeopardizing my friends, my family, and myself."

To many, this was tantamount to an admission of guilt. (Five years later, McGwire admitted to taking legal body-enhancing supplements.) Sosa, too, when asked in the same hearing about drugs, categorically denied using them. But suspicion remained. Sosa followed his sixty-six-homer season with sixty-three, fifty, sixty-four, and forty-nine home-run years. Oddly, his fifty and forty-nine years led the league but not his sixty-three or sixty-four years, which finished behind McGwire and Bonds, respectively. Suffering from an assortment of injuries and being, he felt, hounded by drug accusations, Sosa grew surly toward fans and the media, left the Cubs with a sour taste in a lot of people's mouths—including, presumably, his—played one mediocre season in Baltimore, and then retired from baseball in 2007, at age thirty-seven.

Steroids are said to help build muscle mass during workouts and speed recovery. Doctors aren't sure of the side effects, though most caution that they can certainly be dangerous to one's health. One wondered, was it these three players or their pharmacists who were primarily responsible for splintering seats in the bleachers and the upper decks?

It is believed here that no amount of drug use can add to the terrific hand–eye coordination needed to hit a home run. One might hit the ball somewhat farther with increased strength, but not meet it solidly. It seemed that Sosa, McGwire, and Bonds were superior players, and long-ball hitters, even before there was any suspicion of drug use. It is this writer's view that all three deserve to be in the Baseball Hall of Fame.

"You can't teach timing in hitting a baseball, especially when you're talking about hitting a ninety-three-mile-an-hour slider," said Tony La Russa, manager of McGwire's St. Louis Cardinals. "And if it was just muscle and strength generating those home runs, then you'd have every weight lifter and offensive lineman come off the street and start hitting balls over the fences."

For all the pyrotechnics of the McGwire-Sosa home-run extravaganza, perhaps the single most electrifying moment of the 1998 season at Wrigley Field occurred on May 8, a cloudy, rain-threatened spring afternoon.

A husky, twenty-year-old rookie right-handed pitcher named Kerry Wood looked so youthful it seemed he did not yet shave. His boyish appearance, though, belied a powerful, whirlwind pitching motion. Wood was beginning his fifth big-league career start, against the Houston Astros, a good-hitting team that would end the season first in the National League West division. Wood struck out the first Houston batter to face him, Craig Biggio, on a third-strike swing and miss. Wood fanned the next batter, and the next. In the second inning, he struck out two batters, before Dave Clark made contact and flied out.

There was a murmur in the stands as well as in both dugouts. Wood's fastball was sizzling at or near one hundred miles an hour, and his breaking ball was diving away from right-handed batters and into left-handed batters as swiftly and madly as a balloon with its air suddenly escaping. The Cubs scored in the second inning, for a 1–0 lead.

Opening the Houston third inning, shortstop Ricky Gutiérrez grounded into the hole between short and third. The ball bounced

nineteen, shared by David Cone, Tom Seaver, and Steve Carlton, and the major-league record was twenty, held by Roger Clemens.

In the seventh inning, Wood recalled, a light rain began to fall. "I thought the umpires might call a halt to the game," he said. "I hoped they wouldn't. Honestly, I just felt I was playing catch out there. I took in everything. I was able to look around and enjoy the fans that were doin' it up. Not too many times when you're out on the hill does the game slow down that much where you can really take it all in. Everything seemed to be going in slow motion. . . . I really didn't know how many strikeouts I had, but I knew it was a shutout—we were winning 1–0. You keep track of things like that."

In the ninth inning, with the Cubs now leading 2–0, Wood made Bill Spiers, pinch-hitting for the pitcher Reynolds, swing and miss at a third strike. Strikeout number nineteen, tying the National League record.

Biggio was next up, and he grounded out.

Up came right fielder Derek Bell, a right-handed batter, who struck out, flied out, and popped out. The count went to two strikes. Wood wound up and fired a low curveball that broke from the inside of the plate to the outside. Bell chopped helplessly, for strikeout number twenty, ending the game and tying Clemens's all-time record.

Former Cubs third baseman Ron Santo, in the broadcast booth, said he felt goose bumps. "I've never felt that way before," he said. "That's the first game I've ever seen that the hitters had no chance." Recall that Santo faced Sandy Koufax when the Dodgers' left-hander threw a perfect game against the Cubs in 1965.

The 15,758 spectators of the game—the crowd was relatively sparse perhaps due to the threat of rain—witnessed one of the most dominating pitching performances in the history of base-ball. In fact, *Sports Illustrated* at the time called it the best ever.

"I've had at least twenty-five thousand people come up to me over the years and tell me they were in the ballpark and saw the game," Wood recalled. "Don't know where they all could have been hiding."

Woods finished the season with a 13–6 record and 233 strike-outs, third in the league. He was named National League rookie of the year. He started the third and final game in the play-offs against the Atlanta Braves, in Wrigley Field. Wood pitched five innings, gave up three hits and one run, and left the game with the Cubs behind 1–0. The Braves went on to win 6–2, behind Greg Maddux, who had carried a shutout into the eighth inning.

off the outstretched glove of Cubs third baseman Kevin Orie. Gutiérrez was safe with what the official scorer called a single (some in the press box disputed it, believing it should have been ruled an error). It would be the only Houston base hit of the game.

Brad Ausmus struck out, and pitcher Shane Reynolds bunted Gutiérrez to second. Wood balked Gutiérrez to third, but Biggio grounded out for the final out of the inning. The only other Houston base runner in the game would be Biggio, who was hit by a Wood pitch in the sixth inning, and he advanced no farther.

Meanwhile, Houston batter after Houston batter was going down on strikes. Wood struck out the side in the fifth, in the seventh, and again in the eighth.

Fans in the bleachers held up κ signs, emblematic of his strike-outs. Wood now had eighteen of them, tying the major-league record for a rookie pitcher. The National League record was

Wood developed elbow problems in his pitching arm and underwent Tommy John surgery that kept him out of the entire 1999 season and limited him in 2000 to an 8–7 record with 132 strikeouts, 101 fewer than in his rookie season.

Madison Avenue in Chicago is known to local baseball fans as the demilitarized zone. The closest thing to trench warfare the city knows, it is a dividing line not just for the city's street-numbering system but for Cubs fans and White Sox fans, with loyalties split between Wrigley Field on the North Side and Comiskey Park on the South Side—a distance of some ten miles. And emotions remain heated whether the teams are winning—which they have

done infrequently over the last half century—or are in last place, as the Cubs were on June 16, 1997, or in fourth place, as the Sox were that same year. Rarely is a fan of the Cubs and White Sox the same person.

There are stories of Cubs and White Sox fans coming to blows in bars and on city streets, and of fans of one team or the other

refusing to darken the door of the rival ballpark. One day, Bette Gleason, the sister of the late Chicago sportswriter Bill Gleason, a family of South Siders, chanced to accept a free ticket for Ladies' Day at Wrigley Field. The family patriarch, Joe Gleason, told her, "It's worse than if you left the church."

White Sox owner Jerry Reinsdorf went to Wrigley Field to watch a City Series game in the early 1990s and "was cursed and spit at," he said, and needed security guards to get him out of the ballpark. He has never returned.

Santo was traded to the White Sox in 1974. He remembers a sign that greeted him in Comiskey Park: RON SANTO—WELCOME TO THE MAJOR LEAGUES.

The last time anyone took a Cubs–White Sox game seriously—at least in relation to the record book—was when the Cubs and the White Sox played in their lone World Series against each other, in 1906. Time flies, and ninety-one years later, in 1997, they played each other again—this time in the first interleague regular season games that counted in the standings. There would be yearly alternating three-game series, first at the Sox's park and the following year at Wrigley Field. Major League Baseball had begun interleague games to boost attendance, and they succeeded, with natural rivalries playing for keeps and before generally full houses—the Yankees and the Mets, the Dodgers and the Giants, the Reds and the Indians, the Cardinals and the Royals, the Astros and the Rangers.

The look of the players on the greensward of Comiskey Park was clearly an homage to yesteryear. Each team wore commemorative uniforms—the White Sox in white caps and the white home baseball suit of 1917, the Cubs in the navy blue and gray of their 1911–12 teams.

The Cubs won that first game, 8–3, but the Sox took the final pair. The next year, in Wrigley Field, when the starting White Sox lineup was announced, it was, to no one's surprise, booed, though there was a scattering of cheers. Obviously some White Sox fans had braved insult from their ilk to maneuver into, for them, the less-than-sainted crosstown ball field. Before full, throaty houses, the Cubs swept this series in three straight day games, 13–7, 7–6, and 6–5 in twelve innings.

In 1999, Sosa and McGwire hooked up in another season-long homer duel, with the Cardinals first baseman edging out the Cubs right fielder, sixty-five to sixty-three. The new manager of the Cubs, Jim Riggleman, didn't help the fortunes of the team: last

place again. Don Baylor became the Cubs' new manager in 2000, and it was last place again.

"Sure, there's a long, long history of losing that we're burdened with," Baylor said early in the season. "You're reminded of it all the time. Even grandmothers come up to me and say, 'Will the Cubs ever win in my lifetime?' I tell them, I tell my players, 'Guys, that was the old millennium. We're in the new millennium.'"

In 2000, other troubles boiled for the Cubs. When Sosa demanded a 2001 contract extension, the Cubs balked and awkwardly attempted to trade him. After the Cubs finished the season at 67–95 and in last place, thirty games behind the NL Central champion Cardinals, Andy McPhail, the general manager, let thirty-six-year-old Mark Grace go as a free agent. A standout first baseman for thirteen seasons, Grace was miffed. While knowing it was a "business decision," he remarked upon joining the Arizona Diamondbacks, "It's good to be on a team at last that's committed to winning," suggesting, to be sure, that the denizens of Wrigley Field weren't.

The Cubs finished in third place the following year, but fell to last place and thirty games behind in 2002.

Hope, though, springs eternal, if not also internal, in the hearts of Cubs fans. In 2003, the Cubs unveiled yet another new manager, Dusty Baker, who for the previous six seasons had managed the Giants in contention each season, and in 2002 led them to a National League pennant, though they lost the World Series to the Anaheim Angels in seven games. Three young starting pitchers, a healthy Kerry Wood, Mark Prior, and Matt Clement, and potentially effective though mercurial Carlos Zambrano, produced visions of a strong rotation. That wasn't all. Veteran slugging outfielders Sosa and Moisés Alou and three new acquisitions, first baseman Eric Karros and second baseman Mark Grudzielanek from the Dodgers and Aramis Ramirez from the Pirates, looked like the start of a feared batting order.

The Cubs were beginning to look lethal.

LEFT: Cubs "superfan" Ronnie "Woo Woo" Wickers carries his glove as he walks past the Wrigley Field sign welcoming Dusty Baker as the new manager of the Chicago Cubs, November 19, 2002.

RIGHT: Mark Grace singles in two runs versus the Milwaukee Brewers, July 23, 2000.

2003–2010

THE FOUL BALL THAT WILL LIVE IN INFAMY

Well, the FBI is now saying that Al Qaeda may be planning an attack on a U.S. sports stadium. See, I don't think Al Qaeda, though, has any idea about our sports. You know what their big plan is? To hit Wrigley Field during the World Series.

—Jay Leno, quoted in the *New York Times*, April 4, 2010

In their annual, seemingly quixotic quest to end their ninety-three-year world championship drought, the Cubs in 2003 got off to a rollicking start. They walloped the Mets, 15–2, in the opener in Shea Stadium, went on to win thirteen of their next twenty-two games, and found themselves solidly in first place in the NL Central division.

Now, unfortunately, they were confronted with 140 more games in which to win the division and head for a world championship. That was something Cubs historians knew hadn't happened since 1908, when the Ottoman Empire went into permanent decline.

The Cubs had a lamentable if tantalizing history of starting fast, like the racehorses known as morning glories, then fading as the race and the shadows grew ever longer. The June Swoon is as famous in Chicago as Al Capone, or Oprah.

New manager Dusty Baker addressed the issue of the large number of day games at Wrigley Field, compared to other team's home schedules.

You certainly have to add that to the equation, if they are the only ones who haven't won in a long time and still playing mostly day baseball. You wish they'd add some more night games in the summertime.

But it's true that most players play most of their games at night, starting in the minor leagues. For the most part, we're the swing shift, the three-to-eleven people.

———————————

But, it was suggested, since the Cubs play eighty-one games at home—all but eighteen of them day games—don't they have an advantage in being able to adjust to the difference better than visiting teams?

"Not necessarily," Baker continued, "because they only play three games at a time in Wrigley Field, and then they're gone."

Ah, but some of those games are played after visiting teams have, as Baker said, trouble sleeping because day games in Chicago give opponents ample time to party on Rush Street, among other areas.

Even the slugger Sammy Sosa, who was enjoying success on the current schedule, went on record saying the Cubs would be better with more night games. He'd taped a newspaper headline to his locker the season before: "Let There Be Night."

"I don't know," said Rey Sánchez, the Mets shortstop who played seven seasons for the Cubs, from 1991 to 1997. "It doesn't appear that day games hurt Sammy too much."

If the heat supposedly wilted the team, then why didn't all the players wilt? Greg Maddux and Fergie Jenkins and Bruce Sutter were Cy Young Award winners while hurling half the season in Wrigley Field; Bill Madlock was a two-time National League batting champion there. And how to explain the remarkable careers of future Hall of Famers Ernie Banks and Billy Williams and Andre Dawson, and also of Ron Santo, a nine-time All-Star, all toiling magnificently under the sultry Chicago summer sun?

"You have to turn the situation into a positive," said Sánchez, viewing the matter with the perspective gained from experience. "As a professional, you have to make your adjustments. You have to go at a slower pace in the heat. Maybe you only run 90 percent to first base on an easy grounder. Maybe you don't work as hard outdoors doing extra work, but build yourself up indoors. The body adjusts. And you have to understand—if you party, it's not going to take you over the edge." That is, it will deplete, not enhance.

On an April evening before a night game in Chicago in 2003, the wind blowing fiercely off Lake Michigan and the temperature barely above freezing, Baker sat in the dugout in a Windbreaker and gloves.

He was asked if the weather—the cold, not the heat—would prove detrimental to the fortunes of the team. This was a reversal of the usual complaint about playing in Wrigley Field.

"You've got to deal with the elements," Baker said, apparently dusting weather excuses from the bench. "There are ten million people in Chicago, and they deal with the elements. The Cubs can too."

The jury was, of course, still out on whether they could.

On June 8 of that year, Wrigley Field was the site of not only a highly unusual ball game, but one that could be considered a masterpiece.

The Cubs played host to the New York Yankees in an interleague, regular season game. This game should have been bottled and put in a time capsule. If Rembrandt had painted a ball game, this would have been it. The game was all it had been touted to be and more, like a winning lottery ticket, like a first kiss.

It showcased the forty-year-old Yankees starter Roger Clemens, trying for the third time to reach the historic career milestone of three hundred victories. The twenty-five-year-old

and FDR competed for the most headlines. In the beach-weather seventies, the sun shining sweetly after days of miserable gray and rain, the breeze off Lake Michigan rippling the pennants on the stadium rooftop, there was standing room only on a perfect day for a ball game.

The felicitous tension happily distracted attention from the sour left by a widely reported Sammy Sosa incident earlier in the week. The jubilant right-field icon was discovered to have used an illegal cork-filled bat, which is alleged to help propel baseballs farther than bats made entirely of ash and maple.

The game was scoreless into the top of the fourth. Wood was striking out Yankees hitters as though he were caught in one of Walter Mitty's dreams. The Yankees went ahead 1–0 in the seventh, and Clemens was removed from the game after giving up a single to Sosa and a walk to Alou. But Eric Karros walloped a home run off reliever Juan Acevedo, and the Cubs took the lead, 3–1. Wood pitched into the eighth, striking out eleven, and the Cubs won, 5–2. The young ace achieved a personal milestone, winning his fiftieth career major-league win. He had only 249 to go to equal Clemens.

The Cubs were in a tight race for the division title all season long with both Houston and St. Louis. In early September, however, the Cubs essentially halted the Cardinals' three-season run in the play-offs by winning four of five games with them at Wrigley Field. The Astros stayed close, but the Cubs finished the

Cubs players swarm closing pitcher Joe Borowski (48) as they beat the Atlanta Braves in Game 5 of the NLDS, 5–1, at Turner Field in Atlanta, October 5, 2003, clinching a trip to the National League Championship Series.

Cubs pitcher Kerry Wood took the mound with determination, as if to say, "Not so fast, old-timer."

Both were strikeout artists, one perhaps the best pitcher of his generation, the other with the potential to be his successor, and both were also burly Texans who, it seemed, could lift a piano and move it across a room.

These two historic teams were playing the second game of a weekend series. It was the first time the two teams had met in meaningful games since the 1938 World Series, when Seabiscuit

season with an 88–74 record for first place, one game ahead of Houston and three in front of the Cardinals.

In the National League Division Series (NLDS) against the Atlanta Braves, the strong work of starter Wood and closer Joe Borowski and a clutch single by center fielder Kenny Lofton gave the Cubs a 4–2 win. They went on to take a dramatic five-game series for the franchise's first postseason series title since they won the World Series in 1908.

A lot of the credit for the upswing in the Cubs' fortunes went to their manager, Dusty Baker, a toothpick invariably clutched in his teeth, perhaps as a cogitation aid.

Karros, who had been unhappy early on being platooned at first base with Hee-Seop Choi, now extolled the manager.

"Dusty called me into his office and told me not to think of myself as a pinch hitter or a bench player. He said, 'This season is not a sprint, and you're going to get a lot of opportunities. Especially playing all day games in Wrigley Field. We're going to use everybody, like having two teams.'"

Following their victory over the Braves, the Cubs faced the Florida Marlins, a Wild Card entry, with the National League pennant on the line. The Marlins were led by standout pitchers Josh Beckett and Carl Pavano.

Despite losing the Wrigley Field opener 9–8 in eleven innings, the Cubs took a 3–1 lead in the best-of-seven series. One more win and they would be on their way to the World Series for the first time since—well, all Cubs fans knew what *since* meant. It was, for most, when their grandfathers were children or even yet to be born.

But in Florida the Cubs lost Game 5, 4–0, on a two-hitter by Beckett. Now the Cubs led by only three games to two, and the series returned to Wrigley Field for Game 6. Cubs loyalists as well as Cubs executives and players expected—hoped? prayed?—that a World Series would soon follow.

On a neon crawl above a tavern on the corner of Clark and Addison kitty-corner from Wrigley Field, a question was posed: IS HELL FREEZING OVER? This was a response to a front-page headline in a preseason *Sports Illustrated* that predicted the Cubs would win the pennant.

But not so fast.

Fans streamed into the ballpark for Game 6. The exhilaration, coupled with the expected anxiety, if not full-fledged fear, was palpable through the city all day long. The game began in the cool Chicago night.

The Cubs were sailing along on the strong right arm of their remarkable kid pitcher, Mark Prior, and leading by 3–0 when the Florida Marlins showed up, perhaps to the surprise of some, to bat in the eighth inning. No problem. Six more outs and the Marlins would be history. So, too, would the old Cubs curse.

The full-capacity crowd of 39,577 was cheering and stomping and giving standing ovations to everyone including the vendors. Oh, what a night! Prior got a fly out to start the inning. Juan Pierre followed with a line-shot double. But so what? Prior was in command.

And then, oh what foul winds began to blow off Lake Michigan! After one out—and five outs left for the Cubs' trip to the World Series—Marlins second baseman Luis Castillo lifted a lazy fly ball down the third-base line that left fielder Moisés Alou hustled over to grab before it landed in the stands. A gaggle of fans, arms upraised, surely believed that they had as good a chance of securing a souvenir as Alou had in establishing the second out of the inning. After all, a ball hit into the stands is the province of the fans, no? As it turned out, the answer for Cubs fans from that time forward was no.

A fan wearing a Cubs cap reached for the ball, which bounced off his hands. The poor spectator, who would become infamous in Chicago—unfairly, in this writer's estimation—was Steve Bartman, twenty-six, who worked in suburban Chicago at a human resources consulting firm.

Alou screamed interference, ranting to the umpires that he could have caught the ball. The ball was ruled, however, to be on the spectators' side of the wall. No interference. Visibly upset, Prior threw a wild pitch—Pierre hustling to third—and walked

Cubs fans celebrate after Chicago beat the Atlanta Braves 5–1 in Game 5 of the NLDS at Turner Field in Atlanta Sunday, Oct. 5, 2003.

Todd Hollandsworth of the Florida Marlins scores behind Cubs catcher Paul Bako during the infamous eighth inning of Game 6 of the NLCS, October 14, 2003, at Wrigley Field.

Castillo. Iván Rodriguez singled to left, scoring Pierre: 3–1 Cubs, Castillo to third. Men on first and third.

Miguel Cabrera hit a ground ball to the Cubs' shortstop—a sure double-play ball—and Alex Gonzalez closed his glove before catching the ball. One could almost see the steam coming out of Prior's ears. Bases loaded. Derrek Lee doubled to left, scoring two

runs to tie the game, 3–3. Baker went to the mound to remove Prior and replaced him with Kyle Farnsworth, another hard-throwing right-hander. Farnsworth issued an intentional walk, loading the bases again, and then gave up a sacrifice fly, allowing the Marlins to get ahead, 4–3. Another intentional walk to load the bases again, and another double, clearing the bases: 7–3. The

fans grew quieter and quieter. Almost stealthily, left-hander Mike Remlinger replaced Farnsworth and yielded a single to Pierre, who was batting for the second time in the inning, before registering the final out of the incredible, heartbreaking sequence of events. The score now stood at a stunning 8–3 in favor of the visitors, which is how the game ended.

In Wrigley Field, the joy of an amusement park had been suddenly transformed into the gloom of a graveyard.

But look, the fans figured, we've got Kerry Wood, our best pitcher, going against the Marlins tomorrow night. All's well that ends well; this according to the Bard, yes—but according to the Cubs? Perhaps.

Wood had gone 14–11 over the season, led the league in strikeouts with 266, and thrown the fastest fastball in the major leagues, averaging 95.4 miles per hour. What's more, he'd earlier beaten the Braves in the NLDS and pitched well against the Marlins in Game 3, the extra-inning win for the Cubs.

In his postgame news conference, speaking to the legions beyond the ballpark, Baker said, "We need the fans. We need their positiveness. We need their noise. We need them pulling for our team like they've never pulled before. This is probably one of the biggest games in Cub history. As for our team, we have never done anything easy."

Did this sound like a man grasping at straws? The team was indeed on the verge of a monumental collapse. What else could he do? Well, he could start his rested ace, Wood.

The full-capacity crowd of 39,574 and the several hundred packing the rooftops of the bunting-festooned apartment buildings across from the park for Game 7 couldn't have been more responsive to Baker's urging from the night before if he had stood at home plate and exhorted them over the public-address system.

When the Cubs took the field before the first inning, the throng jumped to its feet and cheered, chanting, "Let's go, Cubs!"

The cheering continued when Wood got two swift strikes on the Marlins' leadoff hitter, Pierre. They were quieter when Pierre lined a triple to right field and Rodriguez drew a one-out walk. Shortly after, the crowd quieted still further—one could barely hear a whisper—after Cabrera's three-run home run into the left-center-field bleachers. First inning, and the Cubs were already behind 3–0.

But all that changed in the bottom of the second when Karros singled and scored on an infield out and Gonzalez doubled and

Kerry Wood—yes, hurler Kerry Wood—hammered a homer into virtually the same place that Cabrera did, to tie the score.

Talk about "positiveness." The joint exploded with exultation.

Moisés Alou homered with a man on third to make it 5–3 Cubs. This is more like it! Uh-oh: The Marlins fought back, scoring three more runs in the fifth—Wood came out, Farnsworth came in—to take the lead, 6–5.

Florida made it 7–5 in the sixth, 9–5 in the seventh, and though the Cubs scored one run in the bottom of the seventh, the score stood at 9–6 as the Cubs came to bat in the ninth, their last chance. Was a miracle possible?

Well, Aramis Ramirez, leading off the inning, was hit by a pitch. One man on. The crowd stirred. Randall Simon pinch-hit for Karros and went down swinging. Gonzalez did likewise. Two outs. Catcher Paul Bako was the last hope, the last desperate hope. Bako swung and flied out, ending, well, everything.

In the saddest of all possible worlds for Cubs fans at this point in the twenty-first century, the Marlins would play the Yankees in the World Series. Hardly any consolation for Cubs fans, but the Marlins were victorious over the Bronx Bombers as well, four games to two.

But it should be remembered in that final inning of the Cubs' final game of the season, in the Cubs' last futile at bats, a chant, or a plea, or simply a recognition of enduring love and affection, started up and rolled through the crowd, through the grandstand and the box seats and out to the bleachers: "Let's go, Cubs! Let's

Cubs fans patiently wait outside Wrigley Field hoping to catch a home-run ball as the Cubs face off against the Arizona Diamondbacks in the NLDS, October 6, 2007.

go, Cubs!" They were all standing, every last fan, it seemed, cheering on their darlings in this last gasp of hopeless hope.

It would echo for them through the long, hard, bitter winter ahead.

Bartman, pelted by debris from other fans and escorted out of the park by security guards, became such a figure of ignominy in Chicago that he would not again be seen in public, receiving death threats and inspiring rumors of having undergone a face-lift to disguise himself. But immediately after the game, he issued a statement through an intermediary:

I had my eyes glued on the approaching ball the entire time and was so caught up in the moment that I did not even see Moisés Alou, much less that he may have had a play.

Had I thought for one second that the ball was playable or had I seen Alou approaching, I would have done whatever I could to get out of the way and give Alou a chance to make the catch.

Bartman apologized to Cubs fans: "I am truly sorry from the bottom of this Cub fan's broken heart."

In later days, Governor Rod Blagojevich, defending Bartman, in a fashion, said, "Nobody can justify any kind of threat to someone who does something stupid like reach for that ball."

And Florida governor Jeb Bush, tongue in cheek, offered "asylum" to Bartman and an oceanfront retreat in Pompano Beach for a three-month stay if he needed to get out of Chicago.

While the Cubs retained the nucleus of the team that had missed going to the World Series by five outs the year before, they seemed to never get a good footing in 2004, despite attendance passing the three million mark—3,170,155—for the first time in history. (It would continue to surpass three million each season for the rest of the decade). Fortunately, owing in part to a weak division, the Cubs actually contended for the 2004 play-offs.

One hope for good days had been the return of Greg Maddux, who, at thirty-eight and entering his nineteenth big-league season, had won sixteen games while losing eleven for the Braves in 2003. His ERA of 3.89, however, was his highest since 1987, his first full season with the Cubs.

Did he still have it? Steve Stone, a Cubs television analyst and former Cy Young Award winner, said, "I remember watching a game on television some time ago and Maddux got a first strike on twenty-three consecutive batters. That means he was ahead in the count right away, and had the hitters hitting his pitches, instead of struggling."

In spring training, Maddux said, "Now people ask me, 'Why didn't I have a better year last year?' Well, I won sixteen games. So what they say goes in one ear and out the other."

Maddux, who still looked in some ways like "your friendly neighborhood paper boy," as Paul Sullivan of the

Derrek Lee is greeted by teammate Milton Bradley after hitting a two-run homer, September 7, 2009.

on, Maddux, now a four-time Cy Young Award winner, took the mound seeking to become the twenty-second pitcher in 128 years of major-league baseball to win three hundred games. He had a 10–7 record, was tied for most victories by a Cubs pitcher this season, and had won his last two starts.

Affectionately called Mad Dog by his Cubs teammates and the finest National League pitcher of his generation by many more, Maddux began by slipping a called strike past the Phillies' lead-off hitter, Jimmy Rollins. But the euphoria was short-lived. On the very next pitch, Rollins smashed a drive that just cleared the right-field wall, only a few feet over Sammy Sosa's upturned eyes.

As Rollins rounded the bases, it seemed as if the deeply disappointed and shocked standing-room-only crowd had been bound and gagged. The silence was palpable.

Maddux threw a ball to the next batter, Placido Polanco, and the generally cool Mad Dog uncharacteristically snapped his glove in disgust as he caught the return throw from his catcher, Paul Bako. Polanco grounded out, but Maddux delivered the second home-run pitch of the inning, this one to Bobby Abreu. The Phillies got an unearned run in the fifth, and Baker took Maddux out after six innings, with the Phillies ahead 3–2. In the next inning, the Cubs scored four runs and won the game, 6–3, but Maddux was not involved in the outcome. He would have to wait another week, and go on the road, before beating the Giants in San Francisco, 8–4, to win number three hundred. Maddux ended 2004 at 16–11—he pitched one more season for the Cubs—and would conclude his magnificent twenty-three-year career with 355 wins (and 277 losses), eighth on the all-time list.

On September 25, the Cubs led the NL Wild Card play-off entry by one and a half games over the Giants and the Astros, and both of those teams lost that day, giving the Cubs a chance to take a commanding two-and-a-half-game lead, with only eight games remaining in the season.

Alas, closer LaTroy Hawkins couldn't hold a lead in the ninth inning against the Mets, surrendering a game-tying three-run homer to rookie Victor Diaz on a two-out, two-strike pitch. The Cubs went on to lose in extra innings. The defeat seemed to cause a team-wide depression. They lost to the Mets the next day and dropped six of their last seven games in the stretch run. "This last week's been like a nightmare," Baker said at season's end. "It seems whatever you do doesn't work."

The Astros won the Wild Card.

Chicago Tribune described him when he was a twenty-year-old Cubs rookie in 1986, pondered a remark by Joe Torre, the Yankees' manager from 1996 to 2007. Torre had said, "Greg Maddux is an artist. When you swing at one of his pitches, it's a ball, and when you don't, it's a strike."

Still true? Maddux was asked. He thought for a moment. "Well," he said, "maybe not so often."

On August 2, a sticky, ninety-degree afternoon, and with a near-capacity crowd of 39,032 in Wrigley Field cheering him

One great change for the Cubs occurred on the last day of the season. Sammy Sosa left the game early and then lied about it publicly. Increasingly unpopular with fans and some of his teammates, Sosa was traded to Baltimore. The 2005 Cubs had been picked as serious contenders that year, but with pitching aces Wood and Prior disabled at times, the team finished in fourth place, twenty-one games out of first place, winning just seventy-nine games. But it wasn't Derrek Lee's fault. The six-foot-five right-handed first baseman, obtained in a trade with the Florida Marlins, was a strong candidate to win the Triple Crown for much of the season. He hit with a quirky waggle of the bat over his right ear, as if there was a log lying across home plate that he was preparing to subdivide, and then raised his left leg like a cancan dancer when the pitch approached the plate. Lee finished first in the league in batting average, .335, second in homers, 46, and seventh in RBIs, with 107.

Two months before the end of the 2005 season, Ryne Sandberg was inducted into the Baseball Hall of Fame in Cooperstown, New York. In his acceptance speech on a hazy, hot Sunday afternoon, Sandberg related the following tale:

———————————————

A man comes upon a bottle on a beach, pops the cork, and a genie appears. The genie grants the man one wish. The man says he wants to see peace in the Middle East and hands the genie a map of the region.

After studying for hours and hours, the genie replies, "This is impossible," and suggests that the man give him another wish.

"I always wanted to see the Cubs in a World Series," the man says.

"Hmm," the genie replies. "Let me have another look at that map."

———————————————

While the joke was mordant, Sandberg added that he was happy to play for two Cubs teams that made the postseason, but told devoted Cubs fans he was sorry that "I could not help get them to a World Series." As baseball fans knew, it was not for lack of effort on Sandberg's part.

In 2004 and 2005 there were two positively, unequivocally incredulous occurrences, the hardball equivalent of the cow jumping over the moon, the Martians lining up to order lattes at Starbucks. The first event stunned fandom; the second, on the very heels of the first, made people wonder if this was simply a coincidence or evidence of an invisible celestial hand.

Two of the three franchises in baseball that had gone the longest without winning a World Series *won them*: The Boston Red Sox in 2004, after an eighty-six-year drought; and, of all teams, the Chicago White Sox—the crosstown nemesis of the Cubs—in 2005, after a fallow and frustrating eighty-eight years.

As in a weird game of musical chairs, that left only the Cubs standing, or staggering. Forlorn but not forgotten. And if ever the cliché "Hope springs eternal" applied to anyone, it was the Cubs, spring after spring after spring, for nearly one hundred of them.

Manager Lou Piniella giving umpire Mark Wegner an earful, 2007.

"One thing's for sure," said Dusty Baker in 2006, at the Cubs' spring-training site in Mesa, Arizona. "The law of averages is on our side.

"It's got to happen," he added. "This team has to win it one of these days. And I'd like to be here when it happens."

Did the White Sox winning the season before create an added incentive for the Cubs?

"Guys aren't thinking about the White Sox," said the Cubs' hitting coach, Gary Matthews. "We're concerned with the North Side."

Maybe so, but . . . "I wouldn't call it jealous," said Baker, referring to the White Sox. "I mean, it was great for the city of Chicago, but you just wish it was you."

Though Carlos Zambrano emerged as a good young pitcher, winning sixteen games, hardly anything else was positive for the Cubs, who ended up in last place that season.

Baker, a hero to the fans just three years earlier, did not have his contract renewed. The Cubs sought a fierier leader than Baker, who appeared too laid-back—especially after the Cubs weren't winning—and the front office chose Lou Piniella to lead them. Former manager of the pennant-winning Cincinnati Reds, as well as manager of the Yankees, Mariners, and Devil Rays, Piniella was famous for his short fuse and the jaw-to-jaw disputes with umpires in which he sometimes kicked dirt to make a point and threw his baseball cap to the ground and kicked *it* to make an even more salient point. But there were two sides to Piniella, who

was also nicknamed Sweet Lou for his sometimes sunny disposition and infectious laugh.

The Cubs invested in the free-agent market and signed pitchers Ted Lilly and Jason Marquis and outfielder Alfonso Soriano, the latter to the richest contract in Cubs' history: eight years, $136 million.

The moves worked, to a degree: The Cubs won the NL Central, but in the Division Series they lost a three-game sweep to the Arizona Diamondbacks, scoring just six runs.

Many, however, predicted that 2008 would be the year that the Cubs won it all. It's an old song, but some, particularly Cubs fans, seemed not to tire of warbling it. The Cubs indeed headed into the All-Star break with the league's best record, and tied the league

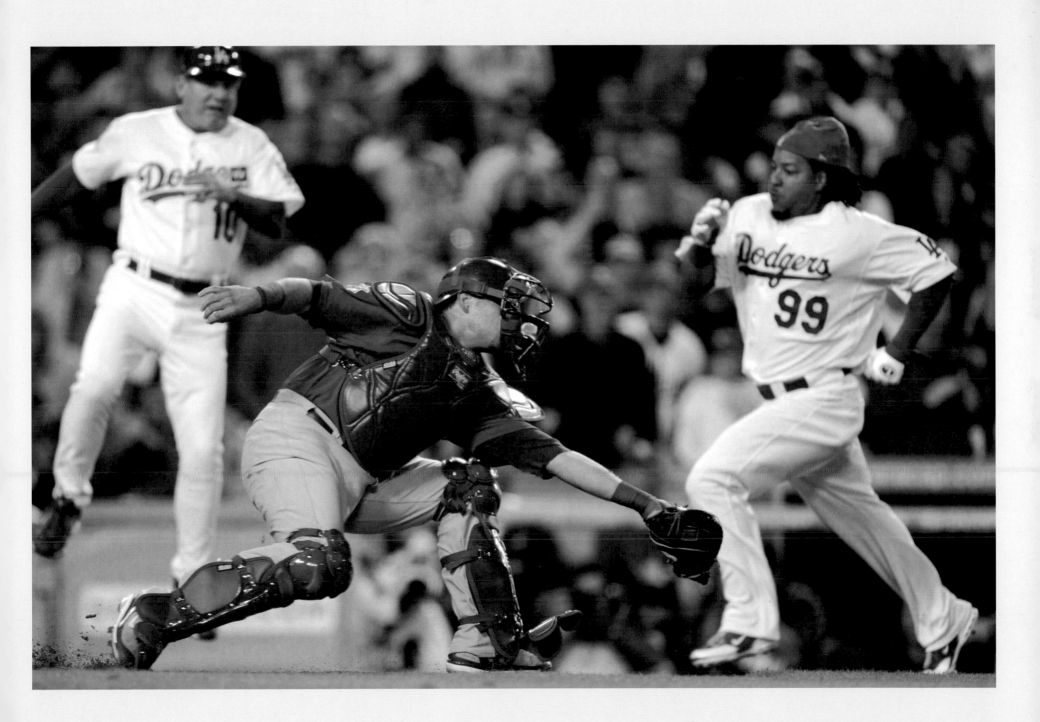

record with eight representatives to the All-Star Game, including catcher Geovany Soto, who would be named the league's rookie of the year.

On September 14, Zambrano pitched a no-hitter against the Astros, and six days later the team clinched the division title by beating the Cardinals in Wrigley Field. It was the first time the Cubs had gone to postseason play two years in a row since they qualified for the World Series in 1907 and 1908. The 2008 Cubs had won ninety-seven games and were heavily favored to beat the Dodgers in the NLDS.

The Cubs took the lead in Game 1, but James Loney's grand-slam homer off Ryan Dempster put the Dodgers ahead, and for good. The Cubs' defense was filled with holes—in Game 2, each of the four infielders made an error—and the offense was hardly better. The Cubs were swept again in three games and again scored a total of just six runs.

Thus went another "season of destiny," another collapse on the road to the World Series.

Soriano, who had gone one for fourteen in the series, was asked what he would tell the fans. After a moment's thought, he said, "I'd tell them, 'Be patient.'"

Though Cubs fans are experts in patience, they could hardly be faulted for getting tired of waiting.

One mid-May morning in 2009, Piniella was reclining in his seat behind his desk in his compact clubhouse in Wrigley Field. He told me:

Before I took the job as manager here, I didn't realize that the Cubs had gone so long without winning a World Series and hadn't even *been* in a World Series since 1945. It's hard to believe. But I've been made painfully aware of it. Before I got here I wasn't fully prepared mentally for the impact of that history. In my first conversation with the general manager, Jim Hendry, I told him that my number one concern was winning. But in my first six weeks here, we were under .500. And I told him, "Winning, hell, I want to get out of here alive!"

People are always coming up to me and saying things like, "I've been a Cubs fan for sixty years—when are you going to win?" I tell 'em, "I'm trying as hard as possible to get it done."

I asked if he'd gotten any unusual advice from fans. I mentioned former governor Rod Blagojevich, who was under indictment for a variety of abuses of his high state office and had had his phones bugged by the FBI.

"Oh, he's a huge Cubs fan. He's been in my office here a number of times. Likes to talk baseball. He's even given me some lineup suggestions."

Were they helpful?

"I gave them some thought, but I can't tell you that I've used any of them." Piniella evinced a slight grin.

"When I was named National League manager of the year [in 2008], the governor called me at home to congratulate me. That was very nice. I'm sure our conversation was taped."

He was asked if he believes the Cubs have been cursed.

"I don't believe in curses," he said. "People said the Red Sox had been cursed. They said the White Sox had been cursed. They both won the World Series. The Cubs are due—though I don't know how long it'll be."

When you hear the Cubs being called "lovable losers" and "cuddly," what comes to mind for you?

"It's something you need to get away from. To succeed in

baseball, you have to be tough. You have to deal with the ups and downs of a long season. If you accept 'lovable' and 'cuddly,' you're basically accepting losing."

Immediate goals? "To win the division again. First things first. No Cub team has gotten to the postseason for three straight years. Now that would be an accomplishment."

It didn't happen. Among other mistakes, the Cubs invested in a three-year, thirty-million-dollar deal for outfielder Milton Bradley. But from nearly the beginning of the season, Bradley appeared disgruntled and had issues with fans and team members. He complained about, among other things, being booed and heckled by bleacher fans who, he said, "hated" him. After he staged a tirade following a fly out, Bradley was told by manager Piniella to leave the dugout and go home. There was a confrontation later in the locker room. On September 20, Bradley was suspended for the rest of the season by general manager Jim Hendry after an interview with the media that Hendry termed "disrespectful" to the club. All that might have been relatively

acceptable if he hadn't also been disappointing in competition, at times appearing distracted in the outfield and hitting a mediocre .257 with twelve homers and only forty runs batted in. Bradley was traded to Seattle in the off-season.

On June 19 of the 2009 season, Kerry Wood came out to the mound once again at Wrigley Field—except this time he was wearing a Cleveland Indians uniform. After several seasons of injuries and surgery to his pitching arm, Kerry, having been relegated to relief pitching for the Cubs and being the team's closer, asked for a two-year contract, but the Cubs turned him down. So in December 2008, the thirty-one-year-old Wood accepted an offer from the Indians.

When he took the mound in an interleague game at Wrigley Field, the capacity crowd, in a moving scene honoring one of its past heroes, gave Wood a standing ovation.

The Cubs stayed in the Wild Card hunt until being eliminated in the final week of the 2009 season, finishing second in the division.

At season's end, there was a change, however. But not on the playing field. The Cubs' owner, the Tribune Company, which had declared bankruptcy, sold the team to the Ricketts family, led by Tom Ricketts, the chairman. The Rickettses were longtime Cubs fans, and wealthy, having earned their billion-dollar fortune primarily in investment banking. The Ricketts family was placed at number 371 on the *Forbes* list of the four hundred richest people in America. The purchase of the Cubs was estimated at $845 million.

In a news conference before the start of the 2010 season, Ricketts spoke about Wrigley Field.

"We want to be proud of Wrigley Field," he said. "We want to be proud of what we've done in the off-season." More than ten million dollars was spent on additions and improvements, including the restrooms, the clubhouse, one-way glass in the batting tunnel allowing fans to watch Cubs hitters in the batting cage under the stands, and renovation of the back of the scoreboard for the first time in seventy years. "It's a one-hundred-year-old building. I knew when I redid my house halfway through it would have been easier to tear the whole thing down. The fact is, we love Wrigley. It's about preserving Wrigley. It's what we signed up for."

But Tom Ricketts may not have been prepared for the controversy of a sign. He sought to generate more revenue by erecting a Toyota advertisement, a 360-foot-wide illuminated sign, behind the left-field bleachers. But, as Ameet Sachdev, a *Tribune* reporter, noted, Wrigley is a baseball stadium that fans "seem to view as their own personal shrine."

Fans protested, in letters to the newspapers, in letters and phone calls to the ballpark. The rooftop owners across Waveland Avenue were incensed, saying it would obstruct their view. Preservationists said it would stick out "like a sore thumb" at the historic ballpark. The battle was on! Ricketts, who said the sign could be worth two million dollars over three years to the Cubs, tried to play hardball. "I have a lot of other dollars that can be invested in Wrigleyville—or not," he said. (Wrigleyville is the neighborhood around Wrigley Field.) Would the city buckle to the threat? The city's Commission on Chicago Landmarks, which has final say on alterations, was to review the team's permit to erect the sign. Wrigley was then the only major-league ballpark with landmark status. (Fenway Park received landmark status in 2012, the one-hundredth anniversary of its construction.)

The hullabaloo was reminiscent of the uproar about installing night lights in Wrigley Field. In mid-May, the commission approved the sign (in exchange for a four-year moratorium on

Cubs center fielder Marlon Byrd, 2011.

outfield signs at the park), but the sign couldn't be put up until the City Council Building Committee gave it a thumbs-up, or down.

While all this was going on, the Cubs were, well, being the Cubs. Despite being picked by the sports pundits to challenge the Cardinals for the division title, they struggled in the first part of the 2010 season and were ten games under .500 by the end of June.

The Cubs had traded the malcontent Milton Bradley to Seattle in the off-season and got center fielder Marlon Byrd, who wound up making the All-Star team. Derrek Lee, who would be traded before the season was out, and Aramis Ramirez, among others, had off years. And Carlos Zambrano (he of the five-year $91.5-million contract) suffered a meltdown in June when he got into a shoving match with Lee in the dugout after he gave up four runs in the first inning and blamed his fielders. He was suspended for several weeks for actions "unacceptable," said Jim Hendry, and the volatile pitcher was made to undergo anger-management counseling. He returned to the pitching rotation and won his last eight games of the season.

Ryan Dempster pitches to Russell Martin of the Los Angeles Dodgers in Game 1 of the 2008 NLDS at Wrigley Field.

But the big news, perhaps the biggest surprise, was that manager Lou Piniella, who had announced that he was retiring at the end of the season after his fourth year as the Cubs' manager, hastened his departure. As the headline in the *New York Daily News* had it, "Early Adieu for Lou." On August 22, he said that he wanted to spend more time with his ailing mother. Some cynics saw it another way: "He fled the Cubs," one said. "Can't blame him." The Cubs were then twenty-three games under .500, despite two rookie standouts, shortstop Starlin Castro, who would hit .300 for the season, and nifty outfielder Tyler Colvin, who on September 19 suffered a freak accident. While running down the third-base line, he was struck in the chest by a splintered bat from teammate Welington Castillo. That piece of the bat, acting like a spear, entered just inches from Colvin's heart and collapsed one of his lungs. He was rushed to the hospital, and it took him nearly two months to recuperate.

Third-base coach Mike Quade took over as interim manager of the Cubs, and from August 23 to the end of the season, the team seemed to wake up, going 24–12, the second-best record in that period in the National League. Still, the Cubs finished next to last in the Central Division, sixteen games behind the first-place Cincinnati Reds.

seasons in the Cubs' minor-league system, and it was expected that this would seriously wound, if not sever, Sandberg's ties to the Cubs.

Of the thirty teams in the major leagues, the Cubs had the third-highest payroll at the start of the 2010 season, nearly $147 million (only the American League Yankees and Red Sox were ahead of them), and yet they finished with the eighth-worst record.

Attendance had slipped, but the Cubs still drew the seventh-best attendance, again topping the three-million mark, at 3,062,973 (only about 100,000 below their play-off season of 2009), for an average of 37,814, or 92 percent capacity.

It was more of the same for the Cubs in 2011, only different. Which was normal. A game against the interleague rival Yankees—rare in itself since the two clubs meet each other only one series every several years—saw the outfielders having to battle not only the sun, not only a twisting fly ball, not only the brick fence and the tangled ivy, but a flock of seagulls that had either lost its way from nearby Lake Michigan or was seeking a closer, on-the-cuff view of a ball game.

There was a cry from Peter Gammons, the longtime baseball writer from Boston, who called Wrigley Field a "dump," a description he has never used, as far as is known, for his beloved Fenway Park, which has similar timeworn characteristics.

On the other hand, Carlos Peña, a Yankees catcher who had never seen Wrigley Field before, disagreed with the criticism of the park. Yes, the clubhouse is cramped; yes, the dugout is tight. But "it's part of the gig," he said. "Part of the enchantment of this place is that it is old, and we don't have the best facilities. Its imperfections are what make it perfect."

New full-time manager Mike Quade had high hopes (hardly an odd sentiment for Cubs managers), but the team struggled to even finish above .500 (hardly a new issue for Cubs managers). Yet even good days sometimes turned sour. For one, the volatile Carlos Zambrano pitched seven crisp innings, allowing one run, before being lifted for a reliever against the division-leading Cardinals, a game in which the Cubs lost 3–2 in the tenth inning. "We're playing like a Triple-A team," groused Zambrano. "This is embarrassing." It was one of the better games the Cubs played all season.

Paul McCartney, of Beatles fame, played two concerts in Wrigley Field, on July 31 and August 1, and drew sellout crowds.

At season's end, the fifty-three-year-old Quade, who had never played in the major leagues but had managed in the minor leagues for seventeen seasons, was named manager for the 2011 season. It was a disappointment to the runner-up for the job, the Cubs Hall of Famer Ryne Sandberg, who had managed for the previous four

The band played thirty-six songs, one of which was the classic "Helter Skelter," which McCartney graciously refrained from dedicating to the frequent play of the Cubs.

In all, it had been another long season in which Cubs fans would, as Soriano suggested, have to "be patient." It was now 102 years since the Cubs' last world championship, and counting.

But once again hope, in its ever-idiosyncratic Cubs way, sprang up at Wrigley Field, with the signing of a new president for baseball operations, the highly touted, well-groomed Theo Epstein, who, as Dan McGrath described in the October 26, 2011, *New York Times*, was a "37-year-old one-time boy wonder." Epstein was the general manager of the Boston Red Sox when they won the World Series twice in 2004 and 2007. "The Red Sox hadn't won in 86 years when we took over," said Epstein. Now he was taking over a team that hadn't won a World Series in 103 years.

"We didn't run from that challenge" (in Boston), "we embraced it," Epstein told reporters at a news conference upon his signing a five-year Cubs contract. "There's a gap between where we are and where we want to be, but the goal is to lay a foundation for the long-term success and begin playing baseball in October regularly." The Red Sox began to founder, and the "one-time boy wonder" proved expendable in Boston. Enter the Cubs.

One of Epstein's first acts in office was to fire manager Mike Quade and replace him with Dale Sveum. Epstein began overhauling the team, nearly completely, and pretty much conceded the 2012 season, as the Cubs flirted with the worst record in baseball for the first half of the year, and improved, as it were, to a dismal season-ending record of 61–101, ensconced in fifth, or next to last place, in the NL Central division, thirty-six games behind from the first-place Cincinnati Reds. Among other moves, Epstein traded Cubs stars such as pitcher Carlos Zambrano, who wore out his welcome with his erratic behavior, and thirty-five-year-old pitcher Ryan Dempster, who wanted a multiyear contract, as well as deciding not to resign former all-star third baseman Aramis Ramirez, who wanted a contract beyond his value, in Epstein's view. Epstein was making salary room to pursue other free agents, as well as allowing young newcomers like right fielder Bryan LaHair and first baseman Anthony Rizzo, along with shortstop Starlin Castro, to develop as mainstays of the future.

An intriguing contretemps developed in May when it was reported that Joe Ricketts, the billionaire father of Cubs chairman Tom Ricketts, was funding a $10 million political action

committee aimed at challenging President Barack Obama in the presidential race that fall. Ricketts had sought to work with Mayor Rahm Emanuel on a proposed $300 million renovations project to Wrigley Field in which the city would cover about half of it. When Emanuel, a close friend of the president's and his former chief of staff, learned of this, he was reportedly incensed, and refused to take Tom Ricketts's phone calls. Tom Ricketts, not unwisely, sought to distance himself from his father. "I love him a ton," said Ricketts, about his dad, "but the team is owned by myself and my siblings."

In the summer of 2012, the novelist John Grisham wrote a book titled *Calico Joe,* about a Cubs rookie phenom who gets tragically beaned (it recalls to a degree the Adam Greenberg episode) and soon is gone from baseball. But a line near the end of the book is achingly familiar to Cubs fans, though maybe now even more so with the advent of Epstein: "Wait till next year, the Cubs were famous for saying," wrote Grisham, "but now they meant it."

The 2014 season began on a promising note, for some. The "Restore Wrigley Field" movement by the team's hierarchy resulted in an agreement by the Cubs and City Hall to renovate Wrigley Field. The ball team wanted new luxury boxes, new advertising signs in left and right field, and a general overhaul of the interior of the park. The cost: an estimated $300 million over a period of five years. The city, which holds the landmark status of the park, agreed to the signage as long as taxpayers didn't have to foot the bill for the renovations. The signs may inconvenience the rooftop gawkers across from the ballpark on Sheffield and Waveland Avenues, blocking their idiosyncratic views. "We're not a museum," said Cubs owner Tom Ricketts, "we're a business." Mayor Rahm Emanuel said, "This framework allows the Cubs to restore the Friendly Confines and pursue their economic goals, while respecting the rights and quality of its neighbors. . . . It will have a long-lasting positive effect on Chicago." That, of course, remained to be seen. Meanwhile on the current diamond:

The Cubs won their first game of the 2013 season, beating the Pirates 3–1, and were thus in first place in the National League Central Division. It was, typically, short-lived. By the end of April they found themselves mired in last place (and they would spend the rest of the season either at the bottom of the standings or close to it). At one point in that month, the Cubs did manage to tie a regular-season record that had stood since 1890. Two Cubs pitchers, Edwin Jackson and Michael Bowden, combined to throw five wild pitches in one inning, in a 10–7 loss to the Giants. Meanwhile, not only did the front office announce that it was renovating Wrigley Field, it also stated that it was in a rebuilding mode with the team and the players. To long-time Cubs fans, the refrain was not unfamiliar—about as old as the old ball park itself.

View of Wrigley Field and the skyline beyond from behind home plate, 2003.

1921

TO THE PRESENT:

THE MONSTERS

OF THE

MIDWAY AND OTHERS

It ranks as one of the most spectacular events in the history of Wrigley Field, and it has nothing to do with baseball. On December 12, 1965, the Chicago Bears were playing the San Francisco 49ers in the next-to-last game of the National Football League's regular season. Every fall and winter for fifty years, from 1921 to 1970, Wrigley Field was home to the North Side football team. In 1965, a fleet, dazzling rookie halfback from the University of Kansas named Gale Sayers broke into the pros in unforgettable fashion.

In a preseason game against the Los Angeles Rams, he scored two touchdowns, on a seventy-seven-yard punt return and a ninety-three-yard kickoff return, then

PREVIOUS SPREAD Hall of
Fame Chicago Bears end Bill
Hewitt (56) laterals the football
to Billy Karr (22) for the winning
touchdown in a 23–17 win over the
New York Giants in the 1933 NFL
Championship Game, December 17,
1933, at Wrigley Field.

BELOW Bronko Nagurski of
the Chicago Bears works out at
Wrigley Field, 1943.

made a surprising twenty-five-yard left-handed pass for another touchdown for the Bears' victory. Next, he scored both of the Bears' touchdowns in a loss to Green Bay. He followed that with two touchdowns in a victory over the Rams. Seven days later, Sayers scored four touchdowns, including a ninety-six-yard kick-off return, as the Bears beat the Vikings, 45–37. These were, more or less, simply warm-ups for the December 12 game.

Playing on a muddy field that gave little traction to other runners, Sayers scored a record-tying six touchdowns, as the Bears crushed the San Francisco 49ers, 61–20. His scores came on an eighty-yard pass reception, rushes of one, seven, twenty-one, and fifty yards, and an eighty-five-yard punt return. For the day, Sayers totaled a phenomenal 336 combined yards.

"It was the greatest performance I have ever seen on the football field," exulted George "Papa Bear" Halas, the Bears' coach, who had been watching NFL play for forty-six years, or since the league's inception.

The comic Bill Cosby watched Sayers run and observed, "He would throw the right side of his body to one side of the field, and the left side of his body kept going down the left side. And the defensive men didn't know who to catch. They just stood there. Then they looked to the referee for help, because there's got to be a penalty against splitting yourself. But there's not. I looked it up in the rule book."

Sayers went on to be rookie of the year and continued his stupendous career until injuries cut it short, retiring in 1971. Six years later, at age thirty-four, he became the youngest player ever elected to the Pro Football Hall of Fame.

The Bears didn't win a title during Sayers's career, but they did win eight league championships during their nearly fifty years in Wrigley Field to earn the nickname the Monsters of the Midway, even though the Midway was a plot of park on the South Side of the city. The Bears moved from Wrigley Field to Soldier Field for the '71 season, because the league required that every team stadium should seat fifty thousand or more, and Wrigley Field held only forty-seven thousand for football.

In 1921, the Bears had transferred from Decatur, Illinois, where they had been known as the Staleys (which produced a range of starch products in that city). In Chicago, the team was renamed to identify with the baseball team that played in Wrigley Field.

In the early years, the Bears played with the stands that were in place from the baseball season. Eventually, they added a large portable bleacher section that spanned the right- and center-field areas and covered most of the existing bleacher seating and part of the right-field corner seating. The football field ran north to south, or from left field to the foul line at first base. The remodeling of the bleachers created a very cozy fit, to say the least, for a football field. The corner of the south end zone was literally in the visiting baseball team's dugout, which was filled with pads for safety. One corner of the north end line ran just inches short of the left-field wall.

Legend has it that Bronko Nagurski, the great Bears fullback, slammed into the wall on a touchdown run in a game in the 1930s. He went back to the bench and told Coach Halas, "That last guy gave me quite a lick!"

Perhaps. It was said that Nagurski was so tough and strong, he was the only man who could run interference for himself. Some fifty years later, with Nagurski gray-haired and bowlegged, his cleft jaw still prominent, I asked him about crashing into the wall. "I couldn't put the brakes on in time after scoring the touchdown," he said. "I don't know if I cracked the wall. I have a feeling it was cracked before, but I did hit it pretty hard."

At least Nagurski wore a helmet, albeit a leather one. Dick Plasman, an end for the Bears, didn't wear a helmet at all, one of a number of players in the early years of football, at least into the '30s, who played bareheaded. He had a reason: The leather chapeaus in those days would drop disconcertingly over players' eyes, like the broken visor of a knight's helmet.

In a game one fall Sunday in Wrigley Field, Plasman raced into the north end zone for a pass. Skull untrussed and hands outstretched, he followed the flight of a ball he would not catch. He never considered the outfield wall that jutted inches away. In later days, the field would be resituated and mats hung on the wall. Too late, though, for Plasman's pate. He crashed headfirst into the bricks. When he woke up a few days later, in a hospital bed, his head was finally covered—with bandages. He recovered to play until 1947.

In an interview with him years later, I asked Plasman about modern-day players. He said he believed they were bigger and smarter and faster than those in his day. Did that mean he'd have worn something on his head if he had played today?

"Yes," he said. "Earmuffs."

Through the years, the Bears have had numerous outstanding teams, and players, including the first star of the new T-formation offense, quarterback Sid Luckman. His record-breaking touchdown passes—he once threw for seven touchdowns in a game—led the Bears to victories in four out of six NFL championship games in the 1940s (before the Super Bowl), including a 73–0 win over the Washington Redskins in 1940, still an NFL record for the most lopsided result in a game. Other stars for the Bears in Wrigley Field included center Clyde "Bulldog" Turner, running back George McAfee, tight end and future Bears coach "Iron Mike" Ditka ("Success isn't permanent, and failure

isn't fatal," he once philosophized), and linebacker Dick Butkus, a six-time first-team All-Pro selection and one of the most bone-crackling tacklers in pro football history. A *Sports Illustrated* cover story of him in 1970 was captioned "The Most Feared Man in the Game." "When I went out on the field to warm up," Butkus said, "I would manufacture things to make me mad. If someone on the other team was laughing, I'd pretend he was laughing at me or the Bears. I'd find something to get mad about. It always worked."

It apparently worked quite well. "If I had a choice, I'd sooner go one-on-one with a grizzly bear," said running back MacArthur Lane of the Green Bay Packers. "I pray that I can get up every time Butkus hits me."

The Bears had a rivalry with the crosstown Chicago Cardinals extending back to the early 1920s (before the Cardinals moved to St. Louis in 1959, and later to Arizona). One of their most memorable games, in Wrigley Field, ended with a loss for the home team. On December 14, 1947, the Bears and Cardinals were tied for first place in the Western division, each with an 8–3 record. It was their fifty-second meeting since 1920, but never before was so much on the line in any one game: It was the last game of the

TOP: Gale Sayers by award-winning illustrator Murray Olderman.

BOTTOM: Officials signaling a Bears touchdown during a Western Division playoff game versus the Green Bay Packers, December 14, 1941. Chicago crushed Green Bay, 33–14.

regular season, and the winner would go on to play the Eagles in Philadelphia for the NFL title.

Both teams were confident they'd win and began selling tickets for the championship game to be played a week later. The Cardinals were tougher than the Bears had anticipated. They intercepted four of Luckman's passes and put on a strong offensive display with quarterback Paul Christman connecting for 329 yards on passes, primarily to end Babe Dimancheff. In fact, just sixteen seconds into the game, the two combined on an eighty-yard touchdown pass play, stunning the Bears, and the Cardinals were en route to a 30–21 win and capturing the championship trophy.

Other events in Wrigley Field included games of the Chicago

Sting of the North American Soccer League. The soccer pitch, unlike the football field, ran east to west, or from right field to the foul territory on the third-base side.

On January 1, 2009, the National Hockey League played its 2009 Winter Classic in Wrigley, with the Chicago Blackhawks hosting the Detroit Red Wings in an outdoor game on a portable, flooded rink.

Such artists and groups to play in Wrigley Field include Jimmy Buffet, in 2005; the Police, in 2007; and Elton John, Billy Joel, and Rascal Flatts, in 2009. Rodeos, circuses, and the Harlem Globetrotters performances have all taken place in Wrigley Field.

On November 20, 2010, Northwestern University, situated in the Chicago suburb Evanston, and the University of Illinois, located in downstate Champaign, played a Big Ten football game in Wrigley Field, the first football game played there since the Bears left in 1970.

The field was reconfigured in an unusual way. All offensive plays on this cool fall afternoon headed toward the west end zone, and all kickoffs toward the east end zone. It was done for safety reasons. The end of the east zone was six inches from the brick right-field wall. Every time there was a change of possession, the sellout crowd of 41,058 witnessed the oddity of the players turning around and repositioning themselves so the action headed west—toward the third-base dugout. For the University of Illinois, it seemed that whatever changes were made were for the best. The Illini walloped Northwestern 48–27, with junior Illinois running back Mikel Leshoure rushing for 330 yards, including two touchdowns.

The return of football to Wrigley Field by Illini athletes would inevitably recall for historians the professional debut of the Chicago Bears, and on that North Side turf, of perhaps the most storied player ever for Illinois, Harold "Red" Grange. So fast and strong and elusive he was nicknamed the Galloping Ghost, Grange was one of the most renowned athletes of the 1920s. "He had blinding speed, amazing lateral mobility, an exceptional change of pace and a powerful straight-arm," wrote the sportswriter W. C. Heinz.

In college, Grange once scored four touchdowns of ninety-five, sixty-seven, fifty-four, and forty-four yards all in the *first quarter* against Michigan. When the famed sportswriter Damon Runyon was in the press box in Philadelphia to watch Illinois play the University of Pennsylvania, he saw Grange score three touchdowns, the first for fifty-five yards the first time he carried the ball. Runyon could hardly believe his eyes and compared him to the biggest stars of the twenties. "Grange . . . is three or four men and a horse rolled into one," he wrote. "He is Jack Dempsey, Babe Ruth, Al Jolson, Paavo Nurmi, and Man o' War."

After his junior year of college, in 1925, the six-foot, 175-pound Grange opted to turn pro—a highly unusual thing to do in those days, and he did it for the staggering sum of one hundred thousand dollars. The pro league had been in existence for only five years, and it still had trouble getting space in newspapers and crowds to the game.

"People don't realize today how the colleges fought against pro ball," Grange told me in a 1982 interview. "They were afraid that the pros would dominate the game. After I signed, my coach at Illinois, Bob Zuppke, wouldn't talk to me for three years. I'd have been more popular with the colleges if I had joined Capone's mob rather than the Bears."

On Thanksgiving Day, 1925, thirty-six thousand fans—the largest crowd ever to see a professional football game at that time—packed Cubs Park to watch the Galloping Ghost. On a slick, muddy field, Grange didn't do a vanishing act as the opposing Chicago Cardinals tacklers keyed in on him on every play. "From the start," wrote Lars Anderson in *The First Star*, his biography of Grange, "it became clear that the Cardinals weren't going to allow Grange to run wild. . . . " When the Cardinals punted, they generally kicked away from Grange, though he did amass fifty-six yards in punt returns. And there were no touchdowns by Grange, or anyone else. The game ended 0–0, with Grange at right halfback rushing for sixteen yards in thirty-six carries.

Ten days later, the Cubs Park pro football record was shattered when Grange and the Bears played before seventy thousand people in a game against the New York Giants in the Polo Grounds. Grange played five games in ten days as crowds around the country came to watch him fly with a football. The professional game, with that enormous boost from Grange, emerged as a sport to be reckoned with.

Grange went on to a stellar professional football career both as a running back and a defensive back and was a charter member of both the College Football Hall of Fame and the Pro Football Hall of Fame.

When Grange was seventy-eight and living in a gated community in Indian Lake, Florida, in one of several interviews, I spoke with him by phone.

He interrupted the conversation to say he was looking out the window in wonderment at joggers passing his house.

"I think they're crazy," he said. "If you have a car, why run?"

OPPOSITE: Chicago Blackhawks practice on the ice at Wrigley Field for the 2009 NHL Winter Classic versus the Detroit Red Wings.

ABOVE: Bears Hall of Famer Red Grange, circa 1925.

WRIGLEY MEMORIES

SCOTT TUROW, a former Federal prosecutor in Chicago, is a practicing lawyer who has written ten books that have sold 22 million copies. He grew up in Chicago and its northern suburbs, attending many Cubs games along the way.

Scott Turow throws out the first pitch at Wrigley Field.

My dad's father was an immigrant from Russia, and even as an immigrant he was hooked on the Cubs and baseball. He would listen to the Cubs on the radio and, between innings, run outside and yell in Yiddish over the fence to discuss the prior inning with a friend who had also come from Russia. My father was a die-hard Cubs fan, and he passed that affliction on to me.

I was born on May 12, 1949, and grew up on the North Side of Chicago, in West Rogers Park, near Sherwin and Albany streets, a five-mile bus-and-elevated-train ride from Wrigley Field.

My dad delivered babies and was rarely around, so some of my most treasured memories are of going to Cubs games with him, because it was a big deal that he took the time at all. It was something he was really interested in, and to be able to share something like the Cubs with him became important. We literally talked about the Cubs until he died. I didn't have a perfect relationship with my father, but he was one of the most hardworking human beings I've known. I realized as an adult what an effort it was sometimes for him to make the time to get to Wrigley.

We had season tickets for weekends and holidays for a few years in the early sixties. Second row, behind the visitors' dugout. I probably went to my first game at five or six with my dad—I still have a picture of myself at six in a Cubs uniform, which I think was taken on my birthday—and I started going regularly at about eight or nine, always with my father. I got bit bad as a kid. Wrigley is imbued in my memories from those days.

To be completely honest, being in a crowd that large at six years old was pretty frightening. I can remember not wanting to lose track of my dad. I was not completely at ease there, even though I wanted desperately to be there and never thought of declining to go. Entering the ballpark caused a sensory overload for a young child. We were sitting really close, so you had to be careful with the batted balls. It was perilous, but it was so neat. The visiting players were literally five feet away. I loved watching Willie Mays and Hank Aaron walk out of the dugout. They didn't say a damn word to the fans.

We saw Don Cardwell's no-hitter in 1960. (The Cubs had just gotten him two days earlier from the Phillies.) We saw Hank Aaron hit more damned home runs than I can count. I hated him so much as a kid, but when I grew up I realized what an incredible ballplayer he was. He had a great arm, could steal bases, could hit for average. Deep down I resented the fact that he was an all-around better ballplayer than Ernie Banks. I could only finally admit that in my twenties. As kids, we would play softball in a neighbor's yard and would take turns being Ernie Banks. Sometimes Ernie Banks was on both teams.

A running joke between my dad and me was that although my dad had pretty good hands, in the years we spent sitting behind the dugout, balls screaming over our heads, we never managed to catch a foul ball. There were one or two that I recall glancing off his hands.

But then, before one game, I was down there in our seats by myself—I must have been closer to ten or eleven and my dad was probably getting hot dogs or something—and a guy pitching for the Cardinals named Bob Grim saw me watching batting practice and flipped me a ball. He did it without even looking at me; I don't think the players were supposed to do that. I swear, you can still put that ball to your nose and smell the tobacco juice. When my dad turned eighty I gave him the ball, though I told him it was strictly on loan. He died less than a year later. It's in my study now.

Throughout my childhood, I went to Cubs games with some regularity. Sometimes it was just a couple of games and sometimes a dozen. But I got there every year. None of those years were great years for the team. It was a big deal when they finished in seventh place ahead of the Phillies. But I loved them. I always thought they were going to win. There was no reality principle involved. I loved them and was disappointed every time they lost. It was hard to fathom that Ernie Banks couldn't carry the team by himself. But there was never any pitching! My father was a hard-bitten cynic. If I saw him on a morning when they were on the West Coast, I'd ask him how the Cubs did the night before, and he'd say, "They won—they didn't play."

By the time I was sixteen I would go out to games by myself. In September 1966, the Cubs were playing the Pirates, and my best friend and I were both about to go off to college. We decided to watch a game as one of the last things we would do together. Wrigley Field was the place I'd chosen to spend my last day at home with my closest friend.

I remember where I was in '69 when I realized the Cubs weren't going to catch the Mets. I was on vacation with my parents, and I was standing on an escalator in Philadelphia. And I don't even remember how I realized it. But it was horrible. When you look back at that roster, it's confounding that that team did not win.

I felt betrayed when the games became popular enough that you couldn't just walk into the stadium anymore. Even when they started drawing a million people, there'd be plenty of seats in the ballpark. Then things changed. It was really more of a phenomenon of my adulthood, after I finished graduate school and moved back to Chicago in 1978.

I've been to at least a few games every season since then. I can't imagine a season passing without getting to Wrigley. When you're a lawyer, someone always has tickets to a game. When I was a federal prosecutor, I'd usually sneak out of the office and catch a day game rather than take time from the weekends with my kids. Nobody ever cared about that in that office. Trial lawyers work incredible hours, maybe three thousand a year, so if someone shows up with tickets, no one holds it against you if you go. I'd just get on the L and go to the game in my suit.

One of the most memorable games for me was in the play-offs in 1984. My brother-in-law got a chance to buy play-off tickets—I think they were $125. In 1984, $125 was a lot of money to me. My ex-wife, God bless her, said yes, which was a very kind thing for her to do. We went to the second game. It was miraculous. I ran into a friend outside the ballpark, and he said, "Bunting! Friggin' bunting at Wrigley Field!" (He meant, of course, the red, white, and blue banners hanging behind home plate that were hung only during the play-offs and were therefore such an odd sight at Wrigley Field.) Everyone had their brooms and was yelling, "Sweep, sweep!" And we all know how that ended. It was fun while it lasted.

The Cubs have broken my heart more times than I can count. It's hard to say whether '03 or '84 or '69 was the bitterest loss. I realized in '03 that the part of me engaged with the Cubs is the six-year-old who first went to games with my dad. When the team plays, that six-year-old comes out of hibernation, and when a game like the one in 2003 happens, it's devastating. I guess I'd put all three of those games on an even par.

My experiences at Wrigley Field changed dramatically after my career as a novelist took off. I threw the first pitch for a game in June of '93. The Cubs were playing the Mets. My publisher arranged it. It probably wasn't worth much as a publicity event, but my publisher knew how much it would mean to me, and it did. My friends from the U.S. Attorneys' Office mocked the hell out of me, but I practiced a fair bit. On a slope of lawn at the house where I lived, I would pitch to my thirteen-year-old daughter. I have an entire album filled with photos of that pitch at Wrigley.

They took me out and walked me around the field. The grass put a country club golf course to shame. It was just perfect. But the most striking thing about the experience was that I really understood the magnificence of the architecture of Wrigley Field from the mound. I felt as if I could reach out and touch every person in the stadium. Standing on the pitcher's mound at Wrigley Field was a remarkable moment.

The Cubs infielder Eric Yelding caught my ball and said, "That's the first damn strike we've had in three weeks." That felt good. Bobby Bonilla, who was playing for the Mets at the time, came charging in from the outfield and asked me to sign a copy of my latest novel, which he was reading. That was also very gratifying.

A friend took me to the team's first night game, in 1988. We had great seats, right behind home plate. A night game at Wrigley Field—no one could believe it. The stands were filled with all these old-time fans who had been there only in the daylight, and suddenly, boom! It's nighttime at Wrigley Field. But then it started raining, and it was as if God was saying no to lights at Wrigley. I had been against lights in Wrigley Field, because I thought it would mar the sacred edifice, but when I got out there I thought, "Oh, this is pretty neat." It was a whole new way to appreciate the ballpark.

I've sung the seventh-inning stretch twice from the broadcast booth. Former Cubs president John McDonough was a big fan of my books. I met him at a dinner, and he said, "How would you like to sing?" I just said, "Wow." Being with Ron Santo in the radio booth was a lot of fun. He was a sweet, genuine man.

The one thing about Wrigley that never gets mentioned is that the Cubs have never won the World Series while playing there.

We all love Wrigley so much that we don't want to say that out loud. But if there's a curse, the ballpark is part of it. It's a weird thing—you have to wonder about the ballpark's role in all these years of failure. The dimensions have tempted the Cubs forever to build power-hitting teams, but you have to wonder if that's the wrong strategy.

Still, I love being there. It's a great place. Of course, I'm in my sixties now, and people call me up with tickets. Often I sit in a skybox, but that doesn't change anything. I still just want the Cubs to win! I've lost patience with the lovable loser thing.

Once, I told former Cubs president and general manager Andy MacPhail about how my father rooted for the Cubs his entire life and that for the one pennant they won, in 1945, he was overseas fighting in World War II. He lived and died without seeing them win a World Series, and he literally spent probably 10 percent of his time on the Cubs.

Then I asked Andy, what is the hardest part of your job? He said, "I'm sick of these guys who call me up and say, 'My father died last week, and he never got to see the Cubs win a World Series.' I'm here trying to change that." It was a very funny conversation.

I remain dedicated. I had lunch with George Will a few years ago, and when I asked him about the Cubs, he said, "I quit that." Two years later, in '03, the Cubs were in the play-offs, and there was George and his son. I don't kid myself. I'll never jump ship. I approach most years with no great optimism, but I'll always watch and I'll always listen.

Always.

RYNE SANDBERG is a Hall of Fame second baseman who spent sixteen years in the major leagues, most of them with the Cubs. His number, 23, is one of the few retired by the team.

I was a late-September call-up with the Phillies in 1981 and had six at bats. I got one hit, which came at Wrigley Field. It was the second game of a doubleheader. I came in for Larry Bowa, and I was facing Mike Krukow. It was toward the end of the season, and the Cubs were way out of it. I think we played in front of about ten thousand people. There was no fan interest. Not like we know it today. I remember getting pitched and mishitting it somewhat, and it was a little flare to right field off the end of

the bat. I took it. I always thought it was ironic that it came at Wrigley Field.

I wasn't very impressed with the field. It seemed very old, nostalgic. It was old and outdated compared to what I'd seen. It seemed smaller than what it looked like on TV. I was surprised by it in a lot of ways, for the most part not for the good. There was only a minimal weight room. The facilities were very downscale compared to what I'd seen traveling to the other stadiums. But it became my home field, and I was very happy to be in the major leagues.

I had my sights set on being a Philadelphia Phillie and playing at Veterans Stadium, which was built in the early seventies and had Astroturf, which was a cool thing back then. Maybe in some ways Wrigley wasn't cool to me. I saw how dead the stadium was in those late-September games, and I got good advice from people who said I was going into a situation that was hoping to change and that I could be part of that change.

When I came over to the Cubs, I developed a fondness for Wrigley Field almost immediately. It became my home park. Because of the day games, I saw the ball well and I seemed to hit well there. I think for the most part, players tend to see the ball better and the strings better in the daylight than under the lights. For a couple of years, I lived close enough to Wrigley Field to walk to the stadium. I lived at Park Place apartments—the tall building in center field. I was a nobody, so no fans stopped me and asked for my autograph or anything like that. The team was only so-so popular then.

People were almost wondering back then whether Wrigley Field was too old and if it should be knocked down. It didn't have lights, which started to become stranger as the years went by. It felt second tier, teamwise and with the facility. It just didn't seem as cool and hip as it does today, and with only minimal changes. Now it's antique and what the new ballparks are taking pieces of because it's cool. Today Wrigley is the place everyone wants to be, and that started in 1984.

In '82 and '83, my first two years with the Cubs, there were days with many, many good seats available, but in '84 that all changed. It became a national attraction, I think all because of WGN and Harry Caray and that season we had. In '84 we made a team pact to use Wrigley Field to our advantage. We agreed to not let the nightlife interfere. With all those day games, you need your rest to make it through the season and be successful; let the

Ryne Sandberg acknowledges the crowd after winning the home-run contest prior to sixty-first All-Star Game in Chicago, July 9, 1990.

other teams enjoy Rush Street and the nightlife. They were only there for three days, and we might be there for a ten-game home stand. We used the whole Wrigley scenario of day games to our advantage. Getting your rest is the biggest thing to winning there. Ballplayers aren't used to having nights off. As the home team, we decided not to let it be an interference. It came from the manager and the veteran players. And that season, we fed off the excitement of the fans, with it being a full house all the time.

That season started things for me and brought my game to another level. Most memorable was June 23—my number, so I'll never forget the date. It was a game of the week against the Cardinals. Nationally televised. Great atmosphere. Heavy buzz in the stadium. I remember going up there in the bottom of the ninth with nothing to lose and everything to gain, with two outs. I elevated a split-finger fastball, swung underneath the baseball, which was very out of the ordinary for me—to aim for the bottom of the ball—because it usually results in a fly ball. But Bruce Sutter's pitch goes down and hard so much, I actually swung underneath that ball and connected and tied the game. Sutter was probably the best closer at the time. Two innings later, same thing: two outs, down two runs. I aimed below the baseball again. He was such a ground-ball pitcher. The whole day, I was five for six with seven RBIs and two home runs off Bruce Sutter.

I surprised myself that day, that I was capable of doing that. My manager at the time, Jim Frey, had been talking to me in spring training about being more of an impact player and using my size to hit the ball out of the park once in a while. That had never been my strategy. I was line drives, gap-to-gap hard ground balls and using my speed. That day exemplified what he was talking about. Before that game I was in second place in the All-Star voting. The next week, I passed Steve Sax by a long shot and I was an All-Star for the first time. All because of that game.

That game created a lot of excitement for us and made us realize we were a good team. After the game, Whitey Herzog said, sarcastically, that I was the greatest player he'd ever seen. He was giving a jab to the media, someone who asked, "What do you think of Sandberg's performance?" He said, "What do you want me to say? He's the greatest player I've ever seen." As a young player, I took it to heart. All that combined kind of drove me to winning the Most Valuable Player that year.

The last home game at Wrigley was against the Cardinals once again. A Sunday game, and we were going on the road for a week

with a six-game lead, and we were going to clinch on the road. After that last game against St. Louis, which we won, we were in the locker room half undressed and Jim Frey comes out and says, "Hey, guys—nobody's leaving the ballpark. We need to go out there and give them a wave." We went out in long underwear and flip-flops and half-cutoff shirts. It was amazing. No one had left, and everyone was standing, clapping. We went on the field and it got louder, so we did a little parade around the field and went back in. It was like the fans were celebrating that we were going to clinch and they were going to miss it, which we did, I think three days later in Pittsburgh. It was awesome. It was the first time I'd been involved in winning at the major-league level.

It was too bad we didn't clinch at Wrigley, but the biggest thing was just clinching because of all the history and the stories we'd heard through the years about the Cubs' past teams and collapses. We had a history lesson in that. That was nonstop from the All-Star break: When are the Cubs going to collapse? What bad luck is going to turn on them? The biggest thing was just clinching and getting the monkey off the Cubs' back. It never bothered us that much; we had veterans who had been on winning teams before—Ron Cey, Gary Matthews, Larry Bowa—they kept everyone in check. And we had a good team. So it all took care of itself.

That September, we were in the dugout during a game and someone spotted one guy on a rooftop across the street. It was a full house for the first time in years. He said, "Hey look, there's a guy watching the game from the rooftop!" One guy. In the play-offs there might have been ten or fifteen guys on the rooftop, and then starting in 1985 we saw the evolution of that. What started as a couple of lounge chairs and one or two barbecues eventually became state-of-the-art bleachers and buffets and tickets being sold and the whole works. The fact that the one guy was up there was so funny at the time. It was, "Oh, look at this guy."

Our two play-off games against San Diego were just an unreal atmosphere. I'd never experienced anything like that before. We saw the buildup from the last month of the season to that point.

PAUL LIBIN has won ten Tony awards and produced more than 250 Broadway, off Broadway, and touring productions. He is executive vice-president of Jujameya Theaters and former chairman of the Broadway League. In 2013 he recieved a special Tony Award for Lifetime Achievement in the Theatre.

I still remember going to my first Cubs game at Wrigley Field as a kid and going up through the grandstand and coming out and seeing the park. I'd never seen grass more green. And the ivy on the walls . . . It was a spectacular moment. I'm sure the grass in Humboldt Park was as green, but I always remembered how vivid it was at Wrigley as a youngster.

In those days, you were introduced to baseball by hearing it on the radio. In your mind you conjured what it was like to actually be there. I have a memory of passing Wrigley Field on a streetcar from the outside and seeing that wonderful round corner at Clark and Addison with the big red sign. It's still there.

I remember the first time I got there, I saw across left field the apartments on Sheffield Avenue and thought, "God, what it would be like to live there! You could see every game! You could rush home from school and see the game!"

When the Cubs won the National League pennant in 1945, I was ready. I was going to go to the World Series. There were five or six of us. I can't remember everyone involved, but the plan was that we were going to go to Wrigley Field and sleep outside the park to get bleacher tickets, because back then you could only get them on the day of the game.

We were telling our parents, "We have to go to the World Series! We have to go to the World Series!" Our parents said it was too dangerous. Finally one parent said it was OK, so all the parents said it was OK. We got blankets and bags of sandwiches, and I remember we had a portable radio, which back then was a monstrous thing with heavy batteries and tubes and things.

I'm thinking we were seventieth or eightieth in line. Ahead of us and behind us were a bunch of old-timers. Through the night, no one slept. There was a little talking, a little kibitzing, a little relaxing, but no one slept. There was a lot of talking and storytelling. Like all kids, I knew the batting averages and who all the pitchers were.

We were getting excited, but then at nine A.M. the police came and said we were in the wrong line. They said we had to be around the way, on the other side of the stadium, if we wanted to get into the game. By that time, there were so many people in that other line that there was no way we could get tickets.

There was a pretty violent reaction. Our first thought was that maybe someone took care of the police so they'd get first crack at the tickets. But then we thought that it wasn't the cops who did it, it was the management of the Cubs. Finally we made a vow that the Cubs would not win the World Series or another pennant. All of us outside the park, we made a blood vow.

I was a little Jewish boy in Chicago back in those days, but I married a wonderful Irish girl. And when the Cubs were close to winning the pennant in 2003, she said, "You're going to lift that curse?" I said, "Yeah, I guess so." But an hour or so later, I said, "No, I'm keeping the curse!" And look what happened! The curse stuck!

I haven't been to Wrigley since that day. I've lived in New York for sixty years, and I split my loyalties between the Yankees and the Mets. But I want to visit Wrigley again. I just want to experience it again. It would be a way of absolving bad behavior on my part.

Even without being there in so long, I remember it well. There is something uniquely "baseball" about the Cubs and Wrigley Field. It's one of the bastions of baseball that has not changed in modern times and has been there even as all the other cities build and rip down stadiums. It remains a landmark institution.

Wrigley Field is beautifully shaped. The equalization of left and right field, with bleachers framed above the ivy-covered wall creates the essence of a perfect stadium. Most importantly, it allows baseball fans a perfect view of each moment of every game from every seat.

Paul Libin

JOAN ALESIA is a Chicago native who spent thirty-seven years at Chicago's CBS affiliate slotting commercials. She has been a Wrigley Field season-ticket holder for more than fifty years.

I've been a season-ticket holder since about 1960. I attended games with my mother for about twenty-five years and now my niece for the last twenty-five years. I usually wear a Cubs or Wrigley Field sweatshirt if it's cold and a Cubs hat to games—in pink or the customary blue. I'm still waiting for the World Series shirt. I guess not in my lifetime.

It all started with my mother, who was a Cubs fan. My whole family was. There was no choice for me. Until 2008 I went to all weekend, night, and holiday games. Now, living in the suburbs, I attend all the weekend games and holidays. I've gone to about twenty-seven games per year for the last forty-five years. That's 1,215 Cubs games. And I've been aggravated at only 1,210 of them.

My first seats were between home plate and first base, but the team moved me a few rows back. But I still liked them. Then fifteen years ago they moved me again, about twenty-five rows behind home plate. We had beautiful seats but they took 'em to give to their clients—the big shots. They didn't care how long we'd been going. The clients were more important.

But no matter where you sit, you have good seats, being it's a smaller park, unlike all those other parks today that are so spread out. It seems like Cubs fans are very faithful fans. No matter what, we're there. Look at Pittsburgh or Cincinnati—they can't fill their stadiums. If we have a twenty-game losing streak, we still fill the house. I don't know if you call that stupidity or what. All I know is that if someone said I couldn't go anymore, I'd be very sad.

I like the little bit of remodeling they have done at Wrigley Field, but I also like its old charm. It's nice they have new stadiums, but Wrigley is more intimate, and that adds something special. You feel more at home and like you know everyone, even when you don't. I don't care if they never have a new stadium. I like what we have. There's always a warm feeling in there.

My least favorite thing about Wrigley is the food. We keep thinking they'll get good food and they never do.

I guess the most memorable game I've seen was the Bartman game. Poor guy. It wasn't his fault. I blame Dusty Baker. He could've used his pitchers differently. And Gonzalez made that error. I don't blame Bartman, but everyone needed to blame someone. They had a chance the next day and still didn't win it, so I guess we deserved to lose. We finally had a chance after one thousand years, and it didn't come through. It was very disappointing.

I've seen three no-hitters: Don Cardwell, Milt Pappas, and Burt Hooton. Cardwell's was the most memorable because it was the first one I saw. It was May 15, 1960, I remember that. We had just gotten him. It was a doubleheader, and we lost the first game. We were going to go home but decided to stay, and it was a no-hitter.

I always say I'm not going next year, and then when it's time, I say, "OK, we'll go again." You know you don't mean it when you say it, but you always go back because you think this might be the year. Then again, you get tired of saying, "Wait till next year."

Cubs fans surround Don Cardwell after his 1960 no-hitter against the St. Louis Cardinals.

JIM BOUTON is a former major-league pitcher who achieved early success with the New York Yankees. He is the author of *Ball Four*, a memoir of his major-league career.

I grew up in Newark, New Jersey, as a Giants fan. I played stickball and mimicked all the batting stances. We went often to Polo Grounds to watch them play.

When I was about eight, I spent a summer in Park Ridge with my grandparents. At some point, my brother Bob and I realized we could go see our heroes play at Wrigley Field, so we went to a Cubs-Giants game. We got to the park a couple of hours before the game, and when we saw the Giants in the dugout, we made our move.

We thought the best thing they could get as the visiting team was some encouragement from fans back home, so I laid across the dugout as my brother held my ankles, to let the Giants' players know that they weren't all alone there.

I was upside down but knew the Giants well enough to recognize them anyway. I saw Alvin Dark and told him the whole story, as kids will do: "My brother and I are here from New Jersey, and we're cheering for you." Then I said, "You think I could have an autograph?" He looked up and he said, "Take a hike, son."

Later, my brother asked, "Did Alvin Dark say something to you?" And I told him, "Alvin Dark actually said something to me! He told me to take a hike!" Later that afternoon we burst in the front door when we got home and my brother said, "Guess what, Dad? Alvin Dark told Jim to take a hike!" It was such a thrill to have one of our favorite ballplayers talk to us. It didn't matter what he said.

Now whenever anyone wants to brush someone off in my family, we say, "Take a hike." It's been a lifelong family put-down. That's the thing I've always remembered about Wrigley Field. I wrote about it in *Ball Four*. A few years later, someone ran into Alvin and asked about the story. He said, "I didn't even know Jim Bouton then." I've since run into him several times. He's always very nice to me. We just laugh about it. It helped that I told the story in a way that got across I was not offended by what he said.

Before my sophomore year of high school, I moved with my family to Homewood, Illinois. I'd go back to Wrigley Field a few times, when I was starting to dream of pitching professionally. I wanted to see what major-league pitching looked like. I wasn't really a Cubs fan though. I wasn't a Giants fan either. I stopped rooting for them when they moved to San Francisco in 1958. It seemed like the right thing to do.

I co-wrote a novel with Eliot Asinof, *Strike Zone*, in the 1990s. It's the story of a game fixed by a homeplate umpire, and it happens at Wrigley Field. I picked Wrigley for its history. It just seemed like the right place to do it. I flew to Chicago and spent a day at the ballpark reporting for the book, talking to players and listening to the chatter around the batting cage.

It's amazing they haven't won for as long as they have, but statistically, if you have that many teams for that long, one of them just won't win the World Series. It was true of the Red Sox and now it's true of the Cubs. They're like the old St. Louis Browns or Washington Senators. It'll be a great story when they do win it. But the fans are impressive. They stay loyal. I think it's because people love an orphan, a stepchild, a dog with a limp. They're more lovable.

Fans ride a moving ramp to upper-deck seats at Wrigley Field, on July 22, 1956. The moving ramp was the first of its kind to be used in a major-league ballpark.

GEORGE WILL is a Pulitzer Prize–winning conservative columnist, journalist, and author.

At about age seven, in 1948, a year I think Mr. Wrigley took out ads in the Chicago papers to apologize for the team, I plighted my troth to the Cubs, damn fool that I was. Baseball was in the air—literally—when I grew up in Champaign. It was a radio sport then and we could get Cardinals, Browns, White Sox, and Cubs games. For some reason I chose the Cubs. It was radio that did it. It was an age too tender to make a life-shaping decision. All my friends who became Cardinals fans grew up cheerful and liberal, and I grew up a bitter conservative.

Starting in 1950 or '51, my parents would take me up to Wrigley Field once a summer in our blue 1949 Plymouth. We might have gone to the Shedd Aquarium or the Museum of Science and Industry also, but the point was to go to Wrigley Field. They wouldn't have done it without considerable begging.

Today, of course, it looks quaint. Back then, when there were Ebbets and Briggs and Shibe and Forbes fields, it looked state-of-the-art. It was just exciting to be in proximity to these interglacially famous baseball players.

What makes it special is how many generations have watched baseball there. A whole bunch of Civil War veterans must have watched baseball there. Just think of all the millions and millions of footfalls on those steps from the concourse to the seats. I've been to ball games in three different Philadelphia parks and three different Pittsburgh parks. I hope Wrigley Field is the only place I ever see a Cubs game.

I know if I change my loyalties, they'll win the next year just to spite me. I'm fond of the Nationals—I've lived in Washington DC since 1970—but the Cubs are an addiction. I remember when the 1994 strike started and they were talking about replacement players, Andy MacPhail said what people love is the ballpark and the logo. A lot goes into this complex chemistry of the loyalty of fandom, and the ballpark is crucial.

All my memories of Wrigley Field are disasters. I sat in a luxury box with Andy MacPhail at the Bartman game. Mediocrity doesn't get better with age.

George Will with his son Geoff and former Cubs president Andy MacPhail, 2004.

LARRY BELL is the owner and founder of Bell's Brewery, which grew from his basement to become the nation's fifteenth-largest brewery.

My grandfather wrote a song for the Cubs in 1941 for Charlie Root Day called "Watch the Cubs Play Ball." My grandmother would play it on the piano for us when I was growing up. I still know the words.

On Opening Day we always got to play hooky. Mom packed lunches and Dad packed a flask, and the next day my mom would write a note—"Larry had an upset stomach." It was just what you did for Opening Day. The last one we attended as a family was in a very important year and one of the Cubs' best Opening Days ever: 1969.

We sat on the third-base line, but we were down to the Phillies 6–5 in the eleventh, and my dad said, "OK, let's go, we have to get home." We started for the exit and were back behind first base when Willie Smith hit a two-run homer to win it and the place went crazy. It was the best Opening Day in history! Swedish Covenant Hospital had a contest about the best Cubs experience, and I wrote that up. It was great. I had myself in tears. But some kid won.

The park doesn't look different from what I remember as a kid. It really doesn't. The seats are different and there are the lights now, but my favorite thing as a kid is still my favorite thing, and that's coming up the steps on Opening Day and taking in the first sight of the grass. I get goose bumps still.

In 1967 I came to a doubleheader with my brother Roger, and he was listening to another game on a transistor radio. He stood up and said, "The other team lost! We're in first place!" Soon they changed the flags on the scoreboard and everyone went crazy. The Cubs in first place! That just didn't happen.

I spent most of the 1969 season in the left-field bleachers with my brother and the Bleacher Bums. We would leave Park Forest at five A.M., get in line at six, and wait for the park to open at nine thirty. We'd wait three and a half hours to get in. Someone brought a Frisbee, someone brought cards, someone would go to Dunkin' Donuts. But we got to sit with the Bums in left field. You were a pussy if you sat in right field. I remember the Bums found out Lou Brock was afraid of mice, and they brought a cage of white mice to a game and dropped them on the field while he was out there. He freaked out. As I recall, he didn't play very well that day. Those were great days. The Bums wore yellow hard hats, and the leader had a coronet, and they would do all kinds of cheers.

I took some time off from Wrigley after going to college and then starting my business with just one beer I brewed in the

Charley Root, who served up the pitch in the 1932 World Series that Babe Ruth supposedly signaled that he was going to hit out of the park—and did.

basement and sold from my van. I'd go to the occasional game when deliveries took me to Chicago; I'd bring my kids with me and we'd do a day in the city: drive from Kalamazoo in the morning, make deliveries, catch the Cubs game, then go back up to Kalamazoo. I got into it again in 1998 when the Cubs played a one-game play-off against the Giants for the Wild Card. I paid $435 each for three seats behind home plate. It was worth it. It was pandemonium after we won. You'd think we had won the Series. It was just exciting to watch the Cubs clinch something.

The next year I bought season tickets for seats down the left-field line. People ask me where I sit, I say three sections from Ferris Bueller and twelve rows behind Bartman.

That Bartman game felt like it was going to be a dream come true. It was electric in the stadium. We were going to witness history. We did witness history, but not the history we wanted. We'd seen the Cubs do this kind of thing before, so when the Bartman play happened, you know, the feeling was "Oh my God, this is bad." They brought Bartman up one aisle away and then down the stairs right behind my seats. There were full cups of beer flying over our heads at the poor guy. People were standing on their seats and chanting, "Ass-hole." Security was all around him because people were trying to punch him. It was nuts.

The park feels the same to me as it always has—spiritual. I dream about Wrigley Field. The best one I've had recently was when we were getting close to Opening Day. In the dream, I was having trouble getting to my seats because there were all these boxes in the way—a new Chinese dumpling stand was opening at Wrigley Field. I was excited, because I love Chinese dumplings. When I woke up, I knew we were in for quite a year.

I love the tradition. I love that we haven't done a lot to sell out and don't have to listen to a lot of music that gives me a headache. We still have the Dixieland band and "Take Me Out to the Ball Game."

Since I was a boy, if there's a lull in conversation, my mind goes to the Cubs. One year I want to try going to every game in the season. It might kill me. I already have so many scars on my heart from the Cubs. The last game I attend every year, I sit in my seat until they kick me out. It takes me a couple of months to recover from a bad season.

I like watching the ivy grow in May. I stand in the seventh inning and look around and see if there's someone I know. It's a community. It's Cubs love. Even when we're not winning, it's Cubs love. I love being able to walk over here. It's the neighborhood.

My condo is on the forty-fifth floor of a fifty-five-story building that stands over the center-field wall. In bed at night, all I have to do is lift my head a little and I can see the back of the scoreboard, and I know all is right in the world.

Seeing the Cubs win the World Series is my goal in life. I think about my dad—he died at seventy-six and never saw the Cubs win the World Series. It's like, "Come on, guys, you have to do this once."

I was diagnosed with prostate cancer in the fall of 2007, and the doctor wanted to do the surgery in October. I said, "Doc, the problem is, the Cubs are in first place and we're probably going to the play-offs. Can we postpone it until November?" I think he thought I was a little crazy, but he agreed. We got swept, but I didn't regret it. If we were going to the World Series, I was going to be there.

When the Cubs are in town, the neighborhood certainly becomes a big beer garden. When the Sox fans come, it gets pretty hot. The Cardinals fans come up here and we get into it with them, but the Sox fans are aggressive. The Cardinals fans make me crazy, but at least they're not violent.

JIM KAPLAN is a former *Sports Illustrated* baseball writer and the author of 19 books, most recently *The Greatest Game Ever Pitched: Juan Marichal, Warren Spahn and the Pitching Duel of the Century*. George Will called Kaplan the "poet laureate" of fielding. Also a bridge columnist, Kaplan and his wife, poet Brooks Robards, divide their time between Northampton, MA, and Oak Bluffs on the island of Martha's Vineyard.

"Is he Jewish?"

This is a question Jews ask about any athlete whose name sounds even vaguely *landsman*. Though we're proud that Jews dominated boxing in the 1930s and basketball in the first half of the twentieth century while contributing significantly to racquet sports and swimming, my candidate for the greatest day in Jewish sports history was a baseball game I attended at Wrigley Field between the Cubs and Dodgers on September 25, 1966. Two Jewish lefthanders faced each other for the only time: the Dodgers' Sandy Koufax, then the best pitcher in the game, and the Cubs' Ken Holtzman, a twenty-year-old rookie having what amounted to his baseball Bar Mitzvah that day.

Opponents knew that you had to reach Koufax early to beat him. In the first inning, Don Kessinger walked and Glenn Beckert tripled to left for a run. After Billy Williams struck out and Ron Santo grounded out (Beckert holding at third), Ernie Banks reached on an error by second baseman Jim Lefebvre to score Beckert. Randy Hundley fanned to end the inning with the Chicago line reading two runs, one earned on one hit and one error. The Cubs were happy to score any way they could against Sandy Koufax.

No one expected the lead to hold up, but Holtzman confounded the Dodgers with a good fastball they kept missing and a sharp-breaking curve they could only hit on the ground. Once Koufax found his rhythm, Holtzman was even better. Through eight innings he no-hit the Dodgers, facing the minimum twenty-four batters and yielding just one walk that was erased on a double play.

The Dodgers finally got to Holtzman in the ninth. Dick Schofield singled to center and Al Ferrara, batting for catcher John Roseboro, walked. Hitting for Koufax, Junior Gilliam struck out, but Maury Wills singled to center to score Schofield and cut the Cub lead to 2–1. With all 21,659 of us fans on the edge of our seats, Willie Davis hit a line drive to the right side that looked like a game-tying blow. On a scale of tension, it replicated the Willie McCovey liner that ended the 1962 World Series. As we jumped to our feet screaming, Beckert gloved the ball and tagged Willis for an unassisted double play to end the game. This exquisite agon took only one hour and fifty minutes.

Little did we know that Koufax's career would end that October and Holtzman would throw two no-hitters and go 4–1 with a 2.55 ERA in the World Series. It sufficed just to read the words "two Jewish lefthanders" in the next day's newspapers.

Jim Kaplan

The Cubs have several fans who are celebrities, but probably only RONNIE "WOO WOO" WICKERS is a celebrity because he is a fan. Wickers attends most home games in a Cubs uniform, leading cheers with his trademark "Woo woo!"

Baseball is like medicine. People come and go. Baseball is always there. It gives you love, happiness, and joy, all those things. It's true at all baseball games, but especially at Wrigley Field. To come to Wrigley Field, when you first see the vines and the bleachers, there's nothing like it. I'd never seen grass on a wall before. There's a kindness that is a part of Chicago. It's my home.

I go to almost every home game and have probably been to more than three thousand games. My grandmother took me to my first game in 1949. We took the bus up from the South Side to see Jackie Robinson play. All the South Siders, when the Brooklyn Dodgers came to town, would take the train up and sit in the right-field bleachers. It was really segregated then. All the African Americans were out in right field because that's the way it was. We all wanted to see Jackie play and he knew it, so he would come out and sign autographs before he'd get onto the bus on Sheffield, and he'd give a wave or a tip of the hat. Seeing him gave us a wonderful feeling, because he showed us that we could play as well as any other nationality. When he went out there, it was all about baseball. It was a thrill and an honor to see him. We had Joe Louis, but there weren't that many African Americans playing sports.

I still remember walking into Wrigley Field for the first time. The sun was shining and the vines were just turning green and a joy came over me. It was amazing to be there with all those people. It's hard to describe. When I was a teenager, I would go to fifty or more games a year. If the Cubs were home and I could make it, I was there, sitting in the bleachers for fifty cents. My favorite spot is in left field, about eight rows up.

At one point, the players started leaving me tickets—Bill Buckner, Steve Trout, and Leon Durham. Harry Caray called me Leather Lungs. For a long time I worked at Northwestern University as an overnight janitor. I'd go to the day games, then head up to work. Now I get by washing windows and shoveling snow. When the Cubs get the final out, I start working to save up for spring training.

I go all over the ballpark now: bleachers, grandstand, upper deck, skybox, or I get a standing-room ticket and roam around. I get there at about eight in the morning to see the players.

I didn't plan to become a celebrity. It just happened that way. I was just coming to Wrigley Field and kept cheering the Cubs. I smile and take a lot of pictures, sign autographs, and might occasionally do a birthday party, but I do it for the love of the game. The organization doesn't pay me, but they can't trade me or fire me either. I had no idea sixty years ago that it was going to be like this.

"Woo woo" means "win win." It may be annoying, but it's all in good, clean fun. And the players—Bill Buckner, Dave Kingman, José Cardenal , Jerry Morales, Steve Trout, Andre Dawson, Billy Williams—I've talked to all of them, and they all look forward to seeing me. Or Mark Grace would be over at first and I'd go "Grace woo! Grace woo!" and he'd wave his glove at me.

I was the first person to throw an opponent's home-run ball back. It was in 1967 or 1968, against the Giants. Everyone around me said, "Why did you throw the ball back?" I said, "Because it wasn't a Cubs ball." Now it's a tradition all over baseball. I didn't plan it that way. It just happened. A lot of people ask, what's the best game you saw? I always say, "This one, because I'm still here." But I also saw the All-Star Game in 1962, and the outfield was Roberto Clemente, Hank Aaron, and Willie Mays. That was memorable.

There are no hard times at Wrigley Field, because it's all baseball. Tomorrow the sun will come up and there'll be a blue sky. People say it was bad in '69 or '84 or '03, but it's just timing.

I was grieving in '84, when my girlfriend and my grandmother both died. It was hard for me, but coming to the ballpark kept me together. I went astray and became homeless, but I kept coming to the ballpark and no one knew. I was going "Cubs woo, Cubs woo" and signing autographs and having a good time. It made me forget the other parts of my life.

Wrigley is the same, but the fans have changed. They don't keep score like they used to. Now they just come to the ballpark, have a beer and a hot dog. If someone hits a home run and the Cubs win, that's all that matters. Back in my day, you'd keep score, hang around after and meet the players. But then, the players today don't always take time and sign autographs like they should.

You still get goose bumps here. The sunlight, the green grass, the crack of the bat. People come up here and say, "Ronnie, I read about it, but to actually see it, it's special." When the Cubs win the World Series, I'm going to climb up the left-field flagpole and celebrate. It won't matter how old I am.

Cubs "superfan" Ronnie "Woo Woo" Wickers, 2006.

ERNIE BANKS
"MR. CUB"

JOE MANTEGNA, an actor, has found success on the stage, in movies, and on television. Among his most notable achievements is the play *Bleacher Bums*, which he conceived in Wrigley Field's bleachers.

I grew up in Garfield Park, around Kedzie Avenue and the Eisenhower Expressway, and then moved to Cicero with my family. As an adult I lived all over the North Side, including Cornelia and Halstead, half a mile from Wrigley Field. If I had the windows open, I'd hear the roar of the crowd. I'd hear the roar live through my window, then through the TV set.

Being a Cubs fan is a curse that my father inflicted on me. For whatever reason, he was a Cubs fan, and I never got to the bottom of that. On my block it was hit or miss if you were a Cubs or Sox fan. But there's a picture—it's on my Web site—of me at about eight sitting in front of a black-and-white TV, and you can see it's Wrigley Field on there. Hank Sauer is up to bat.

When you're a kid, you go with the team your father likes. When I was about ten, we went to ten games that summer. And they lost every single one. He asked me to go to an eleventh game, and I refused because I thought I might be the reason they were losing. That was the first time I realized that you could be damaged by following this team, my first inkling that it might be a painful journey—which it has been.

My time at Wrigley was how I conceived the play *Bleacher Bums*. The whole reason was because of this one question: Why the hell do we put up with this? It was so difficult to get people to come to the theater, but I'd look around me at Wrigley and they'd have thirty-four thousand people for a team that was at best mediocre. What is it? Why do thirty-four thousand people come to see a mediocre team? If I could capture what brought them to the park, I knew I'd have a sensation. The play ran for more than twelve years in Chicago, off Broadway, and in Los Angeles.

The universal question is why everyone follows the underdog. Why is there blind optimism? In the face of constant defeat, we look for the silver lining in the dark cloud. It's human nature. There's a whole philosophical aspect. It transcends being about one team. The Cubs are the perfect analogy about fandom and what drives a person to fanaticism. It's not winning. If it was all about winning, everyone would be a Yankees fan. There's something about following your hometown team and hope springing eternal.

Sometimes I sound bitter, but I'm not. It's total acceptance. I'm comfortable with it. I'm totally prepared for the Cubs to be a total failure. People ask me what it will be like when they win, and I tell them I don't think they ever will. And I really don't. I find comfort in that, because if I'm wrong, I'll be the happiest guy in Dodge. If they don't win, I'm the smartest guy in Dodge.

In 2003 they were interviewing me in LA, asking, "How does it feel to be one win away?" I said, "What chance could we possible have?" The interviewers laughed. They thought I was joking. I said, "You'll see." The minute that thing happened with Bartman, it was, "Ah, there it is. There's Garvey's home run or the meltdown with the Mets in 1969." I was disappointed and I was hurt, but I wasn't surprised.

The thing that upset me was all the crap on this kid. That's when I realized these weren't the real fans. They were heaping abuse on this kid for no reason. I didn't even watch Game 7, because I knew they would lose. Some guys came by my trailer wanting to know the score. I said I didn't have it on, because it had ended the day before.

I live in Los Angeles, but I still get to four or five games a year. Wrigley Field is a shrine. If you're going to watch a baseball game, there's no better place. It's a living thing. It's a part of the neighborhood, and it's part of a city in a neighborhood. You can take the bus or the L or walk or take a cab there and come in through a million different ways. Most other places, like Dodger Stadium, if you don't have a car, you're screwed. That's a totally different thing. Wrigley Field is a part of the pulse of that North Side neighborhood.

When I was first living there, in the mid-seventies, it was a tough neighborhood. You could get an apartment cheap across from Wrigley, because who would want to live there? Who would want to deal with all those crowds? No one knew it would turn into this.

I've thrown out the first pitch three or four times. Most significant was in 1998. I threw out the first pitch, then that day's starter, Kerry Wood, signed the ball for me. That ball is one of my most treasured possessions. What was great is we were all in town for *Bleacher Bums*, and my brother and uncle were there, and it was so memorable. What were the odds?

That game was as close as we've ever gotten to something tremendous. We have to grab our Cubs highlights as we can get them. It's always close, but no cigar, but this time he closed the deal. I remember it started slow. The weather wasn't great—it was kind of misty and rainy—and the park wasn't full. It was early in the season and we were playing Houston, which, you know, who gives a damn. As it got to fourteen, fifteen, and sixteen strikeouts, it became clear, "Wait a minute—we're witnessing something here." I sang the seventh-inning stretch, then went in the booth, and you hear me on the tape screaming, "Seventeen! Eighteen!" That's a huge memory.

I love sitting all over the park. Hell, I'll sit wherever anyone gives me a seat. I have particular affection for the bleachers because of those characters out there and the play I got from sitting there. The fact that things worked out so well, I'm forever grateful to the bleachers. But it's a whole other perspective from anywhere else in the park. I used to sit in the first row and harass the outfielders. I'd harass Lee Mazzilli, nice-looking outfielder for the Mets who I hated. I'd try to get creative and swear at him in Italian.

Dan Lauria, who is an actor and a friend of mine, introduced me to Mazzilli a few years later, because he was thinking of becoming an actor. I was so scared he would say, "Wait a minute, you're that son of a bitch Cubs fan who used to swear at me in Italian!" He didn't, of course, but then I told him what I had done. He says, "Are you kidding me? At Wrigley Field everyone was yelling at me. I never gave them the satisfaction of looking at them, because you look at them, you're dead."

I remember back in '84 I was doing *Glengarry Glen Ross* in New York City, a play that changed my career. I remember watching those games against the Padres and Garvey hitting the home run. It was devastating. The phone rang. It was *Time* magazine wanting to know how I felt about the Cubs losing the pennant. I don't even know how they got the number. My first reaction was to go off—"F— this, they blew it again," and so on. But then I decided I wouldn't give them the satisfaction. I said, "Yeah, they got beat, but I'm gonna wear a Cubs hat at the curtain call tomorrow night." And I did. I whipped out a Cubs hat for the curtain call, and the New York audience booed. Then I threw the hat into the audience. It was a catharsis. I was just proud to be a Cubs fan.

Joe Mantegna with statue of Ernie Banks outside Wrigley Field.

RON SANTO played fifteen major-league seasons, fourteen of them with the Cubs. He was a nine-time All-Star but never made the Hall of Fame. In his later years, he was a beloved color commentator for Cubs radio broadcasts. Santo passed away on December 3, 2010.

I was from Seattle, and all sixteen clubs came in and tried to sign me when I was in high school. But I decided there was something about Wrigley Field. I used to watch it on the Game of the Week. I watched all the games, but with Wrigley Field, there was something special. A buddy of mine moved to Chicago my sophomore year of high school, and we kept in touch. He talked about the Cubbies and Chicago and what a great town it was. I guess it was just watching all the major-league games and the way they always talked about Wrigley Field and the way it looked on TV—when they'd scan around, you'd see people were so close to the field. It was like a cathedral. I was amazed at Ernie Banks and the way he hit.

So, all sixteen teams made offers and a lot made higher offers than the Cubs. It was amazing. At eighteen years old, I lived in a duplex in an Italian neighborhood called Garlic Gulch. My father left when I was six, and my stepfather came into my life at twelve. He was a wonderful man. Everyone offered Double-A ball, and every team had twenty minor-league teams back then, so Double-A ball was unbelievable. Every team offered that except the Cubs. Theirs was the lowest offer. But their scout said, "You're going to be a major leaguer, no doubt about it." The scout called and said, "Ron, we know what you've been offered, and the Cubs aren't going to offer that." It wasn't important to me.

I pretty much eliminated the American League, because I liked watching the National League better. The Reds had offered a lot of money, and my father said, "Do you want to take the Reds' offer and be set for the rest of your life?" In those days the amount of money they offered was unbelievable. I said, "No, I just have a good feeling about Chicago." There was something about the Cubs, Ernie Banks, and Wrigley Field.

I went to spring training and was sent to Double-A in San Antonio. The next year I was invited to spring training as a nonroster player and sent to Triple-A. I was called up June 26 and played my first game at Forbes Field in Pittsburgh. We won a doubleheader.

A 1971 Ron Santo baseball card.

Next day we were at Wrigley Field. The clubhouse was down the left-field line back then. I got dressed, and I'm walking out of the clubhouse doorway down the left-field line, and Ernie came right behind me, and we were walking together. I looked into the stands and the bleachers—no fans were there yet—and walking on that grass, I felt like I was walking on air. The energy was unbelievable. I knew then I'd made the right decision.

I ask people when they're at the park for the first time what it feels like, and they always say the same thing, that you just feel the energy. It's exciting. It makes you want to watch a game. You feel good about the game. If I was on the road and I wasn't hitting well when we came home, I always picked it up a notch.

I was away from the game for seventeen years between retiring and doing the radio commentary. When I went into the booth, there was still that same energy I always felt. And I still feel that same way about it, because look at what I've been through—losing both legs, open-heart surgery, bladder cancer—but every time I got back to Wrigley Field, I never thought about a thing but the Cubbies. It's kept me going, no doubt about it.

I always hit better at Wrigley Field. It's the fans and just the feeling of the park. In my day, when the game was over, win or lose, we were in the clubhouse for two hours after game time. When we came out, there were a hundred fans, and we all signed. I could always feel the difference between Wrigley Field and other parks. I had more confidence, definitely. After my first game at Wrigley, I realized I was there to stay.

I became known for clicking my heels after a win in 1969. We were in first place and lost the first game of a doubleheader. If we lost the second, we'd be tied for first. Jim Hickman hit a three-run homer to win it, and I was so excited I ran up the third-base line and clicked my heels three times. I really didn't even remember doing it. I was just so happy. I get home and watch WGN sports, and there I am clicking my heels. I didn't even remember. Next day Leo says, "Ron, the way things are going, how about clicking your heels when we win at home from now on?" I only did it at Wrigley Field, and the fans loved it. When we fell to second, I stopped.

The 1969 season wasn't tough for me, but it was tough for a lot of guys. There's no doubt we were the best team in the National League. But the Mets beat the Orioles in the World Series, and I thought the Orioles were the best team in baseball that year. What we did that year was unbelievable. We drew 1.7 million people. It was so exciting. It was sad, don't get me wrong, but there was nothing we could do. They played over .800 baseball down the stretch. To me they were the Miracle Mets. They just got hot.

The '69 club related to the fans and the Bleacher Bums and everyone. The fans are the best. And I've become one of them. I can't help it. It bothers me a lot when we don't play good. But I've loved every minute of it.

In 1984 I was eating at Don & Charlie's in Phoenix while the game was on, and I kept going back to the bar to watch. There was no doubt in my mind we would win, and I thought that the weight would come off the shoulders of the '69 team with them winning. It didn't happen.

Of course, '03 was just horrible. That was awful tough. We were going to win, were going to the World Series. I was in Arizona getting treatment for bladder cancer, but they were going to postpone the surgery so I could come back to Chicago and do the Series. I was so excited. But it didn't happen. I knew we had a great team, and it seemed like there was no way we weren't going to win. We had two of our best young pitchers going. You just never know about this game of baseball. There's a lot of pressure, because it's been so long, but I wouldn't change the experience I've had here for a World Series with anyone else. I would never. Chicago has been so good to me. I've loved every minute of it.

When I started when I was twenty, we were averaging six hundred thousand fans a year. The sixties clubs, from '66 on, brought the fans back to baseball. With the talent, the way we played, the way we generated interest and related to the fans, we kept the fans coming. Then all of a sudden, it becomes their kids who they bring to Wrigley Field, and then their kids. And when we go on the road, win or lose, we sometimes outdraw our opposition. They never lose their allegiance when they come to Chicago to see the Cubs. The economy shrinks and ticket prices go up, but people still come out. When you look out and you see a full house and every rooftop is filled, there's no more beautiful picture. The energy with the fans is always there.

LES GROBSTEIN is a lifelong Cubs fan who has spent forty years as a Chicago sports radio personality. He has been on the front lines for many of the team's most memorable moments during the last fifty years.

I grew up a Cubs fan, of the Durocher era team with Ernie Banks, Ron Santo, Billy Williams, Fergie Jenkins, Ken Holtzman, Glenn Beckert, Don Kessinger, and Randy Hundley. That was the most popular team—more popular than the '84 team, the '03 team, more popular than anything in my lifetime. And they never won anything.

Durocher got there in '66 and said, "This is not an eighth-place team," and he was right. They were a tenth-place team. Dead last. However, the very next year they went through a metamorphosis and finished third. They were actually in first for a little bit, but they weren't good enough to beat out the Cardinals, who won it, or the Giants, who finished second. They finished third, which was phenomenal for those guys.

The next year they finished third again, then '69 happened, which was the first year of divisions. Everybody thought the team they were going to have to beat was the Cardinals, but the Cubs were way ahead of them. The Pirates were threatening, but the Cubs finished pretty well ahead of them too. No one took the Mets seriously. The Cubs had an eight-game lead in August, and the Mets came out of nowhere, and they just wouldn't lose. Everyone says the Cubs blew it. Well, they lost by eight games. It wasn't even close. The Mets just beat them.

My grandfather took me to Wrigley Field a lot, including my first game, against the Phillies in 1959. Art Mahaffey beat Glen Hobbie 6–3. Everything looked a lot bigger than it did on TV. And we didn't have a color TV, so I remember thinking, "Oh, this is pretty cool." It looked absolutely gigantic in person. I also thought it was interesting that the upper deck was closed. Except on weekends or against really good teams, they kept the upper deck closed.

I remember the vines. The wooden scoreboard. That the stadium is right in the neighborhood, which was neat. The thing I really thought was weird was when you're watching on TV, and you're hearing Jack Brickhouse and Vince Lloyd—I thought when you were in the stands you'd hear them too. I was like, "Where are the announcers?" My grandfather said you only hear that on TV.

I liked the Sox then too, and I enjoyed seeing both teams play,

but it was one or the other. Why I picked the Cubs is unexplainable. I can't even explain it to myself. I've had a lot of Sox fan friends say, "Come on over to the dark side." I go, "Nah, if I switch over, it means I wasn't a loyal Cubs fan in the first place." I'm not going to give up my loyalty, and believe me, there has been plenty that is worth giving up the loyalty for. I went through '69. I went through '84. I went through '89, when they were slight favorites against the Giants and everything Don Zimmer did, his buddy Roger Craig outfoxed him. I went through '98, but they were no match for Atlanta. They didn't even belong in the play-offs, and they were banged up. I went through '03 and that fiasco. And no, it's not Steve Bartman's fault. Anyone who blames Steve Bartman for anything is an idiot. You want to blame Alex Gonzalez for booting that double-play ball that would have ended the eighth inning with the Cubs still up 3–0, that's another story. If he turns that double play, game over. Anyone who blames Steve Bartman, you are an idiot. Quote me on that. You are an idiot.

What irritated me even as a kid was at Wrigley Field, a lot of Sox fans would show up and root for the other team. I thought, "Why the hell are they doing this?" I didn't think that was necessary. I was eight or nine years old. By the time I was ten, I was taking the L to games by myself, but I didn't tell my parents. I didn't start ditching class to go to games until high school. Then I ditched a lot of classes to go to games.

The whole school ditched for Opening Day. I was the only one who would ditch for the second day, the third day, et cetera. I'd go to class, but by fifth period, I'd duck out, walk to the L and take the Ravenswood line to Belmont, switched to the Englewood-Howard line, go one stop north to Addison: ball game.

I grew up in the bleachers, but I would take those passes and pay a couple extra dollars to sit in box seats. At the end of the 1965 season I got myself a box seat behind home plate, and there were a lot of empty seats next to me, so a bunch of my friends who had grandstand seats came down and sat next to me. There was this older woman, she had to be about seventy, and she didn't want my friends down there. She was screaming, "Usser, usser"—instead of "Usher, usher"—"get the kids out of there, they don't have tickets!" They went to the exchange and got the tickets, and they came back next to me and made noise like nobody's business. After about the third inning she got up, waved her hands at us, and left. I was thirteen years old.

By my freshman year of high school I knew I wasn't a good

enough athlete, so if I wanted to be involved professionally, it was going to be with my big mouth. I started taking tape recorders to games and recording them. I'd go into areas where there weren't many people, which was easy to do because the park wasn't filled up much, and I'd do my own play-by-play. Sometimes I'd be around people and they'd ask, "What the hell are you doing?" But some of the older guys actually thought it was pretty cool, and they liked listening.

Pete Marcantonio, the grounds superintendent, would have kids line up along the left-field line and have them put up all the seats so the cleanup guys could sweep. When we were done, we would get a pass for a game. Sometimes we could double up and get two games.

I've probably seen thousands of games at Wrigley. I haven't counted, though, so that's my best guess.

The defining moments for me as a Cubs fan are the meltdowns: a combination of '69, '84, and '03. Eighty-four was absolutely the year. They blew the Mets out of the water and won the division handily. Then there were those first two games at Wrigley Field, and by the way, anyone who thinks because they didn't have lights they had to play an extra game in San Diego, that is not true. They were scheduled to have Games 3, 4, and 5. Anyone can look it up. They would have lost a World Series game, but they never got that far.

For Game 1, I brought my parents, grandfather, and my then wife. It was pretty surreal already, and then Bobby Dernier leads off the game with a home run. It was so surreal. It was the Cubs in the play-offs! The last time they were in the play-offs was seven years before I was born! Up until then, 1945, the year they dropped the big one on Japan, was the last time they were in the play-offs. The stadium was going crazy. And it was 13–0.

After Game 2, all the Padres, including Tony Gwynn Sr., will tell you to this day they pretty much felt it was over. When they landed that night, they were greeted by a big mob. The players and a lot of San Diego fans were pumped up because Royko had just ripped San Diego, saying they didn't deserve a World Series. All of a sudden, the crowd became really belligerent. When the Cubs took the field, the fans were just nasty. It wasn't that the Padres fans were excited their team was winning—they were excited the Cubs were losing.

For Game 5, Durham hit a two-run home run in the first, but later missed a ground ball. He hadn't missed a ground ball all season. I was on the charter going out there, and they were very calm, they didn't seem overconfident or cocky. Now I'm on the charter flight back to Chicago. I'm editing tape for Larry Lujack's show, which I was doing the next morning, and we're probably over the Rockies somewhere, and I feel a tap on the shoulder. It's Leon Durham. He goes [in a high-pitched voice], "Hey man, these guys gonna rip my ass all winter?" I had to think quickly, and I said, "Bull, you hit a two-run homer in the first inning. Without that homer, that error don't mean s—." He goes, "Yeah man, that's right! Thanks, man!" He goes over and taps Lee Smith. "My error don't mean s— if I don't hit the home run. What do you think of that, bitch?" Because they called each other "bitch" all the time. Of course, to this day they still bring up him missing that ground ball.

In '03 they were five outs from the World Series. The mob outside the ballpark waiting to celebrate was incredible. Every time Prior got an out, the place was going nuts. Every out, they were going crazy. I talked to a couple of my White Sox fan friends, and by the eighth inning they were ready to go to the top of the John Hancock Center and jump. When the eight-spot appeared on the board, it took the air out of the building. It was like a funeral parlor all of a sudden.

People were gonna kill Bartman. They didn't do much till the Marlins got their rally going. When the Marlins got their rally going, people were going, "A—hole, a—hole." Security finally hustled him out of there for his own safety. That's the last time we know he was seen at Wrigley Field.

Most of the memorable games I've seen at Wrigley were losses, I'm afraid. The 1979 23–22 loss to the Phillies in ten innings comes to mind. The Phillies got seven in the top of the first, and the Cubs came back for about five in the bottom of the first. The balls were just flying out of there. Kingman hit three for the Cubs, and Mike Schmidt hit two for the Phillies, including the game winner in the bottom of the tenth inning. We were laughing our asses off. It was funny. 23–22! Nobody could stop anybody. Schmidt hit that homer in the top of the tenth and everyone thought, "No problem, they'll get it right back in the bottom of the tenth." Well, they didn't. The Phillies shut them down, and as the Cubs fans walked out, everyone was thinking, "Well, this figures." Whenever they got into a slugfest with the Phillies, they'd almost always lose. In 1976, Schmidt hit four home runs at Wrigley, and the Cubs lost to the Phillies again.

The first ever Cubs–White Sox game at Wrigley Field was in 1998. The game was tied, and Wil Cordero hit a ball with the go-ahead run at first base, and it would have scored, but the ball bounced into the vines. Cordero had to go back to third. Cubs win. The Sox fans went crazy, but those are the rules.

The atmosphere and intensity was unbelievable. The Cubs were having a great year in '98. One game went into extra innings, and finally the eleventh inning. Tony Castillo was pitching for the Sox, and Brant Brown was up for the Cubs, and Brown launched one toward right center. I still have a tape of Pat Hughes saying, "Back to the wall goes Ordóñez," and he's with Santo, they both say, "Gone!" You hear the place just explode. Pat Hughes says, "Brant Brown with a homer in the bottom of the eleventh has beaten the White Sox by a final score of 6 to 5." I played it on the Score several times over the next few days, and White Sox fans were calling my voice mail and *MF*ing me like you have no idea. The fans of the two teams don't dislike each other—they hate each other. Sox fans are on top of hating Wrigley and the Cubs.

It's like the Sox treat the Cubs like a little sister in Chicago. Supposedly, after they won the World Series in '05, they said they were going to back off, but it's only gotten worse. A lot of them have told me they don't want to back off. I respect that. It's part of the rivalry. I'm going to tell you something about the Cubs-Sox rivalry, and this is a fact: I covered the 2000 World Series between the Mets and Yankees in its entirety. All five games. It was a love-in: "Hey, this is cool, it's New York and New York." I saw Mets and Yankees fans high-fiving. It was a love-in compared to what happens between Cubs fans and Sox fans. If there was ever a World Series between the Cubs and Sox, no matter what park you're in, there would be Molotov cocktails. It would be ugly. Let's say the Cubs won the World Series on the South Side. You'd need the National Guard down there. In fact, you'd need the army, navy, air force, and marines.

And if the Cubs won the World Series at Wrigley, it would be Armageddon. But based on everything I've seen in my lifetime, I fully believe my grandson's great-great-great-great-great-grandchildren will come and go and the Cubs won't get to the World Series, much less win one. I've seen too much s—. That thing was over in '84. They pissed it away. It was over in '03. They pissed it away. And, by the way, I do not believe in the slightest in jinxes, hexes, or goats. I believe in incompetence. Look, I was twelve years old when they traded Lou Brock to the Cardinals for Ernie

Broglio. When a child knows this is going to be one of the worst trades in Cubs history—at age twelve!—that shows what a moron GM John Holland was. OK? I should not have known more at age twelve than the Cubs' general manager. They got suckered in and handed a bill of goods by Bing Devine, who knew Ernie Broglio was damaged goods. And Bing Devine would always get pissed off if anyone asked if he knew he was selling damaged goods.

I've seen two no-hitters at Wrigley: Hooton's and Holtzman's. I missed Pappas's because my girlfriend had me take her to the Museum of Science and Industry.

One of the biggest things for me was getting the Lee Elia rant on tape. Everyone has heard it by now. The Cubs were 5 and 13 going into that game. It was a Friday afternoon at Wrigley Field. I'm covering the game for WLS and the Associated Press, sitting in the press box there. They're winning. A kid from Buffalo Grove was making his Wrigley Field debut, a rookie named Mike Marshall. He hits a home run for LA. Back come the Dodgers, they tie the game, then Lee Smith throws a wild pitch in the top of the eighth inning, allowing the go-ahead run to score that held up. Dodgers win by a run.

That was the last year the clubhouse was in the left-field corner. Now that's the grounds crew's clubhouse. In '84 they built the clubhouse under the third-base dugout, where it still is today. Anyway, the game ends, there were maybe eight or nine thousand people there that day, and they're livid. Players are walking down the left-field line to the clubhouse, and a couple of drunks throw beer at Larry Bowa and Keith Moreland and connect. Lee Elia sees all this and starts having a fit. It looks like a couple of players are going into the stands, and some players pulling them back—no, don't do that. The players appreciated that Elia had their back. He goes into his office. He probably should have cooled off longer, but he was pissed. All the LA media and most of the Chicago media went to the LA side to talk to Mike Marshall, with the exception of myself and three Chicago beat writers—Don Friske from the *Daily Herald*, Robert Markus from the *Tribune*, and Joel Bierig from the *Sun-Times*. Us four were the only ones in there. There were no PR people around. If this happened today, there'd be a zillion PR people around, and they'd be on us like maggots, all right? We walk in, Elia sees us and says, "Hey, fellas, come on in." He seemed fine. He probably should have waited and chilled out. He didn't. He looks at us as if to say, "What do you got?" I said, "Another real tough one." He nods his head, and that's when he started with, "We're mired now in a little difficulty. We've got all these so-called f—ing fans that are supposed to be behind you. . . . " About the first three minutes goes through. He goes, "They talk about the great f—ing support the players get around here. I haven't seen it this f—ing year." We all liked the guy and I knew he was burying himself, so I try to get him to stop. I go, "See you tomorrow." He goes, "OK," and I take a step out. Then a few other radio guys come in. They all got the latter part of it but not the juicy stuff. I was the only one who got the whole thing.

At that point on the tape you hear the showers start to run and you hear the hair dryers, because a lot of the players had long hair back in those days. Elia started saying a few other things and I'm thinking, "I have to get the hell out of here." In the left-field corner, I run into Joe Mooshil, one of the guys I worked with at the AP, a legendary writer. I say, "Joe, I know you're in a hurry, but you got to hear this!" He says, "This f—n' better be good." I say, "Joe, just listen!" I played it for him, and he had a cigar the size of a tree trunk in his mouth and it's flippin' around, and he goes, "Holy s—, I got to get in there!" He runs in there, and I headed up to the old press box, which is now the suite mezzanine

level. I'm on the ramp walking down there and who is coming up? Harry Caray, Vince Lloyd, and Lou Boudreau. As they're coming up, I go, "Guys, it's a Friday and I know you're in a hurry to get out of here." Harry goes [in raspy Harry Caray imitation], "You're damn right we are, Les." I go, "I don't care. You guys have to hear this thing. I promise you'll be glad I play this for you." I play it from start to finish. Vince's eyes start rollin'. Harry turns white as a ghost. Boudreau couldn't believe what he was hearing. I hit the STOP button. Vince goes [in gruff imitation], "Jesus, Lou, he's gonna get his ass fired!" And Lou, in typical fashion, says [in strained, higher-pitched imitation], "This is true good, kid!" Harry says, "What's the son of a bitch doing?" They all took off white as a ghost, Harry especially.

I wasn't supposed to call in the tape because the station was too busy and because of union rules. There were fifty-four profanities in the tape, forty-five with the *f* word. I called the station. I said, "Roll tape," but they said they couldn't. I said, "Just do it, I'll take responsibility." I feed it. They played it that afternoon, bleeped out. We had it on the air before anybody.

Elia swears to this day that he didn't realize what he was saying. He was so worked up about the guys getting beer thrown on them. I believe him. I've gone into temper tantrums like that, and sometimes you don't know what you're saying.

Wrigley is a special place. The seats are good in there. They're close. Most ballparks, even the new ones, the seats are far back and higher. If you're in the last row of the upper deck at Wrigley, you're probably lower than in the first row of the upper deck at the newer places.

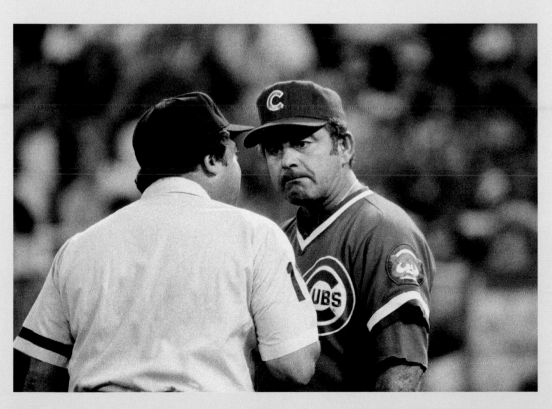

Cubs manager Lee Elia and plate umpire Terry Tatta "discuss" a call, 1982.

ROD BLAGOJEVICH, a Chicago native, was governor of Illinois from 2003 to 2009. In 2011 he was convicted of multiple corruption counts.

The first game I went to was the Cubs and the Houston Colt .45's—the old Houston Astros. Remember them? My dad took me and my older brother. We sat in the grandstand between third base and home plate. My dad was a hardworking immigrant from Yugoslavia and didn't know anything about baseball, so he put on his sunglasses and took a nap. But it was a big deal to me and my brother. It was '64 or '65. I was about eight. I still remember the excitement of being outside the ballpark and seeing the hawkers sell their merchandise.

All we had at home was a little black-and-white TV, and what I'll never forget is seeing the green grass of Wrigley Field for the first time. I'd only seen it in black-and-white. There was this symmetry of the diamond, this pastoral setting right in the city. I'll never forget how green it was—the vivid greenness of the field. There it was, literally in living color. It's an image I'll never forget. For an eight-year-old, it was breathtaking.

It was a Sunday game, a doubleheader. We went after church. It was planned for weeks. Even with tickets being as low as they were, it was a big deal. My dad dutifully took us even though he didn't understand any of it.

We stayed for both games. Billy Williams hit third, Ron Santo hit fourth, and Ernie Banks batted fifth. Billy Cowan played center field. I think Bob Buhl pitched, he wore number 31. Either Dick Ellsworth or Larry Jackson pitched the other game. They traded Larry Jackson for Fergie Jenkins. Did you know that? The Cubs obviously got the better of that trade. Andre Rodgers was the shortstop, Dick Bertell was the catcher. I still remember all this.

The next year I went to a game with my mother and brother and a childhood friend. It was the Cubs versus the Giants. Again we sat in the grandstand between third and home. My mom bought us Cubs caps from a vendor, and she must have spent twenty minutes having us try them on. The people behind us were yelling at her to sit down.

I grew up at Cicero and Armitage. We had to take two buses to get to the stadium. I went to Lane Tech for my first two years of high school and Foreman for the last two. I had the advantage of having an older brother, so I could do things without my mother,

and soon we started going to games by ourselves. We'd take the bus. In '68 and '69 we went to a lot of games.

In '69, when all of a sudden it looked like they could win, that ballpark would fill up. In '67 and '68 you could go anytime you wanted and get a seat; by the sixth inning you could sneak down to the box seats. You weren't supposed to, but they'd kind of let you because a lot of people weren't coming to the games. In '69 everything changed. That team captured the imagination of the city. Sharing them with new fans was an easy sacrifice to make if it meant the chance to see your beloved Cubs winning and maybe going to the World Series.

To me, whether Wrigley is filled up and the Cubs are winning or they're a bad team and no one's showing up, it's just a special place. It's one of the last places where you can step into another era. The attraction baseball has for many, and certainly for me, is its connection to the past. Wrigley Field, Fenway Park, the old Yankee Stadium—they gave people a chance not just to enjoy baseball in the twenty-first century, but these parks are where your father or grandfather went to the games. Whoever thought they'd get rid of the old Yankee Stadium? That's why Wrigley Field is so special.

One of the upside-down things I've had to deal with in this federal prosecution is having my good intentions put back on me. One of those things that I tried to do was good for the Cubs. I was concerned that Sam Zell, who was all about the bottom line, was willing to walk away from tradition. I was eager and determined to work with the Cubs so that when the Tribune Company sold the team, the Cubs would stay in the ballpark.

I had lunch with Zell. He had been helpful to me in a previous run for governor. As an aside as we were leaving, I asked if he had any plans for Wrigley Field. He said, "Oh, it's an old ballpark and we have to tear it down and build a Coors Field–type stadium." I called my chief of staff and said Zell was talking about tearing down Wrigley Field. I wanted to know what my options were. I felt privileged to be governor at the time, that I could do something to help this team I've had a lifelong love affair with. Wrigley Field is the number-three tourist attraction for our state. Did you know that?

It's one of the eight wonders of the world. Of all the places in the world I could spend time at, Wrigley Field would be in the top five. The other ones would be Yosemite, Jackson Hole, Westminster, St. Peter's Square, and maybe the Taj Mahal, though I've never been there.

Illinois governor Rod R. Blagojevich (right) speaks at Wrigley Field. Looking on is former Chicago Cubs player Ron Santo (left) and "Wild" Bill Holden, 2005.

The most memorable game I've ever been to at Wrigley Field was the 23–22 game against the Phillies in 1979. I got there late, which is something I tend to do, in the top of the first, and just as we walked into the park, the Phillies pitcher, Randy Lerch, had just hit a home run and it was 7–0. We were like, "Holy . . . !" It didn't take long to realize it would be a special game, because the Cubs came with six in the bottom of the first. I remember Bill Buckner hit one in the first and Dave Kingman hit three, including one of the longest I've ever seen. It must have landed four or five houses down on Kenmore. Remember Glenallen Hill's home run in 2000 that landed on the rooftop across the street? I think Kingman's was farther. I had no voice after that game from screaming and yelling so much. Bruce Sutter, our fucking—oh, I have to watch my mouth, my daughter's here—our closer, gave up a home run in the tenth inning.

I went to the Bartman game with my daughter Amy. She was seven and I bought my own ticket; I never put tickets on my campaign funds, unlike most politicians. It was 3–0, and I told her—I vividly remember saying this, and I remember thinking about not saying anything, and that maybe I should wait until the ninth inning, but I did it. I probably shouldn't have, but I said, "Amy, we're five outs away. You are five outs away from seeing something that only a handful of people in this park have ever seen." And then as sure as I said that, Castillo hit that foul ball.

We were in box seats a little to the left of home plate. I didn't see the play, but based on the fans' reaction, it was clear something had happened. And then the bottom fell out. We were all shell-shocked. I was a brand-new governor and my political stock was pretty good, but I forgot all about being governor. I was seven years old like Amy. Some guy unleashed these demons. As I walk out of the park, I have media all around me, and they say, "What about this guy?" I didn't know he was being threatened or he had to be escorted out. And I said, "He commits a crime, he won't be pardoned by this governor."

I don't regret saying that. I was a Cubs fan. I wasn't the governor. I wasn't advocating anyone kick his ass, but that's why you call it home-field advantage. The media, the hypocrites they are, they outed him the next day.

After Game 6, I said prayers for my children, my wife, my deceased parents, and that God deliver me from temptation and evil. I said an extra prayer for Kerry Wood because he was pitching the next night. I thought we'd rise to the occasion, but as with so many Cubs fans, there was that little voice. Even when Kerry Wood hit that home run, I still had a bad feeling.

One of the benefits of being governor is the Cubs took my phone calls. Hendry and I would have lunch, and I'd pepper him with questions and suggest off-season moves. I had a staff when I was governor, and I would have them look up the top prospects in the Red Sox or Marlins organizations and go to these lunches prepared, so I could make trade suggestions. It was a chance to be like a kid again. I don't think he did anything I said, but at least he listened. He was very polite about it.

Another advantage to being governor was that when I had a calf strain in '03 or '04, I had an assistant call the Cubs' trainer, Dr. Adams, who said to come on in. Man, when you're governor you can get into these places. Then I tore a hamstring muscle in the summer of 2007 in southern Illinois on this nine-mile route I liked to do, but I had to do it early in the morning or at night because it got so hot. I got hurt, but I ran through it. Dr. Adams had treated me before, so I called him and got treated on the same table where Soriano gets his hamstring treated. I loved it. It was thrilling to be in the locker room. I remember thinking that I'd take the injury just for the experience. I got an MRI by the Cubs' surgeon—my insurance covered it, I didn't get a freebie—and it showed a tear.

I'm a typical Cubs fan. I'm like you and you're like me. There are millions of us. Half the fun is planning ahead. I'm already thinking about what moves we can make.

I didn't go to a game during my trial in 2010. It was my first season without a game since 1976, when I spent the summer working on the oil pipelines in Alaska. I wanted to go. August 3 was my daughter's birthday, and I thought of it, but she went with a friend instead. The jury was deliberating. I didn't think it would be a good idea to be having fun at a game while the jury was working hard deliberating my fate. The Cubs were helpful during the bad times, because baseball gave me some diversion, but I always followed them when I was riding high too.

Most of the games I've been to have been with Amy. Since she was three years old she's been my companion at Cubs games. When I imagined being a dad, I imagined teaching my son to play ball and play catch. When we learned Amy was going to be Amy and not Andy, I didn't have any regrets, from the moment she was born. I'd read a Doris Kearns Goodwin book about how she grew up to be a great Dodgers fan, and I resolved to do that with Amy.

Amy was texting me Cubs scores during the trial. It's fun going to the game with someone who actually cares. I can ask Amy questions like, "What do you pitch to him now, at 3–1?" She once predicted a squeeze play, which I thought was a bad idea. But they did it! She was exactly right.

Wrigley Field is much prettier now. The ballpark only gets prettier. I don't know that I like the signs they're adding so much. But the ballpark looks great. It's just a beautiful place to be, and it has ambience. The atmosphere is magical, and you've got all these people around who are engaged in a very special sport. There's a great vibe.

When I was governor I'd go to the same seats—again, I paid for them—so if I wanted to go at the last minute, I could. It was by the scouts, down there by home plate. As governor you have to be somewhat flexible, so I wouldn't lock in games. Some of my finest memories as governor are going to those games with Amy. When I wasn't governor anymore, one of the unfortunate things was that I didn't get those tickets anymore. I didn't want to call the Cubs, so I went on StubHub and paid the premium price so that we could still get those same seats like it was old times.

I figured it out quick that I could get tickets as governor. It didn't take long. I would have my administrative assistant call Hendry and those guys. It was fantastic. It gave me the chance to be a boy again, to listen to these guys talking about the team. My standing with professional athletes meant more to me than my standing with other politicians.

We want them to win it, obviously, but when they don't, there's always something to look forward to. My fear is, once we win one, it won't be quite that magical to win a couple more.

I prefer day games. Wrigley Field on a bright, sunny day with all that's going on is one of the best places in the world to be. There are only a handful of places that equal it. There's something about the optimism of a bright sunny day. Hope springs eternal.

SHECKY GREENE was born on the North Side of Chicago, in the Rogers Park section, in 1926. He became one of the most popular Las Vegas nightclub comedians of his generation.

When I got out of the service in June of '46, I went to Wrigley Field first thing with an old friend I grew up with in Rogers Park. It wasn't that crowded; it was wartime baseball. I sat in the left-field bleachers and caught four home-run balls—two by Andy Seminick, who played for Philadelphia, and two by Dominic Dallessandro, who was a small center fielder for the Cubs. I'm the only one I've ever heard of who caught four home-run balls.

There's such excitement when you're young about these things. You catch that first ball and, when you've been going to the games all your life, all you can think is, "I got it! I got it!" The first one was hit by Seminick. The second was hit by Dallessandro. After that one, I went all up and down the bleachers yelling, "I got two! I got two!" Then the third one came. And then the fourth one! I almost took off the arm of the guy in front of me to get it, so I said, "Here, I'm sorry, take the ball." He said, "I don't want the ball. Keep the ball." He was mad because I almost killed him. After the game I waited outside the stadium saying, "I got four balls!" No one cared. A week later I gave them away, one to my cousin, one to the kids in the neighborhood, and I don't remember about the other two. It's a nice memory.

Even with everything I've done in show business, catching four balls was one of the great thrills of my life. I've told it onstage, but people always thought I was making it up. It really happened!

As a kid, I didn't go to that many games, because we couldn't afford it. But it was an important part of my life. My dad had a good job until the Depression, but then he became a shoe salesman on the road. He never had interest in anything but the horses. My mother took a job in a women's shoe store, selling handbags and hosiery. It was tough in those years. In the thirties we kept moving to different apartments. We started on the West Side. Then we lived across the street from the beach. But with friends of my brothers, we took the bus from Sheridan Road to Clark and Addison. If there was nothing to do in the afternoon, we'd just say, "Let's go to the ball game." And we would.

I was in awe of the ballpark. I always wanted to know about the guy in the scoreboard who changed the numbers. I wondered what kind of life that was. Did he ever go home? Everything about the ballpark thrilled me. Going to get a hot dog, the guys throwing the peanuts—that's another thing that thrilled me. Guys would throw the peanuts four aisles. I used to say to them, "Why don't you pitch for the Cubs?" It was just thrilling to go to the ballpark. I still remember the food stands on the corner outside the park and all the smells.

I remember watching Charlie Grimm and Gabby Hartnett. Jewish fans always said they were anti-Semitic. We thought everyone was an anti-Semite. Look how they treated Greenberg when he got in. He was such a hero to us. We wanted him to come play for the Cubs. I saw him play at Comiskey Park. We went down just to see him. We had such pride in Jewish sports players. Later I met Charlie Grimm and became very close to him. Charlie came in to see me work a few times, and I'd sit with him and his wife. He was a nice guy. He was wonderful. Not an anti-Semite, as it turned out.

I left Chicago at about twenty-five, and until then I went to Wrigley Field every year. When I came out to Los Angeles, I started to go to the Dodgers games. I got friendly with those guys. I used to go to Eli's, a delicatessen, and I'd bring sandwiches to the ballpark and sit in the box seats, and they'd say, "Put the goddamn corned beef away! It's killing the batters!"

But I always liked Wrigley best. I like the vines on the outfield wall, the scoreboard, the whole thing. I loved Andy Pafko and these guys running into the vines to catch the ball. It's my concept of what a baseball field should be. Dodger Stadium is nice and everything, but in my mind, Wrigley Field is a true baseball field and always will be. I went to the old Yankee Stadium and it did nothing for me. It was just another baseball stadium.

My other big memory at Wrigley happened after I was in show business. I went with my father, and we sat in the right-field bleachers. The guys around us were gambling, saying, "You bet he goes? I got ten to one on a home run!" They would bet on everything. My dad didn't get into it, but he started to raise his hand like he was going to take the bet, and some plainclothes cops grabbed him. They were going to arrest him! I talked the guys out of it. I was in show business and told 'em who I was. They just said, "Get 'em out of the park." That was in the fifties. Those same guys, they're still in the right-field bleachers betting.

I flew into Chicago to be at the first night game. I thought they should've had lights before that point. I thought it was wonderful. That was the last time I was there. I see it on television these days, and it looks the same. They still don't trim the vines in the outfield! I'm glad it has stayed the way I remember it. Certain things in your life you don't forget from when you're a kid. You're so impressed with those things initially, and I'm sure it's the same with New York kids with the Brooklyn Bridge and all that shit, but for me it was Chicago: Lincoln Park, the zoo, and Wrigley Field. Now when I think of Wrigley Field, I think of my youth and remember the kids on the street behind left field waiting to catch the ball and the smell of that goddamn food and the crowds running to get into the ball game. I see me at that age and I see me with those four balls. I see Billy Jurges, Phil Cavarretta, Stan Hack, Augie Galan, and what's his name in right field? The Swede. Ah shit, I can't remember.

OZZIE GUILLÉN played shortstop in the major leagues from 1985 to 2000, including eighteen years with the Chicago White Sox. He was hired as manager of the White Sox in 2004, and managed them for eight seasons, before asking for his release at the end of 2011. He was hired as the manager of the Miami Marlins in 2012.

Wrigley Field is awesome, but to work in the stadium is a pain in the ass. When the game starts, it's a unique way to play baseball.

The fans are really into it, and there isn't stuff and advertisements all over the place. But inside, it's a very uncomfortable place to work. Maybe in the 1870s it was OK, but now it's uncomfortable. And not just for me, but for the media, the fans, and the people working there every day. The people who work there don't say it because they might get fired. And the media, the fucking media, they never say anything, but they don't like it.

The clubhouse is small, and to get to the batting cage you have to walk all the way to where the rats are—and there are rats. I'm not making this up. I've seen them. When you talk to the media, the room is very small; sometimes I have to do my interviews twice. From the clubhouse to the field it's like an hour, and you have to take a cab. I had a guy take a s— in his pants going from the field to the clubhouse during a game in 2008. I'm not going to say the name.

It smells too, believe me. I played in old Comiskey Park and it's the same smell. It's like people drank all night and left their cups there. It's the biggest bar in Chicago. But that's a good thing. And it's in the middle of a neighborhood. I was in Cubby Bear two days ago. It's like the people walking around Wrigley Field at twelve o'clock at night taking pictures of the Harry Caray statue. What the f— did Harry do? If he worked in Kansas City, he wouldn't be shit. Some people go there just to see who is going to sing the seventh-inning stretch and they leave. I celebrated two play-offs

Cubs manager Lou Piniella (left) jokes with Chicago White Sox manager Ozzie Guillen before their interleague game at Wrigley Field, June, 17, 2009.

there—Atlanta and the Marlins. It's the worst clubhouse to celebrate at. It's too small.

One day in 2004 I had to park at McDonald's across the street because Wrigley ran out of parking spaces. I had to walk through the Cubs fans, and believe me, there weren't too many friendly fans out there. I was there with my wife and my family and I had to tell this one guy, "You can call me whatever you want and curse me out, but not when my wife and my family are here." Good thing he understood my point.

If you go to New York and you don't go to the Statue of Liberty or Fifth Avenue, you haven't been to New York. If you go to Chicago and you don't go to Wrigley Field, you are missing a lot. When I say I hate Wrigley Field the stadium, I hate Wrigley Field for the accommodations. But it's fun to go there and be a part of the game—the fans, the seventh-inning stretch; I love the scoreboard, the fact that the walls have no advertising on them. It's just baseball. As soon as the game starts, it's a unique place to be.

The most memorable game I ever had there was Game 6 in 2003. I was the third-base coach for the Marlins. It went from so much noise to very quiet in a second. One pitch, there was so much noise, and the next pitch was silent. Then the next pitch everyone was screaming and yelling again. I had never seen anything like that. That was such a memorable day, because we went in there having to win two games against Prior and Kerry. But we had a better team than they did at every position but maybe right field, where they had Sammy. They were overconfident after beating us in Miami.

A lot of people talk about that kid Bartman. It was right behind me. I never thought Alou really had a chance to catch it. This kid did what everyone in the stands would have. He didn't even reach out for the ball; the ball was right there in his hand. If Alou didn't make that reaction, I don't think any of this would have happened. When Alou threw his glove and pointed at the kid, it became this thing. If Moisés had let it go, people wouldn't have even realized what happened.

When Kerry Wood hit a home run in Game 7, that ballpark went crazy. When I left the dugout to go back to coach third base, the people were yelling and making fun of me like we were going to lose. To me it was fun.

I don't know how long Wrigley Field will last, but it's a marvel of Chicago. I have people from Venezuela who don't even care about baseball, they're just my friends, and they want to go to Wrigley Field.

The people who work there are great. Everyone who works there treats me very, very well. I have friends there. I've got season tickets for a hundred years at Wrigley Field, and every time I go there they hug me, they talk to me, we have fun, we appreciate each other, we make fun of each other.

They're unique fans. The fans are very patient and passionate. And they make a lot of excuses. They say, "We lose because of a fucking goat, we lose because of fucking Bartman." No, you lose because you've had a lot of horses—t teams in your past. That's why you lose. The fans at Wrigley Field are f—d up, but they have fun. They go out there, they boo you, they're fun.

I get booed there more than anywhere except maybe Cleveland. But I look at it like, they boo because they think you're special and they wish you worked for them. They don't boo Brent Lillibridge, but they boo f—ing Manny Ramírez. I've never seen Pablo Ozuna get booed. They don't boo horses—t players.

Wrigley hurts the Cubs because of the hours they play. They play one day at one, the next day at three, the next day at two. For a day game, you've got to be there at eight o'clock and you don't leave till five. Then you have to be in bed at eight.

RICHARD DURBIN, a U.S. senator from Illinois who was first elected in 1996, became the Senate Democratic whip in 2005.

I grew up downstate as a Cardinals fan, but over the years my passion for the Cardinals has waned. A lot of that has to do with Wrigley Field. I started following the Cubs when I became a congressman. When I was elected to the Senate, my campaign manager said, "I have one piece of advice: An Illinois senator should root for an Illinois team." I decided then that I would take on this burden like everyone else. I've been an NL guy my whole life, so the White Sox weren't an option.

When I die, my obituary, if it's complete, will probably include my most famous speech, which lasted sixty seconds on the floor of the House, about saving the wooden baseball bat:

Mr. Speaker, I rise to condemn the desecration of a great American symbol. No, I am not referring to flag burning; I am referring to the baseball bat. Several experts tell us that the wooden baseball bat is doomed to extinction, that major-league baseball players will soon be standing at home plate with aluminum bats in their hands. Baseball fans have been forced to endure countless indignities by those who just cannot leave well enough alone. Designated hitters, plastic grass, uniforms that look like pajamas, chicken clowns dancing on the baselines, and of course the most heinous sacrilege, lights in Wrigley Field. Are we willing to hear the crack of a bat replaced by the dinky ping? Are we ready to see the Louisville Slugger replaced by the aluminum ping dinger? Is nothing sacred?

Please do not tell me that wooden bats are too expensive, when players who cannot hit their weight are being paid more money than the president of the United States. Please do not try to sell me on the notion that these metal clubs will make better hitters. What is next? Teflon baseballs? Radar-enhanced gloves? I ask you. I do not want to hear about saving trees. Any tree in America would gladly give its life for the glory of a day at home plate. I do not know if it will take a constitutional amendment to keep the baseball traditions alive, but if we forsake the great Americana of broken-bat singles and pine tar, we will have certainly lost our way as a nation.

When it comes to baseball, I'm a complete traditionalist. The designated hitter and some of these things don't seem right. Even the lights at Wrigley Field are troubling to me.

To me it's the essential American ballpark. I'm sure every ballpark has its stories, but it seems Wrigley Field has the most. I went to Fenway thinking it could compete. Wrigley Field wins hands down. I felt much closer to the game. In Wrigley you're smack-dab in the neighborhood, and there's something so cool about that. All these other parks are loaded with so much other stuff. Wrigley Field isn't.

ROGER MCDOWELL pitched for five teams during a twelve-season major-league career. He is now the Atlanta Braves' pitching coach.

Wrigley Field was my favorite ballpark to visit when I played. It's where a lot of the history of the game is and was. I still love to go there. I love going out early into the stands, when the smell of the beer and hot dogs from the day before is still in the air. It's a special place. I'll take my digital camera and go around the ballpark and take pictures from different angles and different areas, get some photos I can put up at the house. I like the angles, the seats, especially the seats that don't have views, where you have to look around the poles. That's part of the charm of the old ballparks. I'll go out and sit in the center-field bleachers—that's a great shot to have, facing home plate. I started out going to the farthest seat in the right-field upper deck and left-field upper deck too, taking some pictures.

The newer ballparks, like ours, for example, in Atlanta, it's not where Dale Murphy played or Phil Neikro or Eddie Mathews. At Wrigley Field every great player to put on that uniform played on that surface. I guess I'm a sucker for the history of the game. I like the way the game was played even before I played.

In 1989, I was at Wrigely, pitching for the Mets. It was hot. Really hot. I knew the grounds crew had a hose under the bleachers, and I just took a shot that it was hooked up and that it could reach out to the field so that I could hose off the Bleacher Bums. They loved it. I don't think they minded much, because they had enough beer in their systems even though it was pregame.

Pretty much every game, regardless of how many people were in the stands, the Bums always filled up the bleachers. Whether it was the students or the unemployed or the businessmen, they were all out there. I had about a two-year initiation to get accepted. There was back-and-forth banter with the people in the stands. You had to know that what was said wasn't always meant to be harmful. They were all out there to have fun. If you had a bad night the day before, they let you know it. They're very knowledgeable, and they let you know what they know.

After a couple of years, I started throwing them baseballs and playing catch with them. The best games we played, they would hold their beer out in front of them and I would try to throw the ball in the cup. They always had to move the cup to get the ball. And it was such close quarters up there that my object was always

to get as many people wet as I could. They loved it. Absolutely loved it. To this day there is still a fella there who was the best catcher of them all. He'd take the ball out of the cup and lick the beer off it. There were many times I might throw the ball high and over someone's head and the person behind them might get a cold beer on their lap. Which was my goal.

When I was with the Dodgers in about '92 or '93, I got a big garbage can from underneath the stands and put a hundred dollars in there, a Tim Wallach bat, and a Tommy Lasorda signed ball, and the object was to throw the ball into the can from the bleachers—you got what was in the pot. No one was getting it in, and all of a sudden Orel Hershiser comes running out, and he's got his jersey, and he throws his jersey into the garbage can. Now we've got a Lasorda ball, a hundred-dollar bill, a Tim Wallach bat, and Orel's signed jersey. No one could get it, and it was getting close to game time. There was a little boy, and I threw him the ball and moved the can right below him, and he got it all. Those guys are special out there in the bleachers. That's why people write books about them and sing songs about them.

I don't know the kid's name, but when I was with the Mets I went to dinner at a Bleacher Bum's house once. His mom made dinner. I don't remember what she made or where he lived. It was a day game and he just yelled, "What are you doing for dinner tonight?" I didn't have any plans, so I said OK. I think he was an usher there and it was his day off. To get an invitation like that from someone at Wrigley is a very genuine thing. It doesn't happen anywhere else.

That kind of interaction is totally unique to Wrigley, just because of the proximity of the people in the bleachers to the outfield, where you're shagging during batting practice. There's no other ballpark like that, where you have the closeness to the fans. In the bull pen, which is down the right-field line, they're right over your shoulder, but that's a little more of a sophisticated crowd, a little more upscale. The Bleacher Bums, they're game for anything.

It's hard to say why Wrigley is so unique like that. It might be a midwestern thing. A lot of it I think has to do with Harry Caray. He was a genuine, honest guy who loved the team and typified the disappointment and the hopes. But he was always supportive and a true Cub.

JIM RIGGLEMAN managed four teams in a twelve-year career, including the Cubs from 1995 to 1999.

Wrigley plays different from other fields. It's shorter in left center than some other places, but the wind blows in early in the year, then blows out toward the middle of the season. It plays as a tough place to score runs in the first six weeks of the season. The grass is high, and the wind is blowing in, and it's cold and not comfortable for hitters. It's a great place to pitch. I like that kind of baseball. I think that's good baseball. As the year goes on, the wind starts blowing out and hitters get more comfortable.

It's definitely different: The energy at the ballpark, it's packed every day, it's exciting every day, the loyalty of the fans. It's a special place. It's hard to put into words, but it's unique. Boston has that. Not many other places do. The architecture of the park is not modernized the way the new ones are. It's got that older field. There's just a lot of charm there. It has the nooks and crannies. There are some angles you don't have at other places. There's a closeness behind home plate to the batter's box and the dugouts. It's just a different feel from other parks.

In 1997 we started 0–14. People forget that. It was horrible. Teams will lose a lot of games in the middle of the year, and if you're in last place, that will get brushed aside. It was a challenge to stay upbeat and positive and keep the players motivated and let them know, "Hey guys, today is the day."

The first ten games, we had given up one hundred hits and we had fifty hits. It was as simple as they could hit ours and we couldn't hit theirs. We were playing relatively close games, but the opposition we opened with was the eventual champion Marlins, and we had back-to-back series with the Braves. It was Maddux, Smoltz, Glavine, Kevin Brown, Fernandez, and Leiter—every day we were facing a classic number one–type pitcher.

Fans got on us a little bit, and what's different about Wrigley is when they get on you, there's always a lot of them. They have such a passion, and if they feel like you're part of the problem, you hear about it. They just want it so bad. It's been a long time. They get a little taste of success, and they want you to finish it off.

The thing that came out of '97 is we acquired Kevin Tapani in the winter, but he hurt his hand, and that didn't allow him to pitch until August. At the trading deadline, we acquired Lance Johnson and Mark Clark from the Mets. With Tapani and Clark pitching in August, we saw some light at the end of the tunnel. Tapani won nine games in August and September, and we played better, and we carried that into 1998. We took a pretty good pitching rotation out there in '98.

Kerry Wood's twenty-strikeout game was easily one of the most memorable things that happened when I was with the team. He had shown electric stuff already, but that day everything was in sync and he was just unhittable. It was the greatest pitching performance I've ever seen. People like Ron Santo and Billy Williams were there when Sandy Koufax threw a perfect game against them, and they felt Kerry Wood's game was even more dominant. His fastball was ninety-eight, and his breaking ball was absolutely unhittable.

Through the first three or four innings, you could tell he was overmatching them. It was a good lineup, but he was just over-matching them. It was a good day to pitch. It was a little cold and overcast. Our middle infielders and center fielder could see the pitches, and they said, "This is unbelievable. Guys are missing balls by this much [holds hands two feet apart], and he's buckling knees, and it's classic stuff."

We didn't start looking at strikeouts until the seventh inning. The score was 1–0, and our focus was to win the game. He was a young guy, and we were counting pitches. Under the circumstances, if he had gone 135, we probably would have reluctantly let it happen. But there wasn't a move you could make that wouldn't be encouraging to the other team. To see him leave would have been very uplifting to the other team. He finished with 122, which was more than we wanted, but it was a reasonable number.

You never want your guy to throw 120, but you do it because of the matchup and if it will allow you to win the game. It's not like he got to 118 and we said, "Oh no, he can't go 122 because he'll hurt his arm." It was about the game and trying to win the game. He was dominating the game. Nobody was getting on base since the third inning.

Nobody talked to him in the dugout. Tom Gamboa was the bench coach. At some point Gamboa was commenting to him about how many strikeouts he had. I was just concerned about keeping him at a reasonable number of pitches and winning the game.

Then there was Sammy's home runs. We were just trying to get in the play-offs, and Sammy's home runs were helping us do that. But the other thing he did was take a lot of attention away from other people, which was a good thing. Sammy handled all that attention very well. Everyone else could go about their business and get asked a few questions about a pennant race and move on. What Sammy was doing was answering questions about a pennant race and all his home runs. And he did a great job. He always had a smile on his face. He gave the press what they needed, and that made it a lot better for the rest of the players. People remember his twenty home runs in June, but they don't remember that it was the only month in which we had a losing record. You need contributions from everyone to win.

We were really naive to the whole steroid thing. There was talk around baseball that guys were doing things, but it wasn't looked at that closely. It was almost an attitude of boys will be boys. I think we all were naive to it and closed our eyes to some things and weren't as curious about it as we should have been. Players weren't saying anything; the media wasn't saying anything. We were marveling at the whole thing, but there were no accusations. My only regret would be that what's taken place now should have taken place much earlier, because this stuff started before 1998.

The 163rd game that season, which allowed us to get into the play-offs, was a tremendous night at Wrigley Field. Steve Trachsel pitched great. He walked a few guys, but had a no-hitter going into the seventh. We really played a great game. When the Giants scored three in the ninth, you couldn't help but let that creep in a little bit.

I don't believe the Cubs' history factors into the struggles there have been. Every team is unique unto itself; every team is its own group of twenty-five guys. It's not like they're thinking, "Oh no, the 1963 team will be upset with us." Ballplayers are somewhat self-absorbed. They're concerned with their team, not the team of fifty years ago.

Cubs manager Jim Riggleman, 1998.

BILLY CORGAN is the lead singer and songwriter for the Smashing Pumpkins, a rock band that has won multiple Grammy Awards and sold nearly twenty million albums in the United States.

My grandmother was an every-game Cubs fan. She worked in an envelope factory, and when she wasn't home, she would listen on the radio. Before I was even conscious of what was going on around me, I was watching baseball games with her and picked up on her enthusiasm. I don't remember becoming a Cubs fan. I just was one.

I started going to games with her in the seventies. We'd go on what they called Ladies' Day, which they don't do anymore. I think it was three dollars, and you could bring a kid for free. In the seventies, you could go and you would be looking at two or three thousand people in the stands. If you had even an OK seat, you could sneak down. She was so passionate about baseball, we would be there from the moment they opened the gates. We'd be inside and hanging on the wall and talking to the players to get some autographs, and after the game, we'd stay until they kicked us out of the park. Then we'd stand outside and wait for players on their way to their cars so we could talk to them more. Going to Wrigley Field as a kid was an eight-hour experience.

She was the classic homer. The team could do no wrong. The players were always doing their best, and when they lost, she always thought things were going to get better. She had a rosy view of the team long before that vision became codified with the yuppies in the eighties.

I remember back when I was nine or ten being there really early one day with my grandmother—they were playing the Phillies, I think—and we had one of those moments you always remember. The backup catcher for the Phillies talked to us for twenty minutes by the visitors' dugout. He was surprised how knowledgeable we were about baseball. He told us even though he was a backup what a great experience it was to play major-league baseball. There were probably only fifty people in the ballpark. It was so great. It's hard to imagine that now with how things have changed and all the media attention. To be able to talk to a professional baseball player for twenty minutes who could explain how hard it was to hit a major-league curveball or to be a kid asking, "What's this guy or that guy like?" was amazing.

I've never lost the feeling I first got from walking into the stadium. When you walk up those stairs from the concourse and see the field for the first time, there's something about that place that evokes everything that's pure about the game. With everything that's happened in the last twenty years, it's hard to think of baseball as a pure sport anymore, but Wrigley Field, in symbolic terms, seems to reflect that *Field of Dreams*–type purity.

The pure part of the ballpark is between the bricks. It's the ivy and the grass and obviously the scoreboard. I honestly think they should tear down the stands to turn it into a modern facility around the old ballpark. Then they'd never have to leave the area. There's something about the stadium being in the neighborhood that's so important and so intrinsic to Wrigley Field that you can never kill it with commercialism. It evokes something you can't manufacture. Babe Ruth stood on that field with the same dimensions. There's something about that that speaks to the purity of the game.

You can still get a sense of the simplest part of the game at Wrigley Field. Even the idea of building a wall with bricks—just think about that. That's from a different time. I saw Joe Wallis dead run straight into the wall and concuss himself. He was our center fielder in the late seventies: superfast, not a good hitter at all. Point is, you'd never build a ballpark like that these days.

Wrigley Field has those perfect dimensions. The wall is close enough that it makes a guy want to change his swing just enough on a windy day. There's so much about it that evokes a time when baseball was a simpler sport. It's a pastoral sport, and Wrigley Field is the perfect environment to see a pastoral game in.

I would skip school with friends back when if you got in line for bleachers that day, you could get a ticket. If you were there at nine, you were getting into the game. We'd ditch school and sit in the sun all day. When I got out of school and got weird and gothic and dyed my hair black and gave up on everything that wasn't cool, that was the end of baseball for me for a while. But I remember being in a car with my friends and fishing around on the radio in '84. The Cubs were in the play-offs, and I couldn't resist checking the score. I still couldn't put it down, even though I'd tried. My friends were shocked. They were like, "You like baseball?" It was so uncool.

I met my future ex-wife around 1987. She was a total baseball fan; it was a miracle to find a woman who was as much of a fan as I had been. One day she said, "Let's go to a game," and that reopened the door. We lived right near Wrigley Field, and we'd

Smashing Pumpkins lead singer Billy Corgan singing "Take Me Out to the Ball Game" at Wrigley Field, 2003.

go every time and buy standing-room-only tickets, especially in 1998 when they made a play-off run. That was an exciting time. I was at a game versus the Cardinals when it was clear they were going to clinch. It was an amazing atmosphere. I remember feeling kind of silly: "Why did I have to put something down that I enjoy?" It's hard to explain the mind-set. But I started following the team again.

Wrigley Field and the Cubs will survive, but it's too bad what's going on now. I grew up in a time where it was families going to games and dads talking to kids about baseball. Now it's repressed adolescents, and Wrigley is their place to show off their knowledge. I sound like an old man, but I just don't enjoy going to games in that atmosphere. When the team started winning in the eighties, the yuppies came in and claimed the team as their own. The Cubs became a social qualifier. It was, "Hey, let's go to the game and have a beer." It's not enough for them just to go to the game, the two stockbrokers; they have to show their knowledge that's been ripped off from some ESPN commentator.

I sang the seventh-inning stretch "Take Me Out to the Ball Game" for Game 7 against the Marlins in 2003. I went to two games against Atlanta, the three games in Florida, and the two back at Wrigley Field. I'd never felt the place more electric. It was unbelievable. In Florida I watched the Cubs wipe them up, and as I was walking up the stairs after Game 4, I turned to my friend and said, "We're going to the World Series."

For the Bartman game, I was sitting on the right-field line next to the Marlins' bull pen. The moment that happened, this indescribable sound took over the ballpark. I've played two thousand concerts, and I know the sound of a crowd. That night you're listening to this joyous celebration, and then this hush went over the park, like, "What just happened?" Then ten seconds later there was this devilish murmur, like, "Holy f—, it's the curse." I turned to my friend and said, "The ballpark is going to lose us the game." There were forty thousand people in the park, and they all got negative. The ballplayers pick up on that. The sound in that ballpark went from joyous celebration to instant "Oh my God, we're going to lose," and people became invested in losing, not overcoming. It would have been a great time to overcome the curse.

Right before the seventh inning, someone grabbed me and took me in the booth. I sat behind Thom Brennaman and watched the Cubs disintegrate for twenty minutes, and then I had to sing the seventh-inning stretch. When it came time to sing, it was like singing at a funeral. It was absolutely depressing, but I eked out some message that said, "Real fans believe, win or lose," or something like that. Forty thousand people were there. Thirty-seven thousand were not real Cubs fans.

The Cubs not winning the World Series has gone on for so long that the shadow of it is almost unshakable. I'm annoyed by how the media plays into it, and the fans now are almost too into the negative aspect of it. I've become frustrated with the archetype of the modern Cubs fan—that person is kind of boorish. The last few times I've been to the ballpark, people were swearing so badly, I was cringing for the families around me. And I was sitting in good seats. Baseball is a pastoral game and a family game and a generational game. These days, I'm just as happy to watch it on TV as be in the stands, though I do look forward to someday taking my kids there.

DENNIS FRANZ was born in the Chicago suburb of Maywood in 1944. He has appeared in nearly fifty movies and television series, most notably in his starring role on *NYPD Blue* and in *Die Hard 2*. He was also an original cast member of *Bleacher Bums*.

My father was a German immigrant who came over as a teenager. He wasn't very interested in baseball. But my mother's brothers were very much baseball fans. I fell in love with baseball by playing Little League, where I was coached by my uncle.

I went to games with my dad sometimes, and going to a Cubs game became a big deal for us. We would drive downtown and find a parking space and spend a day at Wrigley. It was something my father and I shared. He turned out to be a real, avid Cubs fan. For us there was nothing better than going to a doubleheader. It was a mutual thing. He was not a baseball follower. He was a soccer fan. He was from a hardworking family and didn't have a lot of time, but going to a doubleheader was the best. It was a real nice bonding for my father and me. I had to be ten or eleven.

One of my mother's two brothers was a Sox fan. The other one was more vocal about the Cubs. There was just something we liked about the Cubs, and when we went to the city, we went to the North Side. We didn't go to the South Side except to go to Maxwell Street.

When you become a fan at a very early age, you find your heroes and you try to be like them. You're hooked. Tops for me was Ernie. I tried to bat like Ernie. I wiggled my finger like him and tried to get that hitch and the giddyup right before he swung. He always had such an upbeat spirit about the Cubs. It was infectious.

The first time I came to Wrigley I was ten or eleven. I still remember the impact it had on me—stepping through the aisles and seeing this field. There was nothing prettier than that field of green in front of me. That baseball diamond and that grass—it was everything memories were made of. It was so beautiful, and all those fans were all around. There was this great greenness of the grass, and it immediately had such a strong impact on me. I got overwhelmed by being in this wonderful stadium with this wonderful baseball field. I've never experienced another baseball venue that I have appreciated on that level. It's a whole different world, a world unto itself. It's like being in the audience when the Rolling Stones come onstage or something. It's so powerful.

When I was older I would go by myself or with buddies during the week. It was a different feeling versus going on a weekend. At day games during the week there was a sense of doing something that you know not everyone can do. It's like getting out of school when everyone else has to go. The people that were there, they were a different kind of fan. I mean, they were there during the week! It wasn't quite as much of a party as during the weekend. They were more serious baseball guys. The weekend was more about entertainment. The weekday games were the guys who lived it.

When I was in *Bleacher Bums* with Joe Mantegna, we spent hours in the bleachers doing research for characters. It was a very interesting time in our lives, to consider that our homework. It gave me a different appreciation for Cubs fans and how devoted they are to the team. We would look for interesting groups and people, then get closer to observe them. We'd listen to them talk and make mental notes of their dialogue and speech patterns, maybe take a few pictures. Then we'd imagine who they were and what they were about, and we'd put fictitious lives together. We invited a lot of them to the show when it debuted. The only guy who hated it was my guy, who was the king or president of the bleachers. He felt we were invading their privacy.

I love the location right in the center of the city. That's old baseball. There aren't many like that anymore. So many stadiums now, you have to go out of the city and to a giant parking lot where there are a bunch of vendors waving you around. At Wrigley, it's right in the neighborhood.

I never wanted to see lights at Wrigley. I'm not a guy who likes change. I like tradition to be tradition. To me it smacked of moneymaking. The sun in that stadium was so beautiful to me. It was just such a visual thing. I didn't want to see that image I had of early baseball in sunshine being played under lights instead, just as I don't want to see roofs over stadiums. If I had my way, we wouldn't change those things.

Do you ever tire of looking at the Chrysler Building in New York? I don't. And I never tire of looking at Wrigley Field. The ivy-covered walls, the dugouts, the scoreboard, it all smacks of old times. It just reminds you that it's always been there. It feels like history. It's a beautiful piece of art that should always remain. It's completely visceral to me and hard to put into words. All of the elements work together. All the other stadiums, there's too much advertising and newness.

SARA PARETSKY was born in Ames, Iowa, in 1947 and raised in Kansas. With the introduction of detective V.I. Warshawski in her 1982 novel, *Indemnity Only*, she became one of the writers who transformed the role of women in the crime novel. Warshawski has appeared in fifteen Paretsky mysteries that have been published in at least thirty countries. She has also written two non-Warshawski novels and several short-story collections. Paretsky, who lives in Chicago's Hyde Park neighborhood, still "lives and dies with the Cubs," according to her official biography.

My love of baseball is rooted in my childhood in Kansas. My dad grew up a huge Dodgers fan in Brooklyn, within walking distance of Ebbets Field. I therefore grew up hating the Yankees, and when the Dodgers moved to Los Angeles, we weren't allowed to mention their name in the house anymore. My dad was one of the first Jews hired at the University of Kansas, so we adored Sandy Koufax because he didn't pitch on Yom Kippur. He was my earliest baseball hero. Even after they moved to LA, I would secretly follow the Dodgers' stats just because I was such a Dodgers fan.

I came to Chicago in 1966, when I was nineteen. I was volunteering for a program where the goal was to help make the summer, and ultimately the civil rights experience of the city, different than the direction it was going. We were working with kids—some in black neighborhoods, some in white neighborhoods—and we were trying to heighten their consciousness, trying to convey the message that even if you don't want to have a conversation with someone different from you, we all need to live together peacefully. It was the summer Martin Luther King moved his family into a tenement here. I was in a program at 70th Street and Damen Avenue, and King wasn't far from that.

The White Sox were the logical team for me to root for, but the Sox didn't return our phone calls when we were looking for tickets for our kids, and the Cubs gave us free bleacher seats every Thursday. We would take forty kids between six and eleven years old on two L trains every Thursday afternoon. Even with the hatred between Sox and Cubs fans—and it was certainly much more volatile in those days—the families never protested us taking their kids to the Cubs games. Most of the parents of these kids worked in the stockyards. These were hard-core Sox fans, but the Sox didn't respect their fans enough to call us back.

I always liked the fact that the park was so accessible. You just hopped on the L and hopped off and there you were. It seemed amazing to me. If we wanted to see the A's play in Kansas City, it was a huge undertaking. You had to always plan ahead because it was a long drive. And just being able to get on and off the train for the Cubs was wonderful. I loved the fact that it felt so urban. I was in a real city. It felt so great. We always sat in the bleachers, though in those days, sitting in the bleachers wasn't the cool place to be. It was the cheap place to be. I have to say, I always felt uncomfortable sitting in the bleachers. I don't like the sun baking me.

What really made me a Cubs fan—I think this would have been sometime in the 70s—happened when I was running, and damaged my ankle so that I couldn't put weight on it for a few days. The only thing on TV during the day, other than the soap operas, was the Cubs.

I became a serious fan from about the late 70s until 1984. I was hooked: Memorizing lineups, watching the games, going to Wrigley whenever I could. I was the marketing manager for a downtown insurance company at the time, and there were 13 of us women who would go to games together. Those were some lean years. I remember Mike Royko always doing his column about the Cubs. And Jose Cardenal and his eyelid problem. Jay Johnstone stands out from those years because he was such a clown. But Bill Buckner was my favorite. He will always be my all-time favorite. He was so dogged, fighting through pain to do whatever it took to play. To this day I grieve over the way he was treated by fans for his flub with the Red Sox.

I really went into mourning when the Cubs lost that series to San Diego in 1984. It devastated me. I had to dial it back. I still followed them, but I couldn't bear to invest so much emotion. They had gotten Rick Sutcliffe at the All-Star break, and he had made such a difference. When I was writing my first book, V.I. Warshawski has a friend named Murray Ryerson, and I described him as looking like Rick Sutcliffe. That's because I was a Sutcliffe fan. It looked like they were going to the World Series. The whole history was about to be put behind us. There was a sense of, "It's gonna happen now." Losing that series was very visceral. I was in love, and my lover died. That's what it felt like. I was in love with the Cubs and the team and players.

I was on the field at Wrigley once. When Disney made this terrible film, allegedly about my character V.I. Warshawski,

Sara Paretsky

OPPOSITE: Wrigley Field, 1963.

FOLLOWING SPREAD: View of Wrigley Field from a right-field skybox across the street from the stadium.

they rented the field one night, and when I was waiting around for them to do something, I went out to right field and lay on the grass. It was when Andre Dawson was playing right field. I loved Andre Dawson. He was such a beautiful player. And I was lying on the grass where Andre Dawson played during the day. It was such a good feeling. You look at that grass—especially when you've had the chance to lie on it—and the only place with more perfect turf is some English royal estate where someone is hand snipping the grass. It's so beautiful.

Then I ran the bases. That has got to be one of the most thrilling memories of my entire life. There were maybe two hundred extras in the stands, and they were all cheering. I'm a terrible athlete. I'm very energetic and committed, but really bad. I thought I must slide into home plate, but I don't know how to slide so I just fell onto home plate. The people were cheering and I thought, "I get it. I get why athletes don't retire."

I've been soured by the Ricketts family asking for the city to spend so much money on renovating Wrigley Field. My sympathy is with anyone who owns the team. The walls are falling down and there are toilets that haven't been flushable since 1920. It really is a pit. It needs to be torn down or seriously renovated. But even if this hadn't come out about Joe Ricketts's conservative politics, this city can't fix its roads and the schools are a mess. We're so in debt. However much we may love our sports teams, we have to fix our roads and schools. Baseball always was a rich man's game, now it's a hyper-rich-person's plaything. Three hundred million dollars to the Ricketts family is like $3,000 to me. Just suck it up and do it.

It has affected my willingness to spend money on supporting my team. I will not spend money on that team. I will not go to the ballpark, even if someone gave me tickets. Let the Ricketts family show that they are willing to spend their own money. I wrote a public renunciation for *Chicagoside*, a local periodical, and I got so much hate mail. I'll probably get more. But I can't bring myself to root for any other team.

Yet, secretly—well, not that secretly or I wouldn't tell you—I still watch the games on TV. Anyone with a hard-luck story will appeal to me. I'm someone with deep loyalty. I would love to have a winning team. If the Cubs started to win—well, now I'm so ambivalent. I can't quite shake my addiction but yet I'm still really ambivalent. I guess I still live on hope, and the thought that if you work hard, good things happen.

BIBLIOGRAPHY

Personal interviews I conducted during my years as a sportswriter and sports columnist that are included in this narrative:

INTERVIEWS

BASEBALL PLAYERS
Ernie Banks
Lou Brock
Phil Cavarretta
Jim Hickman
Ferguson Jenkins
Michael Jordan
Derrek Lee
Greg Maddux
Mark McGwire
Andy Pafko
Ryne Sandberg
Sammy Sosa
Billy Williams
Jim Woods

MANAGERS
Don Zimmer
Dusty Baker
Don Baylor
Jim Frey
Tony La Russa
Lou Piniella
Joe Torre

OWNERS
Jerry Reinsdorf
Philip K. Wrigley

WRITERS
Bill Gleason
Jerome Holtzman
Mike Royko

ANNOUNCER
Harry Caray

FANS (NONBASEBALL PARTICIPANTS)
Barry Holt
Fanetta Johnson
Barbara Snower
Eddie Waitkus Jr.

FOOTBALL PLAYERS
Red Grange
Bronko Nagurski
Dick Plasman

SELECTED BIBLIOGRAPHY

Ahrens, Art, and Eddie Gold. *The Cubs: The Complete Record of Chicago Cubs Baseball.* New York: Collier Books, 1986.

Anderson, Lars. *The First Star: Red Grange and the Barnstorming Tour That Launched the NFL.* New York: Random House, 2009.

Boyd, Brendan C., and Fred C. Harris. *The Great American Baseball Card Flipping, Trading and Bubble Gum Book.* New York: Mariner Books, 1991.

Brown, Warren. *The Chicago Cubs.* Carbondale, IL: Southern Illinois University Press, 2001.

Castle, George. *The Million-to-One Team: Why the Chicago Cubs Haven't Won a Pennant Since 1945.* Boulder, CO: Taylor Trade Publishing, 2000.

Chieger, Bob. *The Cubbies: Quotations on the Chicago Cubs.* New York: Atheneum Books, 1987.

Golenbock, Peter. *Wrigleyville: A Magical History Tour of the Chicago Cubs.* New York: St. Martin's Griffin, 1999.

Green, David. *101 Reasons to Love the Cubs.* New York: Stewart, Tabori and Chang, 2006.

Holtzman, Jerome, and Geroge Vass. *The Chicago Cubs Encyclopedia.* Philadelphia: Temple University Press, 1997.

——. *Baseball, Chicago Style: A Tale of Two Teams, One City.* Boulder, CO: Taylor Trade Publishing, 2001.

Honig, Donald. *The Chicago Cubs: An Illustrated History.* New York: Simon & Schuster, 1991.

Lowry, Philip J. *Green Cathedrals: The Ultimate Celebration of All Major League Ballparks.* New York: Walker & Company, 2006.

Royko, Mike. *One More Time: The Best of Mike Royko.* Chicago: The University of Chicago Press, 2000.

Thorn, John, Phil Birnbaum, and Bill Deane, eds. *Total Baseball: The Ultimate Baseball Encyclopedia, Eighth Edition, Completely Revised and Updated.* Toronto, ON: Sport Classic Books, 2004.

Vorwald, Bob, and Stephen Green. *Cubs Forever: Memories from the Men Who Lived Them.* Chicago: Triumph Books, 2008.

Ziemba, Joe. *When Football Was Football: The Chicago Cardinals and the Birth of the NFL.* Chicago: Triumph Books, 1999.

Plus newspaper and magazine articles from the *New York Times,* the *Chicago Tribune,* the *Chicago Sun-Times,* Newspaper Enterprise Association, *Sport* magazine, *Sports Illustrated,* among numerous others, and online references including Baseball Reference (baseball-reference.com) and Baseball Almanac (baseball-almanac.com).

ACKNOWLEDGMENTS
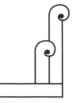

While there is much truth to the widely known dictum by Samuel Johnson—one that I and most writers I know generally subscribe to—that "No man but a blockhead ever wrote except for money," this book was, in addition to an advance on royalties, a labor of love. A lifetime's worth. And with labor, not to mention love, there are invariably other parties involved.

Josh Noel, who not only shared my affection for Wrigley Field and, yes, the Cubs, and, like me, grew up in Chicago, was the perfect person to work with me on it. I've known Josh since, as the saying goes, before he was even born, having been close friends with his father, my Sullivan High School (Chicago North Side) classmate Howard Noel, and Josh's mother, Staci.

I've observed and admired Josh's rise in the world of journalism, to where he is now, a highly valued reporter for the *Chicago Tribune.* He is also my friend. When I agreed to write the narrative for this book, I then asked Josh if he would conduct the interviews for the oral history section. He readily accepted my offer, and I am grateful—and readers of this book will surely share my gratitude—for his devoted work. He did all the interviews except the ones with U.S. Supreme Court justices John Paul Stevens and Stephen Breyer, and President Obama. In both of those cases, I had a particular and singular entrée that proved helpful.

I want to thank David Black, my gifted literary agent, whose insights and gentle prodding and cool wisdom were instrumental for me not only for this book but in other projects on which we have worked.

Likewise, I give a standing ovation to Jennifer Levesque, the editor of this book, whose enthusiasm, professionalism, and sheer editorial talent guided Josh and me throughout the research and writing.

A special thank-you to David Green for the extraordinary photo selections.

And a special thanks for the careful reading of the manuscript by two good friends, Richard Frederick and Jim Kaplan.

Following is a list of others who in a variety of ways aided in the development of this book; if there are some who assisted in one form or another and don't find their names below, my sincerest apologies for the oversight:

Bob Beghtol, Matt Boltz, Earl Burke, Sam Carl, Peter Chase, Ned Colletti, John Diamond, Terry Diamond, Dan Dorfman, Greg Elias, Jerry Feig, Stacie Geller, Alice Gershon, Steve Greenberg, Errol Halperin, Janice Harley, Michael Hawthorne, Barry Holt, Jerome Holtzman, Claire Julian, Yosh Kawano, Stephen Labaton, Ian Levin, Steve Levin, Ted Mann, Billy Marovitz, Karen Mineo, Bill Mulliken, Jimmy Nelson, Gabe Noel, Rhoda Noel, Brett Nolan, Pat O'Connell, Murray Olderman, Tim Pratt, Jerry Reinsdorf, Rob Sanders, Sheldon Schlegman, Bob Sirott, Judd Sirott, Paula Tordella, Hope Wolff, Sarah Wood, and Jim Woods.

One of my favorite dedications in a book is by Don Marquis, in his classic, *archy and mehitabel,* which goes, "dedicated to babs/ with babs knows what/and babs knows why." I do hope that my wife of half my lifetime, the one and only Dolly, knows "with what" and "why" I dedicated this book to her. I know that Josh, regarding the other half of the dedication, shares those same feelings for his dad, the one and only Howsie.

—Ira Berkow

Josh Noel thanks the following people for support, encouragement or assistance during this project: Lauren Stern, Howard and Rhoda Noel, Stacie Geller and Jonathan Frenzen, Gabriel Noel, Michael and Paula Hawthorne, Brett and Gillian Nolan, Adam and Lauren Nevens, Emily Stone and David MacLean, Kerry and Sarah Wood, Claire Julian, Matt Boltz and Ira Berkow.

PHOTO CREDITS

ABOUT THE AUTHORS

IRA BERKOW, a sports columnist and feature writer for the *New York Times* for twenty-six years, shared a Pulitzer Prize for National Reporting and was a finalist for the Pulitzer for Distinguished Commentary. He began his journalism career as a reporter for the *Minneapolis Tribune* and went on to become a sports and op-ed columnist for the feature syndicate Newspaper Enterprise Association. He is the author of twenty books, including the bestsellers *Red: A Biography of Red Smith* and *Maxwell Street: Survival in a Bazaar*. His work has been included in numerous literary anthologies, including *The Best American Sports Writing of the Century* (edited by David Halberstam). Mr. Berkow, who was born and raised in Chicago, holds a BA in English from Miami University (Ohio) and an MSJ from Northwestern's Medill Graduate School of Journalism. He also received an honorary doctorate in humanities from Roosevelt University.

JOSH NOEL writes about travel and beer for the *Chicago Tribune*. He previously wrote about crime for the Baton Rouge *Advocate* and sports for the *Casa Grande Dispatch* (Arizona). He has contributed to *This American Life* and the *New York Times*. His travel articles were collected in the 2013 ebook *Destinations: The Chicago Tribune Guide to Vacations and Getaways*.

INDEX

Page numbers in *italics* refer to images.